D1243022

ATLA Monograph Series
edited by Dr. Kenneth E. Rowe

1. Ronald L. Grimes. *The Divine Imagination: William Blake's Major Prophetic Visions.* 1972.
2. George D. Kelsey. *Social Ethics Among Southern Baptists, 1917–1969.* 1973.
3. Hilda Adam Kring. *The Harmonists: A Folk-Cultural Approach.* 1973.
4. J. Steven O'Malley. *Pilgrimage of Faith: The Legacy of the Otterbeins.* 1973.
5. Charles Edwin Jones. *Perfectionist Persuasion: The Holiness Movement and American Methodism. 1867–1936.* 1974.
6. Donald E. Byrne, Jr. *No Foot of Land: Folklore of American Methodist Itinerants.* 1975.
7. Milton C. Sernett. *Black Religion and American Evangelicalism: White Protestants, Plantation Missions, and the Flowering of Negro Christianity, 1787–1865.* 1975.
8. Eva Fleischner. *Judaism in German Christian Theology Since 1945: Christianity and Israel Considered in Terms of Mission.* 1975.
9. Walter James Lowe. *Mystery & The Unconscious: A Study in the Thought of Paul Ricoeur.* 1977.
10. Norris Magnuson. *Salvation in the Slums: Evangelical Social Work, 1865–1920.* 1977.
11. William Sherman Minor. *Creativity in Henry Nelson Wieman.* 1977.
12. Thomas Virgil Peterson. *Ham and Japheth: The Mythic World of Whites in the Antebellum South.* 1978.
13. Randall K. Burkett. *Garveyism as a Religious Movement: The Institutionalization of a Black Civil Religion.* 1978.
14. Roger G. Betsworth. *The Radical Movement of the 1960's.* 1980.
15. Alice Cowan Cochran. *Miners, Merchants, and Missionaries: The Roles of Missionaries and Pioneer Churches in the Colorado Gold Rush and Its Aftermath, 1858–1870.* 1980.
16. Irene Lawrence. *Linguistics and Theology: The Significance of Noam Chomsky for Theological Construction.* 1980.
17. Richard E. Williams. *Called and Chosen: The Story of Mother Rebecca Jackson and the Philadelphia Shakers.* 1981.
18. Arthur C. Repp, Sr. *Luther's Catechism Comes to America: Theological Effects on the Issues of the Small Catechism Prepared In or For America Prior to 1850.* 1982.
19. Lewis V. Baldwin. *"Invisible" Strands in African Methodism.* 1983.
20. David W. Gill. *The Word of God in the Ethics of Jacques Ellul.* 1984.
21. Robert Booth Fowler. *Religion and Politics in America.* 1985.
22. Page Putnam Miller. *A Claim to New Roles.* 1985.
23. C. Howard Smith. *Scandinavian Hymnody from the Reformation to the Present.* 1987.
24. Bernard T. Adeney. *Just War, Political Realism, and Faith.* 1988.
25. Paul Wesley Chilcote. *John Wesley and the Women Preachers of Early Methodism.* 1991.
26. Samuel J. Rogal. *A General Introduction of Hymnody and Congregational Song.* 1991.
27. Howard A. Barnes. *Horace Bushnell and the Virtuous Republic.* 1991.
28. Sondra A. O'Neale. *Jupiter Hammon and the Biblical Beginnings of African-American Literature.* 1993.
29. Kathleen P. Deignan. *Christ Spirit: The Eschatology of Shaker Christianity.* 1992.
30. D. Elwood Dunn. *A History of the Episcopal Church in Liberia, 1821–1980.* 1992.
31. Terrance L. Tiessen. *Irenaeus on the Salvation of the Unevangelized.* 1993.

JUPITER HAMMON AND THE BIBLICAL BEGINNINGS OF AFRICAN-AMERICAN LITERATURE

by
Sondra A. O'Neale

ATLA Monograph Series, No. 28

The American Theological Library Association and
The Scarecrow Press, Inc.
Metuchen, N.J., & London
1993

British Library Cataloguing-in-Publication data available

Library of Congress Cataloging-in-Publication Data

O'Neale, Sondra A. (Sondra Ann), 1939–
    Jupiter Hammon and the biblical beginnings of African-American
literature / Sondra A. O'Neale.
        p.   cm. — (ATLA monograph series ; no. 28)
    Includes bibliographical references and index.
    ISBN 0-8108-2479-5 (acid-free paper)
    1. Hammon, Jupiter, 1711–ca. 1800—Criticism and interpretation.
2. Afro-Americans—Intellectual life—18th century. 3. Slavery and
slaves in literature. 4. Afro-Americans in literature. 5. Bible in
literature. I. Title. II. Series.
PS767.H15Z75   1993
811'.1—dc20   91-38904

Contents

Acknowledgments

With special thanks to Preston L. Floyd, Robert Hemenway, Marie Morgan, Barbara McCaskill, Lore Metzger, and Martine Brownley—all of whom encouraged me through the years of tedious research that this study of Jupiter Hammon's work, life, and times could make a difference in American literary scholarship and in our grasp of Black experience in the eighteenth century—I dedicate this book—with its message that the hope and potential abiding in the human spirit can overcome any oppressor's plan—to my three children, Teresa, Nancy, and Michael, and to my mother, Edna White.

The research for this study was partially funded by grants from the Office of the Dean of the College, Emory University, and the Office of the Vice–President for Academic Affairs, Emory University.

Editor's Foreword

Since 1972 the American Theological Library Association has undertaken responsibility for a modest monograph series in the field of religious studies. Our aim in this series is to publish two doctoral dissertations of quality each year at reasonable cost. Titles are selected from studies in a wide range of religious and theological disciplines. We are pleased to publish Sondra O'Neale's study of the works of Jupiter Hammon as number twenty-eight in our series.

Sondra Ann O'Neale took her undergraduate degree at Asbury College in Wilmore, Kentucky. Her two graduate degrees in English literature (M.A. and Ph.D.) were taken at the University of Kentucky and earned her membership in Phi Beta Kappa. She has taught at the University of Kentucky, Emory University, and the University of California at San Diego. Currently she chairs the women's studies department at the University of Wisconsin-La Crosse. Dr. O'Neale is the author of several popular and scholarly articles and essays. She is the editor of two forthcoming collections on African-American and other minority women writers.

Kenneth E. Rowe
Series Editor
Drew University Library
Madison, New Jersey 07940

Editorial Procedure

In preparing the edited text, I have consulted James Thorpe's *Use of Manuscripts in Literary Research: Problems of Access and Literary Property Rights* (a 1979 MLA publication); the MLA's *Statement of Editorial Principles: A Working Manual for Editing Nineteenth-Century American Texts* (published in 1967); and Thomas Tanselle's "Some Principles for Editorial Apparatus" (*Studies in Bibliography* 25 [1972]: 41–88). I have designed what I believe is the best possible system for making the text readable while maintaining the integrity of Hammon's style and annotating the content. This includes the following:

1. I have attempted to modernize consistently the punctuation. Hammon's language was similar in rhythm and punctuation to that of the King James Version of the Bible. The overall intention in the clear text is to make his work readable for the twentieth-century reader but to change as few as possible of Hammon's words. (For example, Hammon's use of *hath* rather than *has* has not been changed.) Changing punctuation sometimes becomes a matter of great concern: Hammon's punctuation occasionally created ambiguity. It was then necessary to base a change in punctuation on a close reading of those Scriptures Hammon cited, on Hammon's theological views, and on eighteenth-century usage.

2. Numerous inaccurate or nonverbatim scriptural references, both in the original broadsides and in the Stanley Austin Ransom edition, have been corrected.

3. Corrections and/or updating of spelling (for example, *begining* to *beginning*) have been made and noted in the lists of emendations, with the exception of *shew* to *show, labour* to

labor, and *favour* to *favor,* all of which have consistently been changed.

4. Editorial scholars know that most errant eighteenth-century paragraphing decisions were made, not by authors, but by printers. One passage in the Ransom edition continues for seven pages without a paragraph break. This comparative lack of paragraphing is an important factor in the difficulty of reading the text. I have reduced all paragraphs in Hammon's prose to a sensible length, according to modern standards of grouping subjects and observing topic sentences. These paragraph changes are noted in the lists of emendations.

5. As in the King James Version, Hammon introduced biblical quotes, not by quotation marks, but simply by a comma and capitalization of the first word. Also, Hammon put the scriptural references at different places in his sentences. In general, the citation preceded the quotation; sometimes, however, the scriptural citation followed the quotation, or specific verse citations appeared between the sentences in the quotation. At other times, references were omitted altogether. I have consistently put biblical quotations in quotation marks and I have placed the correct citations after the quotations. Incorrect citations in the Hammon and Ransom texts have been corrected, and missing citations have been supplied. The use of quotation marks and the change in placement of citations have not been routinely included in the lists of emendations. The changes in citation placement are noted in the emendations when the change affected the punctuation of the sentence, when the citation was incorrect, or when there was no citation in the copy text.

6. To conform the passage to the King James Version of the Bible, several changes had to be made from what Hammon had in the original text. This has been done, however, without damage to the text and without violating authorial intentions. Hammon's mind was filled with biblical verse and incident, but when writing he either paraphrased various sections or wrote them down from memory; neither practice was unusual in eighteenth-century prose. For consistency and to reflect the contem-

porary version, all scriptural texts in his essays in this edition have been made to conform to the King James Version. Readers can reconstruct Hammon's paraphrases through the use of the emendations within each chapter. These entries indicate the variations and changes in this edition and show what was in Hammon's original text and in the Ransom and Oscar Wegelin editions.

7. In Ransom's edition, the chapter was printed in lowercase Roman numerals, the verse number(s) in Arabic. Modern-day form of citation (for example, Ps. 1:1) has been followed in the clear text. A number that was expressed as a figure in the Ransom edition but that would today be expressed as a word (18, eighteen) has been written as a word in the clear text. Neither the modernization of the form of the citation nor the change from figures to words has been noted in the lists of emendations.

8. The emendations consist of lemmas (entries, or words) that illustrate how spelling, punctuation, and wording have been changed in this edition in comparison with Ransom's edition (R) and Hammon's original text (H). A caret (ˬ) indicates where no mark of punctuation appears in the edition being cited. A cent sign (¢) represents "etc."

> Sondra O'Neale
> Women's Studies Department
> University of Wisconsin-La Crosse

Introduction:
The First Black Writer in America

On Christmas Day, 1760, Jupiter Hammon, a forty-nine-year-old slave, occasional preacher, and clerk-bookkeeper for wealthy merchants on Long Island, New York, ushered in the advent of African-American literature. A devout evangelical Christian, Hammon had been converted during the earliest stirrings of the Great Awakening. As a writer he used Christianity and its foundation of biblical language, allusion, and imagery to mount a public assault against slavery. He left four poems, two essays, and a sermon, however that offering includes the first, and most comprehensive, statement of Black theology as well as the earliest antislavery protests by a Black writer in all of American literature. But he is usually not lauded for this contribution today. Instead, most critics of Black American literature label him a weak, even shameful, forerunner of the canon, an early Black writer whose concern with salvation rendered him useless for the *real* freedom movement. Because modern critics make a distinction between religious art and the protest tradition when assessing formal aesthetic expression as opposed to indigenous folk creations, Hammon's dual commitment to Christianity and freedom has been either undervalued or ignored.

Thus, as a shrouded legend prefiguring the tradition which he spawned, Hammon has been one of the least understood writers in two hundred years of minority authorial experience. Facts about his life are hidden in the unaddressed history of Northern slavery; and his cries for freedom, which of necessity he veiled in biblical themes, are further obscured by modern unfamiliar-

1

ity with those contexts. A slave all of his life of at least some eighty years, Hammon nonetheless created opportunities to preach among his people, to distinguish himself as a well-known folk, religious, and occasional poet in rural New York, and to become touted as an essayist with invitations to speak and write for both Blacks and whites. Although evidence indicates that he wrote more, Hammon's extant works are extensive for a backwoods plantation slave with little schooling or sustained support from the organized abolition movement, which the next generation of Black writers enjoyed.

Fortunately, Hammon was allowed to acquire the skills of reading and writing—in the early eighteenth-century, as rare and unattainable for a Northern slave as for a Southern one—precisely so that he could assist his masters in commercial endeavors which themselves supported local and regional institutionalized slavery. Thus, while ostensibly beneficial, the training he received merely reimpowered his enslavers. But for Hammon, as progenitor of African-American literature, the real task was apprehension of enough language skill to exhibit an intellectual awareness of the times and to find a metaphorical vehicle for surreptitious discussion of his own enslavement and of the slave state. The result was the first attempt by a member of an oppressed minority in America to present an art of courage and subterfuge—an aesthetic design cleverly marked by scriptural guideposts, rendering it seemingly harmless enough for publication—in short, an art that simultaneously accomplished several subversive objectives. Thus, Hammon began the canon of African-American literature with vital sociopolitical statements: (a) a message to slaves which would adroitly guide them to at least psychological paths of escape through the use of ancient identities more enhancing than those with which slaveholders characterized Africans; (b) a persuasive, though subtle, moral challenge effective enough to touch the conscience of white society; (c) proof that an African slave could indeed publish and distribute his work in an alien world; and (d) the possibility of slave leadership through public and written performance before an integrated audience of slaves and white onlookers (who had the job of "protecting" slaves from this very subversion). Considering these tasks and the social atmosphere organized to thwart their accomplishment, Hammon—befitting his legacy to other protest writers who have used similar tactics through the years—is the triumphant father of African-American literature.

To glean Hammon's work, modern critics must first view the social, historical, linguistic, and literary context of eighteenth-century America and, more importantly, the language, contending doctrines, and pervasive influence of church and religion on the psyche of that era. Ostensibly Christian and para-Christian institutions were not only the prime forces with which the white world defined the slave and exonerated slaveholding; white society's perspective of Christianity's logic and symbolism were the dominant informants of the semantic culture. Critics who say that Jupiter Hammon was too concerned with Christianity to deal with slavery misapprehend these historical contexts. America's slave system was born from contorted interpretations of Christianity. The Northern abolition movement began in a Christian sect (Quakerism), and—as Bruns, Genovese, Jordan, and other historians have observed—Christianity and the Bible were the slaveholder's bulwarks of "moral" support for the slave institution.[1] Thus, as the first African slave to write and to publish in America, Hammon had no choice but to wage war against slavery in the biblical arena.

Most current literary criticism of Jupiter Hammon's work reflects anachronistic thinking and ignores the racism pervasive in all aspects of a slave society, including the burgeoning publishing industry. The awesome restrictions of any master/slave relationship, the peculiar disdain for things African and Black in colonial society,[2] and most particularly, his owners' involvement in the nefarious slave commerce—all indicate that slavery was the incessant crucible of Hammon's life. Just as contemporary critics laud other writers who surreptitiously manage to decry oppression while living in the midst of it, these same critics should give artists imprisoned by American slavery equal latitude of interpretation. Obviously the critic must break hidden codes and patterns to unlock the shackled writers' intended meaning.

Some scholars have been highly critical of the artistic style in Hammon's poetry and prose, of his ostensibly conservative political stance, and especially of the religious framework in which he couched his rhetorical arguments. For instance, J. Saunders Redding (*To Make*) calls Hammon's verse "rhymed prose, doggerel, in which the homely thoughts of a very religious and superstitious man are expressed in limping phrases" (4–5). Redding says that both Phillis Wheatley and Hammon "were extremely religious" and then he makes the incredible statement that "both preferred slavery in America to freedom in Africa" (5). Redding castigates Hammon, implying that the poet was a conservative lackey in an age when most "slave writers were bitterly reproachful of bondage" (6–7): "Many slaves who could neither read nor write but who were nonetheless truly poetic burned themselves out in revolt. To the splendid folly of their deeds Hammon's equivocal statement is an outrage" (7). With brief acknowledgment of the probable difficulty of publishing a militant stance and of the "wisdom" of Hammon's statements about the Revolutionary War, Redding deduces that "summation of his philosophy and a clear–cut statement of his resignation to a life of servitude is found in his words. . . . Hammon's life was motivated by the compulsion of obedience to his earthly and his heavenly master" (7). Redding's strong contentions are stinging, coming from one who is dedicated to making an initial, critical study on the etiology of Black American literary culture. He places Hammon outside the pale of colonial slave experience without reporting examination of that experience and without lending documentation on those (actually unknown) contemporary slave writers whom he implies made such bold literary statements against their captivity.

Of Hammon's style Redding concludes:

> As to literary values, there is not much to choose between Hammon's poetry and prose. Though he was not without the romantic gift of spontaneity, he lacked any knowledge of metrics and

sought only to make rhymes. In prose the artlessness of his construction, the rambling sentences, the repetitions reveal, sometimes at the expense of thought, his not unattractive personality. When he is most lucid there is force in the quaintness of his thought evocative of the highly personal flavor of early American letters. (8)

Redding's harshness is indicative of the common failure to investigate with empathy the realities of slavery in the eighteenth-century American North and to credit the slave writer with enough intellectual humanity to yearn for his own freedom.

While Benjamin Mays' critique of Hammon seems to be more mollifying, in essence he agrees with Redding: "Though Hammon did not believe that slavery was necessarily ordained of God, he did believe that it was for the best interest of Negroes that they be good, obedient slaves" (97). Mays says that Hammon's relationship with God was "compensatory" and "other-worldly" and that his theology was treacherous sophism:

Hammon's ideas of God . . . serve as an opiate for the people. Having received good treatment as a slave, his attitude toward slavery is colored by that fact. His advice, if followed, would lead, and perhaps it did encourage, Negroes to be satisfied with their lot and to look to Heaven for freedom if God did not see fit to give it to them here. (99–100)

"Clearly," Mays reasons, Hammon "was more interested in salvation in Heaven than he was in any form of social reconstruction" (102).

Most modern criticism of Hammon's life and works follows this vein. The early-twentieth-century poet, Thomas Oxley, said that Hammon's "poems are all religious; they are crude and methodless" (37). And in their comprehensive anthology of Black American literature, Keneth Kinnamon and Richard Barksdale say that "his religious fervor seriously impaired his poetry. There is in Jupiter Hammon's verse none of the felicity of thought and verbal imagery found in Phillis Wheatley's poetry" (46). Bernard Bell condemns the first slave poet's work as "lacking the originality, ironic tension, graphic imagery, and

call and response pattern of Black American spirituals" (177).
Like Redding, Bell discounts Hammon's aesthetics:

> Hammon's unimaginative use of the meter, rhyme, diction, and
> stanzaic pattern of the Methodist hymnal combined with the
> negative image of Africa and conciliatory tone of these early
> poems reveal the poet's limitations and the costly socio-
> psychological price he paid for the mere semblance of cultural
> assimilation. (178)[3]

However, the first African slave poet in the modern Western
Hemisphere is not without his supporters. They survey Hammon's offerings by the same criteria (analogy to Negro spirituals,
Christian idiom, sociopolitical caveat, etc.) but draw very different conclusions. Judging Hammon's writing by the light of eighteenth-century aesthetics, Robert T. Kerlin argues that "as 'religious' poetry goes, or went in the eighteenth century—and
Hammon's poetry is all religious—this Negro slave may hold up
his head in almost any company" (21). When editing *Cavalcade*
perhaps Redding had a change of heart, or else it was his co-
editor, Arthur P. Davis, who perceived a basic Hammon tech-
nique. They suggest that in his "Dialogue," "Hammon is double-
talking, and doing it so artfully and with such subtly pointed irony
as not only to reduce the Master's admonitions to absurdity but to
constitute a statement of protest against them" (4).

Historian Sidney Kaplan believes that Hammon's first poem,
"An Evening Thought: Salvation by Christ, with Penitential
Cries," "has all the ringing ecstatic hope for heavenly freedom
with 'tender love' that charges the earliest spirituals of the
enslaved" (171–72). In discussing the same poem, Carolyn
Reese concludes that the religious dogma appearing in Ham-
mon's hymn-poem has secular significance. "His obvious knowl-
edge of classical meter and rhyme is reflected . . . . Jupiter
Hammon should be included among the list of poet-preachers.
Certainly his writings and speeches were as effectual upon the
Negroes as was the work of Michael Wigglesworth upon the
non-Negro public" (34).

Although he derides much of Phillis Wheatley's verse, Vernon Loggins believes that in light of twentieth-century evaluation of folk poetry, Hammon's work has native religious feeling. Like Reese and Kaplan, Loggins likewise concludes that Hammon's verse is analogous to early Black American hymns and sermons:

> Like the spirituals, the poems of Jupiter Hammon were composed to be heard. There is evident in his verse that peculiar sense for sound which is the most distinguishing characteristic of Negro folk poetry. A word that appeals to his ear he uses over and over again, in order, it seems to cast a spell with it. (12)

Loggins comments on Hammon's alternative rhyme schemes, on the effectiveness of his alliteration and repetition, and on the "many examples of syncopation so characteristic of Negro dance rhythms." Then he explains:

> Any impressionable sinners who might have heard Jupiter Hammon chant the poem when in the ecstasy of religious emotion no doubt went away to be haunted by the sound of the word *salvation* if not by the idea . . . . But the most interesting irregularities are the strange rime combinations—such as "word" and "God," "call" and "soul," "sound" and "down." Since we know little about how English was spoken by the Negroes on Long Island in the eighteenth century, we cannot determine how far astray Jupiter Hammon's ear was in hearing exact rimes in such combinations. We can say with definiteness the riming words which he selected are always sonorous. (12)[4]

While these remarks do somewhat counter those negative views of Hammon held by Redding and most scholars of Black American literature, most Hammon criticism, whether commendatory or vitriolic, is devoid of two scholarly considerations: (1) the rise of egalitarian Christianity as the predominant moral and aesthetic force in eighteenth-century America and its pervasive influence on the literary expression of the age; and (2) the biblical fabric of contemporary slave expression—in worship, sermon, art, and song—as the almost exclusive mode of protest expression.

Modern critics who would have had Hammon encourage insurrection should understand the general police state conditions for slaves in colonial New York. Bondmen were subject to a rigid system of laws and regulations purposed to maintain slave control. Because of the size of the state's slave population, these laws were particularly stringent: as early as 1640, New York had the largest slave population north of Maryland (Rawley 345). Between 1750 and 1770 the Black population, through births and rising slave imports, swelled 70 percent (E. J. McManus, *History* 176). By 1785 almost half of the slaves in the Northern colonies lived in New York's territory, especially in such areas around New York City as Long Island, where Hammon lived in a small cove called Oyster Bay (Mabee 17). The only account of the Oyster Bay slave population is in Klingberg's *Anglican Humanitarianism in Colonial New York*. He reports that in 1728 "there were 41 men, 27 women, 17 boys, and 26 girls" who were African slaves in the community (158). Being seventeen years old at the time of this census, Hammon was probably counted among the men. He was also seventeen when missionary Robert Jenney came over from Britain to preach to those slaves owned by Long Island members of the Anglican church. Jenney later recommended that another British missionary, Daniel Denton, come to Oyster Bay to start a school for these Africans. Undoubtedly, Hammon was one of Denton's students.[5]

While many of those included in the increased slave population came during that influx in the mid-eighteenth century, the New York slave trade had continued without interruption since the early seventeenth century. Jordan says that "there were Negroes in the colony as early as 1628" (*White over Black* 83–84). He explains, however, that under Dutch rule, in the colony's earliest years, the Africans were free citizens able to own property. While slavery was instituted among the Dutch, it was a much milder form than that practiced by the British from the last part of that century through the next 130 years.[6]

However, when the British took over control of the New York colony from the Dutch in 1684, E. J. McManus says that slavery entered an era of unprecedented expansion. While the Dutch had imported slaves solely as a commercial venture, through their West India Company the British used local political control—governors, consulates, and customs officials—to initiate and support slave importation. Well over 35 percent of all newcomers to the colonies for the rest of the century were slaves. "The slave trade fast became one of the cornerstones of New York's commercial prosperity in the eighteenth century (*History* 26). Hammon's masters were very much involved in this importation, deriving their wealth from supplying slaves for their section of New York. They were among "the great merchants" who, E. J. McManus says, "imported whole cargoes of slaves, while the smaller merchants specialized in the importation of highly skilled slaves for a more limited market" (*History* 26).

A second and more expanding wave of slave imports hit the colony between 1750 and 1770, precisely during the time of Hammon's first publication. The market was so flooded with an oversupply of slaves that even the bargain minded became users of slave labor because workers could be obtained at distress prices. After 1770 several factors combined to cause a sharp decline in the trade: (1) incessant slave raids had so depopulated the African coast that traders could not fill quotas when the demand returned; (2) as a result, prices became too high for the New York market; and (3) with the market for Africans disappearing, traders looked to the Caribbean and to local transactions. But, most importantly, the economy had generally absorbed all the free workers that it needed and slavery became unprofitable. Several historians agree that this unprofitability, not the altruistic war waged by Black and white abolitionists to end the practice, was the ultimate reason that slavery was gradually phased out in the Northern colonies. They say that had there been an economic need for slaves in the more industrialized North, the institution would have continued just as it did in the Southern colonies (E. J. McManus, *History* 23–39).[7]

As New York's slave population increased, so did its need for slave control. The colony's slave code (which, as with all facets of Northern slavery, has been carefully hidden from popularly known history) began in 1682 when "New York enacted legislation which recognized the slave as a category distinct from the indentured servant (i.e., not serving in perpetuity) and passed regulations which applied only to the black community" (Kobrin 13). The slave code covered all aspects of Black life: legal status at birth, baptism, marriage, prison, curfew hours, special penalties for slaves for all kinds of crime, particularly escape, slave victimization, miscegenation, social functions, free Blacks, relationships with indentured servants, and finally even death and burial.[8]

Another early slave code in 1702 made it illegal for any colonists to transact business with a slave. This was because of the fear that slaves were dealing in illegal contraband that had been stolen from their masters. The code added that "not above three slaves" could congregate except "for their master's profit and by their master's consent" (Higginbotham 119). Slaves found in violation of that ordinance were to be "whipt upon the naked back . . . not exceeding Forty Lashes" (Higginbotham 119). A slave could not "strike a freeman" but a master could punish his own slave provided "he did not kill or dismember him." Each community was directed to appoint "a common whipper" to be paid three shillings per slave (Hurd 280; Higginbotham 119). Kobrin reports that in addition to whipping for various crimes, slaves were summarily punished by branding with hot irons, confinement in stocks and jail, execution, or "transportation out of the colony" (14).[9] The 1702 act had special provisions for runaway slaves. Colonists, especially free Blacks, had to make restitution for time and stolen property if they had aided in a slave's escape. While that act apparently continued until 1726, an appendage was added in 1705 "to prevent the running away of negro slaves" to Canada (Higginbotham 121). And the next year, to assure owners that slave baptism would not initiate slave release, the governors set a seal of law on religious affairs and added that every child born to a

Negro slave "shall follow the state and condition of the mother and be esteemed, reputed, taken and adjudged a slave and slaves to all intents and purposes whatsoever" (Hurd 1:281).[10] In his *History of Long Island,* Benjamin F. Thompson, unable to hide his own prejudice, states:

> In 1706, the negroes had so much increased in number, and become, by vice and intemperance, so disorderly and dangerous to the peace and safety of the inhabitants, that it was found necessary to call in the aid of the civil power to repress or punish their repeated depredations. (1:139)

Written just a few years before Hammon's birth, the governor's proclamation illustrates the overwhelming fear of slaves in Hammon's home territory and the imposing strength of a colonial police system designed to enforce maximum slave control:

> Whereas, I am informed that several negroes in Kings county have assembled themselves in a riotous manner, which, if not prevented, may prove of ill consequence; You, the justices of the peace in the said county, are hereby required and commanded to take all proper methods for the seizing and apprehending, all such negroes as shall be found to be assembled in such manner, as aforesaid, or have run away or absconded from their masters or owners, whereby there may be reason to suspect them of ill practices or designs, and to secure them in safe custody; and if any of them refuse to submit, then to *"fire" upon them, "kill" or "destroy" them, if they cannot otherwise be taken;* and for so doing, this shall be your sufficient warrant. (Thompson 1:139)

Obviously, Hammon was surrounded by a repressive atmosphere that inhibited slave activity and expression. In both 1708 and 1712, administrators passed acts "for preventing, suppressing and punishing the conspiracy and insurrection of negroes and other slaves."[11] Additionally the 1712 law made it illegal for any freed slave to own real estate.

Further, unlike white colonists, Africans were not guaranteed trial by jury. Instead they "might be tried for any offenses in a summary way" (Thompson 1:266). In any court cases the testimony of slaves could be used only *against,* not in support of, another slave (Jernegan, *Laboring* 54). Whenever crimes were of such magnitude that slaves had to be publicly executed, owners were compensated for their losses. These executions were so frequent that in his lifetime Hammon could not have avoided knowing about them. Even in his native Long Island, two slave women, Nell and Sarah, were executed for burning their master's dwelling, and two other slaves, Absalom and Samuel, were executed for robbery (Thompson 2:43). Their crimes should be viewed as political acts because, to the controlling colonists, robbery, arson, or any destruction of property owned by whites were said to be indicative of slave rebellion.

The better-known "Negro Plot" in New York City in 1712, when Hammon was one year old, led to even tighter slave controls. The revolt began with the burning of several governmental structures; then fires continued on a daily basis. Dodd says, "A number of people of color [i.e., mulattoes] were committed to jail as incendiaries, kept in dungeons for some months, and finally condemned to be hanged" (265). Of the one hundred fifty Negroes who were arrested during the revolt, "eleven were burned, eighteen hanged and seventy-one transported" (265). Obviously the euphemism "transported" means that the threat of being "sold down South" because of belligerent behavior was just as real in Hammon's day as in that of Frederick Douglass and David Walker. Nor was it safe for innocent bystanders: "Several negroes, some of whom had assisted to put out the fires, were met and imprisoned and once there, were continued in confinement, because the magistrates could not spare time to examine them" (265). At the time of the riots, historians estimate that there were two thousand slaves living in New York City as part of the total population of twelve thousand persons. Dodd reports that "the panic occasioned by the first disclosures of a plot being formed, was very great" (266). Again the screws of slave control had to be twisted even tighter to keep the "dangerous" 17 percent of the population in tow.

However, 1741 brought another massive revolt. While a series of unexplained fires were again the stimulus of hysteria in the colony, this time there was no clear-cut evidence that a slave revolt was underway. But based on the testimony of one white indentured servant, Mary Burton, eighteen Blacks and four whites were hung, thirteen of the Blacks were burned to death, and seventy of them were again "transported out of the colony" (Higginbotham, 131–35).[12]

Of the "minor" offenses for which a slave in New York could be punished, the crime of cursing seems most absurd. A 1730 law indicates the severity of punishment against a slave who used profane language:

> 1730. *An act for the punishment of negro, Indian, and mulatto slaves for speaking defamatory words.* To be punished, on trial before a justice, by whipping, not exceeding forty stripes; "and the said slave, so convict, shall be sold to defray all charges arising thereupon; unless the same be by his or their master or mistress paid and answered." (Hurd 1:272)

Ironically, modern critics have castigated Hammon because he admonished slaves about cursing and other such minor misdemeanors. In reality he was trying to keep them out of prison and alive.

Within such an oppressive society, naturally all public facilities were segregated (McLeod 166). That, plus the pass system to control "illegal" slave congregation, allowed slaveholders to guard against what was to them the most grievous crime in the colony—a slave's attempt to escape. Moreover, Higginbotham and Hurd found that it was a capital offense for any slave to try to obtain his freedom. Colonial prisons had an unusual number of Black inmates, most of whom were there because of the "crime" of wanting their manumission (McLeod 168). A collection of eighteenth-century runaway slave advertisements illustrates that escaped slaves were most generally from among those who had acquired proficient use of the English language and the ability to read and write. Runaway slaves were next identified by their physical build, skin color (i.e., racial mixture), and clothing (Zook 175–216).

Like most slaves belonging to members of the British hierarchy, Hammon lived in the midst of a tyrannical household run by masters who would expend any amount of money and energy to regain a runaway slave even if his eventual death was the only way by which he could be "possessed." For example, the Lloyds paid bounty hunters to find and return the slave Opium (who could have been Hammon's father) and then more money to find the horse on which Opium had escaped (*Lloyd Papers* 1:144). Similarly, in 1749 one of the Lloyd sons wrote his father that he was in dire need of a particular slave and had to have him returned whether dead or alive: "If Jackson is not Come to Queens Village pray Get Brother Joseph to hire Denton to go to Eatons Neck with his Canoe and fetch him Imediate & I'll pay his Charge be it what it will and would have Denton fetch him Dead or alive for I am in Great want of him" (*Lloyd Papers* 1:425). Like many eighteenth-century Northern slaves who attempted escape or who were sold because of their penchant to do so, Jackson was probably at Eaton's Neck to see a wife or girlfriend, even perhaps children and a family, a normal human pursuit for which so many slaves gave their lives.

Unlike Southern slave breeders, Northern slaveholders discouraged slave childbearing. Marriages between slaves of pure African blood were usually dismissed as illegal. To dissuade, even forbid, Black family settlement, a Black woman of childbearing age was the lowest-priced commodity in the Northern system. Thus many young mothers with new babies were shipped to Southern colonies or to the Caribbean because of their low utility in the New England economic structure. As Hammon's probably unmarried life reflects, the Black male-to-female ratio was about ten to one.

However, the slave marriages which most concerned the arbiters of slave control were those between pure-blood African slaves and white indentured servants. Considered particularly shameful was any relationship between Black men and white women. In one colony, legislators simply "enacted that the white woman so intermarrying" a Negro slave "should serve the master of her husband as long as her husband lived" (Brawley,

Short History 9–20). In Massachusetts an "act for the better preventing of a spurious and mixt issue" required "that a negro or molatto man committing fornication with an English woman, or a woman of any other Christian nation, shall be sold out of the province" (Hurd 1:263). But the converse interracial relationship did not receive the same punishment. Again, the slave was the one who had transgressed: "An English man, or man of any other Christian nation, committing fornication with a negro or molatto woman, to be shipped, and the woman sold out of the province" (Hurd 1:263).[13] Presumably, the English man, etc., would have been an indentured servant.

Jernegan insists that intermixture of races in marriage and childbearing was considered most dangerous because it disturbed the strict class distinctions in the colonies. Blacks alone were always to be on the lowest rung of that class ladder. He says that "a great increase of illegitimate mulatto children in the eighteenth century is one evidence" (*Laboring* 55). Slave masters usually would not allow these children to remain in their households and, as a result, the orphans were often thrown on the state. Undoubtedly this large class of unwanted children was of crucial concern to Hammon when he pleaded with whites to give the education of unwanted slave children a higher priority.

Ostensibly, slaves did have certain rights in the Northern colonies—the right to food and clothing, to care in old age or sickness, to religious instruction, to marry (if the master approved), to have some free time (usually on Sunday), and to testify in court cases involving other slaves (Brawley, *Short History* 55). But in reality they had no legal redress with which to protect these rights. Further, there was little or no protection from victimization. Greene concludes that "an incomplete list of crimes against Negroes would include abduction, selling of free Negroes into slavery, false accusation, adultery, rape and mutilation" (*The Negro* 164).[14]

His findings concur with those of Higginbotham, Hurd, and E. J. McManus (*Black Bondage*) to the effect that there was little difference between the African as slave and as freeman. In fact, as the fear of slave uprisings increased, most of the same

repressive measures were taken against free Blacks as against
slaves because white colonists always suspected that free Blacks
were helping their enslaved brothers to revolt. Moreover, any
errant behavior on the part of free Blacks was used as an excuse
to prevent manumission. A 1767 act in New York declared: "It
is found by experience, that free negroes and mulattoes are idle
and slothful, and often prove burdensome to the neighborhood
wherein they live, and are of evil example to slaves" (Hurd
1:293).[15]

Again the entire desocialization of Africans in New England
life is readily apparent even in Hammon's most immediate
surroundings. Henry Lloyd prosecuted a free Black for alleg-
edly hunting on his property and for trying to repossess a dog
that Lloyd had arrogantly taken from him:

> I have at times for several years been plagued with Tom Gall a
> free Negro of Oyster bay, who comes by stealth to Hunt Deer on
> this place: the last february in the great snow I Discovered him
> but could not till Saturday last find evidence sufficient to prose-
> cute him & had in a manner given over the thought of it, but that
> in my Absence from home last week he or some body for him
> broak into my House, and Stole a Dog from under a table where
> he was tyed. the Dog was formerly his but when he was Discov-
> ered hunting, I took the Dog from him whom to prevent his being
> killed he gave to one of my Sons. (*Lloyd Papers* 1:302–23)

The writer's condescending assumptions—that he had a right to
"take" the dog but that Gall's retrieval of his own dog was
theft—merely reflect Lloyd's economic status. As a wealthy
member of the ruling class he innately believed that his rule
extended to all Africans, not just to those born or bought into
his household.[16]

In fact, the *Lloyd Papers* themselves are a major contribution
to the documentation from which historians of colonial America
conclude that the basis of the national economy in the eighteenth century was slavery—not just for the fledgling South but
for the more established North as well.[17] The slave institution,
along with the profitable spin-offs of rum and molasses, was the

basis of a thriving route among England, Africa, the Caribbean, and the American colonies, and was the source of wealth for New England's shipping oligarchy.[18] Jupiter Hammon lived through four successive generations of "owners" in the wealthy Lloyd family, one of the important spokes in that oligarchical wheel. As one of the few families on Long Island, or for that matter in the state of New York, which had strong familial and commercial ties to Boston, Hartford, New York City, and London, the Lloyds obtained slave labor for their section of the state, prospering greatly from an exchange of goods and human chattel. Their family papers and account books are replete with scores of financial transactions concerning the sale and care of slaves in the island community.[19]

James Lloyd, the American patriarch of the Lloyd family, came to New England "as a teen age youth" in 1670 from his home in Somersetshire, England (Woolsey 7; Bailey 27). He was the third son of John Lloyd of Bristol and could trace his lineage back to Queen Elizabeth's personal physician and to Welsh royal blood. After a short visit to Rhode Island, Lloyd settled in Boston until he married Grizzell Sylvester, who had inherited the Lloyd's Neck property through the untimely death of her betrothed, Latimore Sampson. When the Lloyds settled in Long Island, they purchased the remainder of the 3,000-acre stretch of rich land—suitable for farming, orchards, and timber—and a vast ocean outlet nearby (Thompson 1:432–39). The acreage was originally purchased from Native Americans in 1654 in exchange for "three coats, three shirts, two cuttoes, three hatchets, three hoes, two fathom of wampum, six knives, two pair of stockings and two pair of shoes" (*Lloyd Papers* 1:1; Thompson 2:432; see also Flint 191). Lloyd obtained "the Manorial Grant of the Lordship of Queens Village" from the Governor of New York in 1697, for annual payment of "four bushells of good winter wheat or the monetary equivalent," and renamed the area Lloyd's Neck. At that point the Manor became a separate political entity, representing the British Commonwealth in that section of New York (Bailey 27).

James Lloyd had only intended to use the property for a summer home, but after he died, his son Henry moved the family estate from Boston to Lloyd's Neck in 1711—the year of Jupiter Hammon's birth. Henry purchased sole proprietorship rights from his brother and sister, who remained in Boston with established business interests that were still connected to the Old World. He then headed the clan's economic affairs from Lloyd's Neck, or "Queen's Village" as he called it in his business ledgers, for the next fifty-three years.

Immediately upon his move to Long Island, Lloyd opened a community store where he extended credit to most of the settlers of the Huntington and Oyster Bay villages. Bailey says that the villagers were "Lloyd's labor pool and his customers, and to some extent his suppliers; here young girls as well as men could work for wages or for credit against their purchases" (31). In exchange Lloyd sold his neighbors local or imported merchandise. He kept track of his multiple bartering system in a very detailed set of account books in which the family's dependence upon the slave trade is clearly rendered. Further, Bailey insists that Lloyd's estate was actually the community citadel representing the British government. The Lloyds had power "to hold Court Leet for trial causes" and to arrange their estate as a military fortification when needed.[20] Thus, Jupiter Hammon, America's first African writer, was enslaved directly by an agent of the British empire and that agent was himself merely another British slave trader.

When he was eighteen years of age, Henry Lloyd identified himself in one of his business journals as "a Boston merchant engaged in 'adventures' [commercial overseas ventures]— shares in ships' cargoes or specified goods carried by ships plying *especially to the Island of Jamaica* [italics added]" (Bailey 30). Human chattel was among Lloyd's "cargo," including no doubt Jupiter's mother and father who would have been taken to the Caribbean from Africa where they could be "broken" for slavery, trained to do agricultural work, and taught to speak a modicum of English.[21] This process was fine-tuned, with Lloyd's vessels later shipping slaves up the Atlantic coast.

Those not sold along the Southern route could be molded into needed craftsmen and farm and domestic workers for various colonial purchasers in New York state, especially on Long Island.[22] Undoubtedly, Lloyd's surreptitious remark that he especially shipped between New York and Jamaica was a hint to knowledgeable purchasers that he offered prime, seasoned slaves. McKee writes specifically of that New York dynasty:

> The Lloyds, like so many other persons of wealth, had innumerable dealings which involved the buying, selling and renting of slaves. Henry Lloyd wrote to his father, January 12, 1759, that there was a negro for sale in Boston for fifty pounds sterling, a diligent, hard working fellow who had been brought up in a ship carpenter's yard as a sawyer and borer of holes, and sometimes employed as a smith. He was "to be parted with for no other Fault than going out of nights." (121)

The Lloyds' involvement in the slave trade descended to the sale, repurchase, and resale of slaves from the time they purchased the Africans as children throughout all of the slaves' adult lives. In the same year that Hammon wrote his first poem—1760—Henry Lloyd purchased an eight-year-old slave girl named Hannah for forty pounds. When Lloyd died three years later he left instructions in his will to provide for Hannah's clothing. But his heirs must have sold her shortly thereafter, for in 1785 John Lloyd purchased a slave woman named Hannah who was probably the same child. The terms of the purchase are typical of eighteenth-century New England slavery. Just as the society and the slave masters decreed that she was to be a slave "for her natural life" when she was only eight years old, so they continued to determine her status when she was a woman nearly fifty years old. Her bill of sale reads:

> I John Sloss Hobart . . . sold to the said John Lloyd a certain Negro Wench slave named Hannah about forty eight years of age . . . . I do hereby warrant and defend the said Hannah to the said John Lloyd as and for a Slave during her natural life. (*Lloyd Papers* 2:779)

The first slave mentioned in the *Lloyd Papers* is a female named Rose, whom Henry Lloyd hired out in 1687 to one of his tenants, Edward Higby, for the sum of "a pork barrel per annum." Higby was apparently pleased enough with the bargain that he released Lloyd from a prior commitment to include oxen and brush steers in the transaction (*Lloyd Papers* 1:105). As Rose would have been at least of working age at this time, she was possibly in her late thirties when Hammon was born some twenty-three years later. She probably arrived with Lloyd's first shipment of slaves from Barbados in June 1687. The Lloyds paid Shipmaster James Denham "20 hogshead Molasas . . . and 4 hogsheads 12 teauce rume" for the passage (*Lloyd Papers* 1:112). The purchase was slyly mentioned in Lloyd's entry, "To 40 barrells Oyle for Negros of my wife," and his receipt from "Henry Lloyd of Bristol . . . 1/3 part of Zebulen's Cargo" (*Lloyd Papers* 1:112–13). Rose was rented out the following year, on September 20, 1687.

A male slave, who was given the stigmatic name Opium and who appears most prominently in the *Lloyd Papers* for the next seventy years, was sold with cattle and other slaves through a "buy-back" provision for twenty-five pounds. In the three-month interim (June to September), the slaves were taken through a process of cultural and geographical indoctrination, tested for physical ability and domestic and commercial skill, and taken through a ritual very important to the eighteenth-century slave system—being outfitted in the cheapest appropriate clothing for the colder winter seasons. They were then appraised for salable value by a Mr. John Tutle of Tutle and Moore, Appraisers, along with, according to the *Lloyd Papers,* "eighty-eight head of cattle" (1:114–15).

Opium, the male bringing the highest price (twenty-five pounds), was sold along with Tomeo (sixteen pounds), Gym (twenty-two pounds), and Tony (twenty pounds). But Opium began a lifelong habit of resisting slavery, and the Lloyds had to repurchase him a few days later. He exhibited the same militancy when he attempted to escape from the Manor on horseback in the fall of 1691. Although he was subsequently captured, the exasperated owners had to hire trackers to recover both rider and horse (*Lloyd Papers* 1:144). When James Lloyd's estate was inventoried in 1693, Opium was the only slave mentioned among the meticulously tabulated "valuables." Said then to be worth thirty pounds, Opium was listed with the furniture, dressings, earthenware, and guns. He was the most valuable single item in the estate (*Lloyd Papers* 1:119–26). (Only ninety containers of salt at ninety pounds and one hundred twenty-two pounds of ready cash were of higher worth.)

Between 1695 and 1701, Opium was rented out to the partners Oliver and Brinley and to a Captain Willet at a fee increasing from five to seven pounds per year, bringing the Lloyds a total of fifty pounds cash. McKee used the exorbitant return on the Lloyds' original investment in Opium to illustrate the excessive profitability of slavery:

> Opium first appeared on the Lloyd account books in September 1687 in the form of a debit against Peter Sylvester of Shelter Island . . . . Slaves were sometimes sold on a trial basis and the next entry in the book notes the return of Opium. He was sold again the same year for 25 pounds . . . . Opium could not have stayed sold on that occasion either, for in an inventory of the estate of James Lloyd in 1693 his name appears with the appraised value of 30 pounds. (130–31)

McKee computed the total dollar amount that Opium's labor brought into the Lloyds' coffers: "The total received for him for the eight years was fifty pounds; not a bad return for a slave who in 1687 had been sold for 25 pounds" (131).

Between 1709 and 1710, Opium (the Lloyds by this time softened the spelling of his name to "Obium") is found with the next heir's father-in-law, John Nelson, in Boston. Nelson took Opium so that he could subdue the slave's rebellious tendencies. He wrote the Lloyds:

> Your negro Obium has been retarded partly by reason of the weather & partly for that I was willing that he should be returned to you reasonably cloathed & C he seems to be something unwilling to part with us, but it is in a manner the same familie I tell

him that upon his future good behaviour he may be assured of as
good treatment. He promises his best Endeavors for your Servise
& C. (*Lloyd Papers* 1:187)

In a postscript to the same letter, Nelson lists Opium's clothes
("a Great Coate, Double brested Jackett & a Coate, new and
all line, 2 pr cloth brithces; 5 Shirtes . . . 2 pr stockings") and
then instructs Henry Lloyd to manipulate the slave by pa-
tronizing him while guarding him carefully (1:188). Apparently
Nelson's stint of retraining had not been entirely successful:
"You know how to deal with him. by praiseing or speaking well
of him you may doe with him as you pleace Yett not trust him
too much" (1:188).

With that letter in hand, Opium was returned to Henry
Lloyd, who was at a temporary residence in Newport, Rhode
Island. A few months later Henry Lloyd returned to Oyster Bay
to assume his new status as lord of the manor, and the next year
Jupiter Hammon was born.[23] The *Lloyd Papers* show no further
record of Opium's being hired out. He appears in the Lloyds'
records again in 1732 when he was ill and in need of a doctor's
care (*Lloyd Papers* 1:341). He had been in the Lloyds' service
for forty-five years; considering his high value at the time of his
purchase, when he would have been in early maturity, Opium
must have been in his sixties at the time of this entry. Yet he
appears more than twenty years later, again receiving medical
care, but this time under the supervision of one Jupiter Hammon, whom I believe to be the son of Opium and Rose. In the
two-hundred-year record of Lloyd family affairs, only two
among scores of slaves were kept in continual service to the
family: Opium, for seventy years after his purchase, and Jupiter
Hammon, from birth to death, at least eighty years.

To understand Hammon's battle as a slave writing in the eighteenth century, one must first wrestle with Calvinism as a his-
toric and ever-present force in American society. Students of
Black American literature and theology, moreover, must constantly keep in mind the psychoreligious effects of Calvinism as

an inward dynamism within the mystique of white behavior in the context of American history and thought. In other words, it was no accident that slavery began in seventeenth-century America simultaneously with the birth and uprising of American Calvinism. The presence of one of these phenomena was simply, to some activists in the colonial arena, an authentication of the other.

Slavery was conducive to the Puritans' world view. As the most representative and the most dogmatic sect among American Calvinists, the Puritans held that slavery was a fit analogy of their relationship with God. God was for them a God of force, one who overtook the human mind and will for salvation and sanctification regardless of the subject's choice. In fact, Calvinists ardently believed that all mankind was so totally depraved that no one had enough human, or in this case, divine, goodness to accept God unless God did the initiating. The matter of man's lack of free will, or man as a preordained creature with a fate already prescribed by God, was, therefore, easily translatable to slavery. For those "elect" Anglicans and Puritans—both of Calvinist persuasion—who founded the American colonies, this prescribed fate, better known as predestination, was primary evidence only of their own selectivity. And that selectivity became a religion within itself, one that overrode all other aspects of Christianity and effused itself into the society which they created. Within this value system are the assumptions that God controls man in order to control his universe and that, as his faithful representatives in a Christian society, his chosen men must likewise enforce rules of order to prevent total chaos—a collapse which they feared that mankind without that control was uniquely capable of creating. For most Calvinists in Puritan society, the African—as Black, as savage, as heathen, as ignorant, as animal—represented the ultimate extreme of the "necessary" evil within that volatile chaos. But those attributes with which white colonists defined the African, and delineated him as among the nonelect, were also the very attributes which made Africans their ideal subjects for enslavement. Thus Calvinism, rather than having a basis of devotion to

God, was in fact used for the utilitarian and political control of man.

However, the Word—any word, whether sacred or secular—is an a priori subversive weapon. Turned loose to function on its own within the individual psyche, it is able to disavow the intentions of even those who would manipulate it. Thus even in the seventeenth and eighteenth centuries, the presence of the African and native Indian within the Puritan paradise was a test of the same Scriptural Word upon which the elect had built the perfect representation of God's society on earth. Jupiter Hammon was one of the testers of that Word, always applying it to the same society that purposed to use it to enslave him and his fellow Africans. Hammon knew the Bible well, and he wielded it with a force aimed at those who likewise purported to know it well, especially those who manipulated the Word to affect his enslavement.

Three seventeenth-century Calvinists, two of whom are well-known historical figures, made statements about slavery which can be said to represent the full range of sociopolitical considerations. The lesser-known John Saffin took the political position dominating contemporary thought: that Calvinism and Christianity condoned slavery because the African was incapable of being anything but a brute. He wrote, moreover, that it was un-Christian for a "true" churchman to believe any other Doctrine about the slave institution. At the opposite end of the spectrum was the towering Puritan, Samuel Sewall. He wrote that slavery was an ungodly evil, a curse on the society that would eventually bring down God's wrath. As Jupiter Hammon would do some years later, Sewall selected appropriate biblical allegories and allusions in order (1) to convince his God-fearing public that slavery was a sin of incalculable magnitude and (2) to effect its end.

While Sewall entered the debate in response to Cotton Mather's first pamphlet on slavery and because of the gnawing guilt in his own conscience about it (Towner 41), Saffin joined the fray because of his vested interest as a slave master. The latter evolved his position from the basis of experience and used the Bible as a convenient and socially approved reference to support that position. Saffin essentially attacked Sewall's thesis that American slavery was the same as biblically condemned man-stealing and moreover that it was analogous to the enslavement of the patriarch Joseph (Gen. 37:1–36). In arguing that his slave Adam had no right to freedom, Saffin made one of the most outrageously inhumane statements in American literature. His poem, entitled, "The Negroes Character" states:

Cowardly and cruel are those "Blacks" Innate,
Prone to Revenge, Imp of inveterate hate.
He that exasperates them, soon espies
Mischief and Murder in their very eyes.
Libidinous, Deceitful, False and Rude,
The Spume Issue of Ingratitude.
The Premises consider'd, all may tell,
How near good "Joseph"they are Parallel.

("Brief and candid"54)

Saffin knew that he was articulating the deeply held beliefs of most class-conscious Puritans when he argued that Sewall's call for abolition was against the dictates of God's order for society. He knew they would agree that if there were to be a princely class, then of necessity there must be servants. Thus, to maintain this order, God must even have ordained some men to be slaves.

The first antislavery tract printed in New England, Sewall's *Selling of Joseph,* was a refutation of the biblically based proslavery argument that would be heard continually in colonial American culture. Joseph was the beloved and favored son of Jacob, the Jewish patriarch. Ten of Joseph's brothers, jealous that he was their father's chosen one, sold their brother into slavery in Egypt and told Jacob that he was dead. Persisting in his faith in God for deliverance, and in spite of his enslaved condition, Joseph eventually became the prime minister of Egypt. However, Sewall said that the brothers, and any subsequent "owners" of Joseph, acted without legal or moral claim because "originally and naturally, there is no such thing as slavery. Joseph was rightfully no more a Slave to his Brethren, than they were to him: and they had no more Authority to Sell him, than they had to Slay him." Additionally, Sewall used Exod. 21:16 to equate American slavery to the biblical sin of men-stealing. Saffin objected to this argument on the spurious logic that he had purchased his slaves, not stolen them. Saffin never conceded that slaves should be evangelized precisely because he felt that they were "soulless" beasts without, as he emphasized, the character to know God. Thus he ignored Sewall's other refutation of current proslavery logic—namely, that slavery gave Africans an opportunity to hear the Gospel. To this argument Sewall countered: "Evil must not be done, that good may come of it. The extraordinary and comprehensive Benefit occurring to the Church of God, and to Joseph personally, did not rectify his brethren's Sale of him" (14).

Cotton Mather approached slavery ambiguously. First, he believed that it was a necessary support of the servant/master class system. But he confessed a Christian compunction to "save" the slave, rationalizing that, in fact, God had permitted African enslavement so that Blacks might hear the Gospel. Within Mather's ideal societal structure, the evangelized African was permissible and necessary, provided that the convert remained in the place that God had ordained for him in slavery. Mather tried to reconcile the polarities of his biblical beliefs and the comforts that his sanctioned economic system guaranteed the ruling class by publishing a plan of slave evangelism and socialization that would accomplish the oxymoronic task of freeing men in Christ while keeping them enslaved in the world. The first was a broadside, *Rules for the Society of Negroes,* published in 1693. Written in the first-person plural so that it could be recited by a group of slave "Christians," the nine "rules" provided for separate slave worship services "between the hours of seven and nine . . . that we may not be unseasonably absent from the families whereto we pertain" (6). Among other special restrictions proposed to keep slaves separate from, but still subject to, white Christians, Mather decreed that new slaves desiring to join church fellowship must be brought before the white minister "to be by Him examined, instructed and exhorted" and that "some wife and goodmen of the English in the neighborhood, and especially officers of the Church . . . look in upon us, and . . . do what they think fitting for us" (9). In instructions that set the example for Northern slave codes, Mather added a provision potentially devastating to those slaves who might obtain a yearning for freedom from the same Word intended to make them better slaves: "If any of them ('the other Negro-Servants in the Town') should run away from their masters, we will afford them no shelter: but we will do what in us lies, that they may be discovered, and punished" (8).

Mather issued his second tract, in part as a response to *The Selling of Joseph,* in 1706. But this time his thrust was not directed to Blacks but to "backsliding" slaveholders who thwarted evangelization among their slaves. Not calling for the slaves' equality or freedom, and again in agreement with slave codes, Mather promised slaveholders that baptism would not guarantee slaves their liberty but that the "laws of Christianity that allow slavery . . . wonderfully Dulcifies, and Mollifies, and Moderates the Circumstances of it" (67).

One of the reasons that Saffin's attack was so caustic and Mather's so conciliatory was that Sewall had used compelling biblical arguments to attack slavery. Thus his detractors had to marshal a strong defense. The issue for Saffin was not that he saw Sewall's antislavery commitment as "weak" but rather that their audience would be influenced by the "more relevant" issues of money and class. He thus had to go to an extreme, even fearing that Mather's enslave-but-evangelize ideal would weaken the class system. Sewall was standing on biblical interpretation that would upset the entire societal structure—a structure with which Saffin knew most Puritans, including Mather, did not want to tamper.

In all three positions, the Bible formed the basis of logical persuasion, thus solidifying the parameters of the slave debate at the turn of the eighteenth century. Therefore, those critics who say today that Hammon was too religious to address the issue of slavery must understand that in antebellum America the Bible functioned as the main instrument for slave proponents and abolitionists alike. The atmosphere of controversy articulated by Saffin, Sewall, and Mather regarding (1) the viability of a soulful presence within all men; (2) the possibility that Christ died for the redemption of all souls, rather than for a select few; and further about (3) the right then to enslave one's fellowman, even after he became one's brother in Christ—all pervaded colonial American culture.[24]

By the time of Hammon's birth, just five years after Mather's last volley, both the Congregational (Puritan) and Anglican (Church of England) denominations were committed to Calvinism in joint agreement. In practice and in spirit they were especially agreed on the issues of slavery and class hierarchy. However, while Mather may have suggested that Puritans Christianize their slaves, Anglicans were the ones who institutionalized that Christianization. They tried to accomplish that task through the Society for the Propagation of the Gospel in Foreign Parts (SPG), the missionary arm of the church. Hammon may have received his education from the SPG and a sense of master-class values from the Anglicans. He seems to have gotten his erudite understanding of the essential elements of Calvinism that impinged upon slavery (predestination, election, total depravity, and limited atonement) from the Puritans. But, Hammon undoubtedly obtained the solace of true Christian love and his intensely biblical vision of African freedom and equality from his very politically active Quaker neighbors.

The first Quaker meeting in America was established on Long Island, and the Quaker William Burling of Long Island published an early antislavery pamphlet in 1716. Even the great eighteenth-century Quaker abolitionist, John Woolman, exerting perhaps a very direct influence on Hammon's conversion, intellectual growth, and commitment to writing as a tool for emancipation, twice visited Oyster Bay. The Oyster Bay and Philadelphia Quakers simultaneously published Hammon's *Address to the Negroes in the State of New York* posthumously with a dedication indicating years of fond association.[25]

Several factors within Quaker belief and experience gave members of that denomination a particularly viable background

for empathy with the slave. Quakers had been severely perse-
cuted for their beliefs since the inception of the colonies. Their
community relations at the initial enclave in Oyster Bay were
no different. Trumbull's collection of early legal cases in New
England indicates that Quakers were beaten, imprisoned, and
banished from Long Island and that even non-Quakers who
befriended members of the sect, taking them into their homes
or arranging for their settlement in Oyster Bay and surrounding
communities, were likewise harassed (315–17). Thus, as pariahs, most Quakers, in offering sympathy to African slaves,
were simply reaching out to those who were likewise on the
margins of Puritan society. The Friends' nonhierarchical assemblies created opportunity and compatibility for the slaves' lowly
social state. Friends did not brook ascendant overseers or ministers and they did everything else possible to discourage hierarchy in their fellowship, including advocating unpretentious life-
styles and ordaining women in the ministry.

Ruchames says that Quakers attacked slavery on four major
fronts: (1) that slavery was a denial of the God-given right to
free will; (2) that it was disobedience to the primary biblical
commandment to "do unto others as you would have them do
unto you"; (3) that it was morally unjust before the courts of
God and men to enslave any human being; and (4) that the
African slave was equal to the white person in every capacity
and that any perceived shortcomings were not innate but derived from the effects of slavery (77–78). Many memorable and
forceful American Friends spoke out against slavery before the
mid-eighteenth century, including Burling, John Hepburn,
George Keith, Benjamin Lay, Robert Pile, and Ralph San-
difer;[26] but it was John Woolman who became the most effective catalyst for the antislavery movement in the Quaker fellowship. And it was Woolman who further ignited the Oyster Bay
congregation, an already fiery group that had been advocating
antislavery for years.

According to his *Journal,* Woolman visited the Oyster Bay
community three times with his antislavery crusade. A cadre of
Friends from other colonies and even from England ac-

companied him during his first tour which came to Oyster Bay in May, 1747 when Hammon was thirty-six years old and may have had some freedom to attend. Woolman describes what must have been a very stirring service:

> We reached the Yearly Meeting at Long Island, on which were our friends Samuel Nottingham from England, John Griffith, Jane Hoskins, and Elizabeth Hudson from Pennsylvania, and Jacob Andrews from Chesterfield, several of whom were favored in their public exercise . . . we had also a Meeting at Oyster Bay, in a dwelling house, *at which were many people* [italics added]. At the former there was not much said by way of testimony, but it was I believe a good meeting; at the latter, through the springing up of living waters, it was a day to be thankfully remembered. (*Journal of Life* 21–22)

Woolman visited Long Island twice more, in 1756 and in 1760. While Oyster Bay is not mentioned, he indicates that he visited the same meetings that he had reached on that first tour. Perhaps not coincidentally the honorable Quaker's last Long Island visit in 1760, thirteen years after the first one, was in the same year as Jupiter Hammon's first publication, a poem that was infused with a cry of equality and free will and God's love for all nationalities—all doctrinal positions which Hammon drew from his fellowship with the Quakers. No other denomination in colonial America up to that time advocated and demonstrated such an egalitarian Gospel.

Finally one other "religious" group—this one anti-Christian but certainly amorphous and pervasive within what white colonists believed was a "Christian" society—contributed a great deal to the eighteenth-century perspective of Blacks as a symbolically cursed entity in both earthly and eternal spheres. That "religious" speculation—having perhaps more immediate influence on the provincial view of African skin color than the unimaginative considerations of comparatively dull and far-removed theology—was indigenous witchcraft. Hammon knew that colonial suspicion of the African was rooted in deep-seated hatred and fear within white "Christian" consciousness. He knew moreover that the badgelike "evidence" which brought those nefarious instincts to the surface was primarily the African's skin color. For instance in *An Evening's Improvement* he says, "And we should pray that God would give us grace to love and to fear him, for if we love God, black as we be, and despised as we are, God will love us." And with an urgent plea he repeats that promise in *An Address to the Negroes in the State of New York*: "If we should ever get to Heaven, we shall find nobody to reproach us for being black, or for being slaves."

The slave was a reproach to colonial society, not just because Puritans found it convenient to divide the world and man's corporate and individual sins into simplistic images of Black and white, but more specifically, and pervasively, because the sensational testimony from the many New England trials presented "evidence" that the devil was a Black man. Again both Sewall and Mather were prominent figures in the best known of those trials; and, true to character, Sewall soon disavowed conclusions based on psychic testimony about ethereal states, finally admitting that such evidence was unprovable. He labeled the confessions of admitted workers of necromancy as weak bases for state executions. Presumably if one could not take a man's life on the validity of this testimony, one would have little cause to enslave him on the same grounds. But Mather continued to collect the testimony of condemned witnesses as an accurate and reliable source of information about Satan and his spiritual empire. Mather's publication of that testimony in works like *The Wonders of the Invisible World* was immeasurably damaging to those men and women whom he had earlier proposed to Christianize. As "proof" of his belief in a world of evil that was colored in dark hues, Mather reported the claim of a woman who admitted that she was "possessed," and who claimed to have "seen" Satan as a Black, spectral figure:

> There exhibited himself unto her a Divel having the Figure of A Short and a Black man; and it was remarkable that altho' shee had no sort of Acquaintance with Histories of what had happened elsewhere, to make any Impressions upon her Imagination, yett

the Divel that visited her was just of the same Statue, Feature, and complexion with what the Histories of the Witchcraft beyond-sea ascribe unto him; he was a wretch no taller than an ordinary Walking-Staff; hee was not of a Negro, but of a Tawney, or an Indian colour; hee wore an high-crowned Hat, with strait Hair; and had one Cloven-Foot. (Burr, *Narratives* 261)

Another trial judge, John Hale, said that one defendant, William Barker, confessed to "giving the Devil advantage over me appearing to me like a Black." Hale said that "this [Barker] had before explained to be like a Black man" (Burr, *Narratives* 420). Historian John Taylor, tracing the superstition from England to New England posits that whole communities in the colonies stayed in hysteria because the devil looked like a Black man in the pulpit.

Kittredge also speaks of the pervasiveness of colonial belief in witchcraft's "knowledgeable conclusions":

The belief in witchcraft was practically universal in the seventeenth century, even among the educated; with the mass of the people it was absolutely universal. To believe in witchcraft in the seventeenth century was no more discreditable to a man's head or heart than it was to believe in spontaneous generation or to be ignorant of the germ theory of disease. The position of the seventeenth-century believers in witchcraft was logically and theologically stronger than that of the few persons who rejected the current belief. (372)

The concept of Satan as a Black male was compatible with every scheme of causality within religious and scientific spheres in the eighteenth century. Whether the image was the sociopolitical Chain of Being, or the evolutionary Linnean–Jeffersonian theory of the African as the link between man and nature, or the Calvinists' classification of the Black man as the ultimate symbol of depravity, Blacks were held to be farthest away from God, from "light," from perceptions of absolute truth and educable genius and closest to bestiality, ignorance, and evil. Again few colonists, Robert Calef being the notable exception, challenged Mather's assumptions or publicly made the connection between this witchcraft testimony and African enslavement. Calef said that neither slaves nor witchcraft workers were under Satan's control so much as Cotton Mather himself:

> If any Person pretends to know more than can be known by humane means, and professeth at the same time that they have it from the Black-Man, i.e. the Devil, and shall from hence give Testimony against the Lives of others, they are manifestly such as have a familiar Spirit; and if any, knowing them to have their Information from the Black-Man, shall be inquisitive of them for their Testimony against others, they therein are dealing with such as have a Familiar-Spirit. (Burr, *Narratives* 392)

Calef's *More Wonders of the Invisible World* also aptly illustrates the prevalence of witchcraft testimony in colonial life and the stigma which these reports placed on colonial perceptions of Black skin:

> And that the Devil exhibiting himself ordinarily as a black-Man [298] . . . Know then that this remarkable Indian being a little before he Died at work in the Wood making of Tarr, there appeared unto him a Black-Man, of Terrible aspect and more than humane Dimensions, threatning bitterly to kill him if he would not promise to leave off Preaching as he did to his Coun-trey-Men . . . [399], wherein some scores of Miserable People were Troubled by horrible appearances of a Black-Man, accom-panied with Spectres, wearing these and those Humane Shapes [400] . . . Sometimes, but not always, together with the Spectures there look't in upon the Young Woman (according to her ac-count) a short and a Black Man, whom they call'd their Master, a Wight exactly of the same Dimensions and Complexion and voice, with the Divel that has exhibited himself unto other in-fested People, not only in other parts of this Country. [312][27]

Such was the cultural atmosphere of religion, superstition, and fear in the life and times of Jupiter Hammon. And it was in this almost totally dismal communal vortex that Hammon presented the first literary offerings of an African born and reared in the American colonies. As a slave himself, Hammon attacked slav-ery at its jugular vein—the world of the Bible and of the spirit.

He then translated that attack onto the vital fulcrum of the printed page—no mean feat for a slave who was supposedly preordained to failure, inferiority, and perdition.

An entry in the Lloyds' account books indicates that Hammon was alive in 1790. But, based on eulogistic language in a Quaker reprint of *An Address to the Negroes in the State of New York,* he had died by 1806. As yet, the exact date of his death and place of burial have not been determined.[28] Undoubtedly, critics who read Hammon's canon and assert that he had no regard for slavery are either ill-informed about biblical typology or are even less cognizant of a victim's constraints in an oppressive society when that victim tries to write about and disseminate information on the slave experience. In his prose, Hammon urged Blacks to learn to read and then to read the Bible for themselves because only then could they understand his coded messages about their enslavement. His topics were not so veiled, however, that knowledgeable whites in his more biblically conscious society would have missed them. In haste to apply to Hammon's works, twentieth-century expectations of protests and a critical veneer drawn from the same basic philosophies which enslaved him, modern culturalists have clearly misunderstood his codes, his themes, and his commitment to Black American freedom. Continuing reevaluation of his life and work using not only that biblical code but other contemporary frameworks will undoubtedly enhance modern views of his prominence as the founder of African-American literature.

Notes

1. Lay's *Am I Not* contains comments by numerous abolitionists and ex-slaves on the hypocrisy of white slaveholders who saw in Christianity a means to justify, rather than condemn, slavery. See especially in this volume remarks made by Phillis Wheatley (306–8). Refer also to Agate, 611–12 in Hastings; discussions by Litwack; and K. Miller, *Race Adjustment.*

2. The very color black carried deprecatory connotations in seventeenth- and eighteenth-century New England. Spawning from this atti-

tude were perceptions that Black people were as beasts—void of souls, incapable of forming permanent familial ties, and stunted in artistic and intellectual potential. For additional commentary, refer to Baltazar 5–53, 149–65; Berwanger 266–75; Burr *Narratives* 285–86, 308–12; Clarkson 213–20; Dunston 3–13; Jordan, *Negro vs. Equality* 44–49; Jordan, *White Man's* 4–25, 106–10; C. Mather, *On Witchcraft*, 70–71.

3. Other historians or critics who view Hammon's work as minor or nonrepresentative of the protest tradition in Black American literature include Brawley, *Early Negro Writers* 21–22; *Negro in Literature* 12–14; Higginbotham 140–41; Palmer; and Robinson, *Early Black*.

4. For more on slaves' adaptation of biblical texts and the English language itself in chants and spirituals, see studies by Fisher; Floyd; Katz; Mays (particularly 19–23); Southern; and Thurman. Additional critics who comment favorably on Hammon's works are Costanzo; Jahn; and Porter.

5. Other studies of colonial Long Island include Dodd; Gabriel; Mabee; McKee; E. V. Morgan; Olson; Overton; Pasco; Prime; and Thompson.

6. On the African's transition from citizenship to slavery Jordan contends:

> Yet the first clearly indicated status of any Negroes was freedom, in the 1640's; indeed it remains possible that some Negroes were not slaves in New Netherland until the 1650's. In 1650 two sparring pamphleteers disagreed as to whether some Negroes were actually slaves. Within a very few years, though, the records show indisputably that certain colonists were actively interested in the African slave trade . . . . During the remaining years of the century Negro slavery flourished, and New York eventually came to have a higher proportion of Negroes than any other colony north of Delaware. In New York more than anywhere else, negro slavery seems to have grown Topsy fashion. (*White over Black,* 83–84)

E. J. McManus (*History*) concurs with Jordan's findings and adds that during the transition period a system of "half-freedom" was instituted because there was such an increased demand for slave labor. "This system was introduced into New Netherland by the West India Company as a means of rewarding slaves for long or meritorious service" (13). The "half-freed" men were given passes to enable them to enjoy a type of annual furlough. Moreover the system allowed the Dutch to avoid immediate institution of chattel slavery (8–22).

7. See also Anstey; Burleigh; Greene, "Slave-Holding." McManus concludes that unprofitability was really the impetus for the end of slavery in the New England colonies.

8. Although Hurd says that the slave code actually began in the 1650's (1:270), most historians agree that these particular laws applied more to Native Americans than Blacks.

9. For other sources for slave laws about regulating every activity from congregating and cursing to owning land, see George Fox's essay in Twombly and Moore 232–61; Higginbotham 119; and McKee 100–102. For other discussions on the extent and cruelty of slave punishments, see Greene, *The Negro* 100–153; Hurd 1:270, 272, 293; and Trumbull 67–69, 89–91, 276–78, and 293–95.

10. Many texts detail laws enacted by the colonies assuring the slaves that their baptism would not concomitantly result in their freedom. See Greene, *The Negro* 259–75, and "Slave-Holding," 505–10; C. Mather's *Negro Christianized* in Ruchames, 66–68; and E. J. McManus, *History,* 19–21.

11. More discussion on the repercussions of slave conspiracies include T. J. Davis; Greene, *The Negro;* Kobrin; McLeod; E. J. McManus, *History* and *Black Bondage;* and Quarles, *The Negro.*

12. Aptheker, *American Negro;* Greene (both entries); E. J. McManus, *History* and *Black Bondage;* Quarles, *The Negro;* and Riddell give further background on slave revolts in New York State.

13. Similarly, Greene reports a whole series of executions of Black men because—probably for want of available African women—they crossed the color line to mate with white women (Greene, *The Negro* 156–65). For more on miscegenation laws in Massachusetts, see Moore 208. James Forten, in his "Address to the Inhabitants of Philadelphia against the Colonization Society," implies that even those Northern abolitionists who condemned slavery opposed interracial couples (Ducas 56–62).

14. Numerous studies have been done on the victimization of slaves, particularly those elderly men and women whose masters, finding no further economic advantage in their use, have turned them out to fend for themselves. Refer to Higginbotham 123, 129; Kobrin 15; and Olson, 77.

15. For more on the status of free Blacks, see Dumond 119–25; Greene, *The Negro* 165–66, 290–333; Hurd 1:284; Jernegan, *Laboring* 134–37; McLeod, 152; E. J. McManus, *History* 162–65; and Woodson, *The Mind* 115.

16. Indeed, in the eighteenth–century world view, based on the Great Chain of Being, humanity was a hierarchical configuration in which the white male, like a parent to his child, exerted a decisive

sway over the lives of the Blacks who to him were his inferiors. Refer to Craig 1–32; Jordan, *White over Black* 482–511; Jordan, *White Man's* 194–204; A. O. Lovejoy 183.

17.   The truth about slavery in the North is one of the best-kept secrets in American history and one which needs further contemporary study. See Berlin and Hoffman; Bolt and Drescher; Bragg; Burleigh; H. S. Cooley; Franklin; Greene (both words); Jernegan, *Laboring;* Litwack; McKee; McLeod; E. J. McManus, *History* and *Black Bondage;* Mabee; MacEacheren; Matlack; Olson; Riddell; Saffin, "A Brief and Candid Answer"; Sewall; Woodson, *The Negro;* and Zilversmit.

18.   For more on the slave trade and its commercial route, see Anstey; Aykroyd; Curtin; D. B. Davis; Jordan, *White over Black;* Locke; and Rawley.

19.   See Bailey; Greene (all works); Jernegan, *Laboring; Lloyd Papers;* McKee; E. J. McManus, *Black Bondage* and *History*.

20.   Bailey continues:

> A further confirmatory grant from Governor Dongan of New York, on March 18, 1685, erected the Neck into "the Lordship and Manor of Queens Village," with Power to him and his heirs to hold Court Leet for the trial of causes, and with provision for choosing assessors within the manor according to rules prescribed for townships in the Province. To the royal government, the manors were stabilizing centers—for military defense and for safeguards against the leveling ideas of New Englanders. (27)

In her "Introduction to Lloyd Papers," Dorothy Barck agrees that the Manor was a fortified, self-sustaining outpost for Her Majesty's interest:

> Henry Lloyd and his successors lived with their slaves and tenants on the Manor, which, as regards the necessities of life, was a self-sufficient community, raising wheat, rye, and corn; vegetables and fruits; cattle, sheep, swine, and horses. The trees on the Neck were recognized as its chief source of wealth, and cord wood and timber were cut sparingly and with care not to detract from future profits. The Lloyds were good agriculturalists, actively concerned in grafting fruit trees, improving the breeds of their horses and cattle, and in conserving and enriching the soil by rotation of crops and the use of fertilizers. (*Lloyd Papers* 1:xi)

21.   Greene reports:

> Negroes who had spent some time in the West Indies, or in the
> South, seem to have been found preferable to the "raw," turbu-
> lent Negroes brought directly from Africa. To New England buy-
> ers they possessed advantages over the natives, for often they had
> been "seasoned"; that is, they had become acclimated, were
> more accustomed to regular labor, could speak some English
> and, to some degree, were familiar with Occidental customs.
> (*The Negro* 36)

The Lloyds were apparently typical New York slave traders. In his
Atlantic Slave Trade, Philip D. Curtin says that in a half century of
slave commerce, although businessmen in New York and New Jersey
imported over 4,500 slaves, only 930 were African born: "The rest
were West Indians and even the African-born may have lived for a
time in the Caribbean colonies" (143). (This was of course quite
different from the practice of the Southern colonies, which imported a
high percentage of their slaves directly from Africa, hundreds at a
time.) E. J. McManus concurs: "During the period from 1701 to 1726,
1,570 slaves were imported from the West Indies and 802 from Africa"
(24). Nor was it unusual for Lloyd to include slaves as part of his retail
merchandise. So many "retail merchants acted as slave brokers as a
sideline" that the services of these merchants were "indispensable in
channeling slave labor into productive uses" (E. J. McManus, *History*
31). Without them, neither the trade nor the slave system itself would
have functioned very efficiently" (E. J. McManus, *History* 31–32).

22.   E. J. McManus writes:

> Because of emphasis on skilled labor, the English traders, like
> the Dutch, concentrated on West Indian imports. During the
> first half of the eighteenth century, thousands of slaves were
> transported to New York from Barbados and Jamaica. (*History*
> 28)

See also Aykroyd.

23.   Ransom; Robinson, *Early Black;* Wegelin; and others esti-
mated Hammon to have been born around 1720. However, Lillian
Koppel discovered Hammon's birthdate in the back of a Lloyd ledger,
which said he was born on October 17, 1711. See Ransom 10.

24.   Winthrop Jordan summarizes tensions that had to be reconciled within a Christian nation:

The obligation of English Christians to convert Indians and Negroes was as obvious and undeniable in the eighteenth century as
it had been two hundred years earlier. Yet many of the Englishmen who had settled in America proved reluctant or downright
unwilling to meet this obligation. In part their failure was owing
to practical considerations arising from the necessities of plantation management. (*White over Black,* 80)

25.   For more on Burling and the Long Island Quaker experience,
see Lay; Garrison; Twynham; and Worrall. For information on Woolman's travels, see his journal and essays; Peare; and Whitney (both
texts). Ransom's edition lists all the cosigners of the second printing of
the *Address to the Negros* and identifies the Philadelphia group as
Quakers. The Long Island historical society identified the signers as
eighteenth-century Quakers during my interview at a recent Long
Island Studies Conference.

26.   There is little in current scholarship on the American Quaker's
style of worship or doctrinal beliefs, but there is much on their settlement and history in the colonies and on the abolition movement that
swelled within their ranks until they became the foremost antislavery
force in America. For more on these early Quaker abolitionists, see
Aptheker, "The Quakers," and "They Began"; Bolt and Drescher;
D. B. Davis; Drake; Flint; Frost; Garrison; Berlin and Hoffman; R.
M. Jones, *George Fox* and *The Quakers;* Moulton; Peare; Twynham;
Whitney, *John Woolman;* Worrall; and Zilversmit.

27.   In addition to the works cited, for study on Northern witchcraft in eighteenth-century society, see Levin; MacFarland; C.
Mather, *On Witchcraft;* and Rudwin.

28.   During that recent Long Island Studies Conference, local Long
Islanders graciously took me on a tour of the Lloyd estate, now a
historical site. I, like Wegelin (see Ransom 21–29), was saddened that
I could find no trace of Hammon's burial place or of any other slave
who had served the Lloyd family. Perhaps the Lloyd's Neck community had a separate place for the burial of Black people, a typical
practice in slavery times. However, the location of that site has not
been established.

1. An Evening Thought: Salvation by Christ, with Penitential Cries

Introduction: The Birth of
Black Literature and Theology

The essential theme of Hammon's first poem, "An Evening Thought: Salvation by Christ, with Penitential Cries," is prayer. In any urgent petition such as this one, the petitioner starts with the most crucial needs in the human condition—needs which may not be primarily spiritual. In interceding to God and addressing man in this poem, Hammon therefore has one thought in mind and that is slavery—his own enslavement and that of all Africans in the diaspora. Twentieth-century critics have not recognized this focal point because it is stealthily couched in biblical language, and readers in this age are less aware of biblical meaning. Hammon's contemporary readers understood him, however, and although he was a slave, they allowed him the latitude to protest his enslavement precisely because he used that biblical rhetoric.

For instance, for dispossessed Africans overtaken by the fervor of the Great Awakening, the concept of salvation was all inclusive. Blacks perceived that whites had constructed a colonial hierarchy based on the colonists' insistence that they were the special recipients of the grace and election of God. For American slaves, the concept of salvation was not merely a spiritual one. It included the sincerest yearnings to seek God for all of life's problems, especially the incessant, oppressive confinement of slavery.

In eighteenth-century theological definitions, the meaning of "salvation" was related to the title of Christ as Savior and to that act of redemption whereby a person was "saved" from sin and Satan. "Savior" is the title for the Old Testament Jehovah, who delivered the Children of Israel from bondage in Egypt. Biblical examples include Ps. 106:21: "They forgot God their saviour, which had done great things in Egypt"; Isa. 43:3: "For I am the Lord thy God, the Holy One of Israel, thy Saviour"; Isa. 45:15: "Verily thou art a God that hidest thyself, O God of Israel, the Saviour." The name "Jesus" is a New Testament derivative of Joshua, who was another Old Testament hero central in Israel's emancipation. Eighteenth-century readers were quite knowledgeable about Old Testament personages. They understood that the bundle of ideas inculcated in the term "salvation" implied deliverance from slavery in contemporary homiletics.[1] Thus it was impossible for a slave, writing the first literary expression by an African-American, to have penned the term "salvation" without having slavery—his own ubiquitous crucible and that of African fellows—utmost in mind.

For the colonial evangelical clergyman, salvation was effected at that vortex of spiritual vision when one grasped for Christ as the One Absolute God and Savior who could intervene in every earthly circumstance. As a shepherd-priest, the poem's speaker first asks God to give those who read the poem this necessary vision. Then the speaker admonishes his audience to repent. And next he turns to God with pleas that he mercifully accept that repentance. Thus, the persona fulfills the true functions of a pastor-priest who represents God before men, and conversely, men before God. The speaker maintains these purposes until stanza 16 when God intervenes and speaks to man himself with a convocation based on Isa. 55:1:

> Ho! every one that hunger hath,
>   Or pineth after me,
> Salvation be thy leading Staff,
>   To set the Sinner free.

The phrase "redemption now to every one" is another central refrain of the poem because it expresses the relationship of new contemporary theological thinking (or, as some colonial preachers were calling it, errant theology) to the social practice of slavery. A basic premise of Calvinism—the predominate theological system of the era and the one from which the social mores of slavery in a "Christian" society were derived—was that Christ's atonement was limited, that He died for only that group of people whom God, His Father, had selected for salvation and that all others were doomed to a dismal eternity. This attitude of superior selectivity was a religiously psychological dynamism for the formation of the colonies and was subsequently the "biblical" foundation used to support the enslavement of "unchosen" Blacks.

However, in this his first poem, and as a dominant theme in all of this writing, Hammon is challenging the idea of racial and individual selectiveness. While his work is in some instances influenced by mainstream Calvinism, he seems to have worked out his own brand of Arminianism—namely, that Christ's redemption is available to all who will love and obey Him. The idea that man, and not God, makes the choice about man's eternal status is, of course, Arminian or Methodist doctrine. However, this branch of Protestantism did not come to America until well after Hammon began to formulate and write his doctrinal conclusions. His stance was simply much more compatible with the needs of the disenfranchised and ostracized Africans in American society.

Of equal importance to the concept of "salvation" in the poem's explication is the set of assumptions accompanying religious and social use of the term "redemption" in the eighteenth century. "Redemption" related even more to implications of slavery and emancipation than "salvation." Old Testament Jews called Jehovah the "Great Redeemer" because he "bought" them back from slavery. Some biblical examples of the term as relating to slavery include Exod. 6:6: "I am the Lord, and I will bring you out from under the burdens of the Egyptians . . . and I will redeem you"; Exodus 15:13: "[Jehovah] in thy mercy hast redeemed"; and Ps. 106:10: "And [Jehovah] saved them from the hand of him that hated them, and redeemed them from the hand of the enemy." Later, when forming the tribes into a cohesive community, the patriarch Moses enjoined that if any Hebrew were sold into slavery because of his debts, his blood relatives had the obligation to redeem him:

> And if a sojourner or stranger wax rich by thee, and thy brother that dwelleth by him wax poor, and sell himself unto the stranger or sojourner by thee, or to the stock of the stranger's family: After that he is sold he may be redeemed again: one of his brethren may redeem him: Either his uncle, or his uncle's son, may redeem him or any that is nigh of kin unto him of his family may redeem him; or if he is able, he may redeem himself. (Lev. 25:47–49)[2]

Likewise when Venture Smith, an ex-slave who had spent most of his life in either Long Island or Stonington, Connecticut, published his narrative in 1798 at the age of sixty-nine, he constantly spoke of buying his freedom and that of his wife and children in the language of redemption:

> As Miner [one of Smith's owners in Stonington] did not appear to redeem me I went, and called at my old master Stanton's first to see my wife, who was then owned by him . . . . I never had an opportunity to redeem myself whilst I was owned by Miner . . . . By cultivating this land with the greatest diligence and economy, at times when my master did not require my labor, in two years I laid up ten pounds. This my friend tendered my master for myself. . . . Being encouraged by the success which I had met in redeeming myself, I again solicited my master for a further change of completing it . . . . This left only thirteen pounds eighteen shillings to make up the full sum for my redemption. During my residence at Long Island, I raised one year with another, ten cart loads of watermelons . . . . Various others methods I pursued in order to enable me to redeem my family. (Porter 551–55)

In their exegeses, eighteenth-century theologians were true to the traditional definitions of "redeem" in the Old Testament. In his sermon on 1 Tim. 1:15 ("This is a faithful saying, and worthy of all acceptation, that Christ Jesus came into the world to save sinners of whom I am chief"), the Reverend Daniel

Veysie, an eighteenth-century British minister (British writers provided the overwhelming majority of the reading materials for colonists), delivers a definition of "redemption" reminiscent of its old application in Hebrew law:

> A *Price,* in the common acceptation of the word, is something given in exchange for some other thing: and this price becomes a *ransom,* when it is given for the deliverance of a person who is in a state of bondage or captivity; and the deliverance thus obtained is properly called *redemption.* For redemption, in the original and proper meaning, is somewhat more than mere deliverance; it is a *purchased* deliverance—a deliverance effected by the payment of a stipulated price; which price, as above stated, is properly called a *ransom.* (Veysie 43–44)

Similarly, in a sermon on God's redeeming mercy, another noted preacher of the time, Samuel Davies, cites the Old Testament connotation of "redeem" in a discussion of the word's relevance to Christ and New Testament works:

> Thus you see that taking the word Redemption in a lax improper sense, as signifying deliverance, though without a price, that we may be said to be bought or redeemed by Jesus Christ. But if we take the word in a strict and proper sense, it signifies a particular kind of deliverance; namely, by the payment of a price. . . . Now a ransom is a price paid to redeem a thing that was forfeited, or a person that was held in captivity and slavery. So to redeem an estate, is to pay a price equivalent to it, and so to recover it. To redeem a prisoner or captive, is to lay down a price as an equivalent for his liberty. (Sermon 31, "Dedication to God Argued from Redeeming Mercy" 2:82)

Hammon uses the terms "redemption," "Redeemer," or "redeemed" in each one of his works. His immediate audience knew exactly what he meant because the term was used interchangeably in a religious sense, and, in the eighteenth-century work force, to establish work agreements between employers and employees particularly for the white indentured-servant class, referred to as "redemptioneers." While a relatively few lower-class Anglo-European redemptioneers were kidnapped for the Atlantic passage, most willingly sold themselves into slavery in order to pay their fares. The purchaser then became part of the financial arrangement between the worker and the captain, and often, when a colonist took over the travel bill, he became known as the worker's redeemer. When the worker's labor had accrued to pay the bill in full, the worker was said to have been redeemed. Thus, when Hammon told the slaves that Christ was "Our Great and Mighty Redeemer," his audience understood that he was ascribing to Christ both the will and the ability to free them from slavery. That these semislaves would be freed after seven years of service because their skin was white, while the African had to remain a slave for perpetuity because his skin was black, must have been a sore boil to Hammon and his fellow slaves. Because the term was so familiar in the society, Hammon therefore knew that his readers— both Black and white—understood that he was speaking of earthly, as well as of heavenly, redemption.[3]

The overriding issue was color—the African's skin color and its supposed connotations of evil. As the first African to publish in America, Hammon thus wrestled with intuitive racial overtones within the English language. Like his contemporary, Phillis Wheatley, he could refer to "our dark benighted Souls" (stanza 12) as a description of spiritual death without any regard to the color of the bodies that encased those souls. He knew that in the Bible light and dark referred to the essence of man's spiritual enlightenment, or the lack thereof, not to his physiological hue. His use of the language is metaphorically, not racially, based. His symbolism is no different from that of Dante or Saint John of the Cross who also speak of "the dark night of the soul." Nevertheless, because of the power of the spoken word to create and enforce authority, Hammon knew of the difficult and ironic overtones present when one who is Black, a writer, and a slave uses such color delineations. Thus in his essay, *An Evening's Improvement,* he was able to write that "if we love God, black as we be, and despised as we are, God will love us."

Another one of the poet's recurrent themes steeped in contemporary societal and theological meaning was appropriate nomenclature—assigning a name for God and a name for man. In his dramatic poetry, Hammon has a fictive slaveholder refer to Christ as Master or King, while the corresponding African calls Christ Savior, Redeemer, Servant or, more importantly, Slave. As an example, in the eighth stanza of this poem Hammon, speaking to his slave audience, refers to Christ as "thy captive Slave." His purpose is to identify Jesus with American slaves and to make slaves aware that Christ assumed the most humble position among men in order to effect their salvation.

Hammon's reference to Christ as "thy captive Slave" is taken from Mark's Gospel wherein Christ is presented as Servant to God and to man. A contemporary text, Brown's *Dictionary,* lists the Chief of God's Servants as "Christ who, in obedience to His will, assumed our nature . . . and administers the blessings of the covenant to us" (11). Hammon knew that his Christian era accepted such definitions as standard and that his readers likewise recognized Scriptures like Matt. 23:11: "But he that is greatest among you shall be your servant." The poet enforces his premise that the lowly Jesus would have been more at home with the Black colonial slave than with the white puritanical slave owner.[4]

If the name of God was important to the slave, the name of the slave was certainly important to the eighteenth-century ruling class. Whites in America were very much aware of the power inherent in naming, and they routinely gave slaves names that often implied a pagan or unsaved status. Thus, when he was born to slave parents in America, the poet was named Jupiter after the Roman god and Hammon, a name that was undoubtedly an extension of Noah's fallen son Ham. It was also a derivative of the name of a pagan king, Ammon, found in the Old Testament.[5]

Another early Black American writer, Olaudah Equiano, stresses that slaves must be aware of white society's intent in naming Africans. In his autobiography, Equiano suggests that he was well aware of the psychological attack that was inherent in his captors' insistence upon renaming him. Equiano explains that if his African name had to be discarded he would have preferred a Christian one, as this had more positive connotations in his new surroundings, but the idea was rejected:

> While I was on board this ship, my captain and master named me *Gustavas Vassa*. I at that time began to understand him a little, and refused to be called so, and told him as well as I could that I would be called Jacob; but he said that I should not, and still called me Gustavas: and when I refused to answer to my new name, which at first I did, it gained me many a cuff; so at length I submitted and was obligated to bear the present name, by which I have been known ever since. (P. Edwards, *Travels* 35–36)

Similarly, in his *All Slave-Keepers . . . Apostates* (1737), Benjamin Lay deems those who would traffic in human bodies, systematically shucking these souls of every vestige of their own cultures, to be "Hellish Miscreants," robbing Blacks not only of their identities, as the renaming implies, but also of their souls (Lay 55).[6]

Hammon's emphasis detracts from the idea of a nation or race favored by God. His vision included a spiritual egalitarianism that reached to all the peoples of the world.[7] He knew that America, because of its diversity of races, had the unique opportunity to exhibit that oneness in the Body of Christ. Samson Occom, the renowned Native American evangelist, also lived on Long Island where he converted Montauks to Christianity. Undoubtedly Hammon had heard of his ministry; he perhaps even knew him. Additionally, Hammon observed the hundreds of European immigrants who joined the Englishmen in the New York colony as the melting pot of nations began. He knew that unless slavery was eradicated, the integrated Christian society that he believed the Bible offered to "every one" of "every nation" of "all the world" would be a failure.

Although concerned with racial division and class and color discrimination within the church, Hammon seldom overtly makes Christian love a central homiletic or artistic theme. But in this poem ("Salvation doth increase our Love"), he makes an exception. Evoking biblical themes about united Christian fellowship, he voices a evangelical premise that the Godhead cannot come to the earth in its purest essence unless there is love and harmony among Christians. However, within the context of other thematic statements in this work, he is no doubt implying that professing whites, who insisted upon slavery as a necessary economic support, did not experience true salvation because their love was not "increased."[8]

Hammon's continual emphasis on the availability of salvation for "every nation" is, however, like his use of "Ethiopian" as an alternative ethnic distinction, an urgent cry for the inclusion of African-Americans into full, free, and equal Christian fellowship. This plodding not only belies the Western religious psyche's rigid and almost ritualistic tribal separation, it sprang from the poet's longing for a universal, multiracial Church, both in a mystical union and in local assemblies. Such urging undermined the colonial practice of making Blacks substandard Christians in church membership, in communion, and even in baptism.

Before the arrival of the African, baptism meant equality for all Christian males—extension of the rights to vote, to own property, and to testify at trials. However, by the late 1600's and early 1700's, colonists in New England and the South issued pronouncements notifying their slaves that baptism would by no means result in manumission. In statute after statute the proponents of slavery indicated that they would not allow baptized African Christians any easier road to freedom than uninitiated tribesmen newly arrived in the slave ship's hold. Historians Hurd and Higginbotham cite examples:

[New York statute from 1706:] Be it Enacted by the Governor, Council and Assembly and it is hereby Enacted by the authority of the same, That the Baptizing of any Negro, Indian or Mulatto Slave shall not be any Cause or reason for the setting them or any of them at Liberty. (Higginbotham 127)

[Maryland statute from 1664:] Where any negro or slave, being in servitude or bondage, is or shall become Christian, and receive the sacrament of baptism, the same shall not or ought to be deemed, adjudged or construed to be a manumission or freeing of any such negro or slave, or his or her issue, from their servitude or bondage, but that notwithstanding they shall at all times here-

after be and remain in servitude or bondage as they were before
baptism, any opinion, matter or thing to the contrary notwithstanding. (Hurd 250)[9]

Like many of his white counterparts, Jupiter Hammon, the
slave and occasional preacher, usually preached conservative
theology. When he writes in stanza 1, "Salvation comes by
Jesus Christ alone," he is alluding to one of many heresies that
had crept into New England churches. His close friends, the
Quakers, interpreted salvation as attainable from a divine Inner
Light, universally available to all people.[10] While the orthodox
Puritan, Congregational, and Anglican churches rejected such
quasi-deism, they did entertain the idea that Christian parents
would automatically procreate Christian children. Further,
even in the fervor of the emotional revivals which swept
through the colonies, many still held that church membership or
elite citizenry in a Christian community remained requisite to
salvation.[11] Hammon could not lean toward the Quaker theology of divine Light as sole evidence of Christian experience
because it did not fit his interpretation of the Scriptures. Nor
could he espouse the assumptions concerning predestination
that some in the orthodox camp proclaimed. Knowing that in
social practice Blacks could not qualify for either prerequisite,
the aged writer had no choice but to insist upon the simplest
interpretation—"salvation comes by Jesus Christ alone."

Also central to eighteenth-century Calvinist dogma was the
concept of limited atonement; that is, that Christ's death would
atone for the sins of only a few elect mortals whom God had
preordained to be saved. Inherent in this dogma was the implication that men needed more than God's grace to be saved, and
that they could not receive this grace without divine impetus, or
preselection, to direct them toward it.[12] But in this poem Hammon argues that "The World Redemption have." In other
words, he is shouting, Christ's atonement was not limited and
God's preordination was not necessary. Salvation had been
purchased for everyone. Not only Hammon but also other contemporary Christians saw the dangers for a manipulation of

race and class exclusivity, within secular spheres, in the "salvation only for the elect" doctrine.

In his *Humble Attempt to Reconcile the Differences of Christians Respecting the Extent of the Atonement,* Edward D. Griffin
proposes that the argument of limited or unlimited atonement,
which had greatly divided the Protestant world, is a confusion
of semantics over the terms "believer" and "elect," and that it
arises from a muddling of literal and figurative scriptural language. Griffin clearly saw that the assumption that Christ died
only for the "elect" could easily lead to very racist theology. He
argued that predestinarians saw Christ's friends as the elect
sheep (again, an example of the color-white imagery) and that
"they reason about the sheep and goats as though these terms
denoted the elect and non-elect" (312–23). Griffin challenged
predestinarians: "In the same way they make the seed of the
serpent to mean the non-elect, and argue that the seed of the
woman would not die for the seed of the serpent" (313). Then
he addresses one of the central pinions of racism and slavery in
colonial life:

> Had [the atonement] been for white men and not for black men,
> or for men and not for women, you might have said of the
> Ethiopian that it was not for him, or of this female that it was not
> for her. . . . Had the atonement not been for black men or for
> women, you might have said that it was not for those who were
> foreordained to that complexion or sex; that is you might have
> affirmed the same thing of them as appointed to such a distinc-
> tion, because in the appointment and the possession they are
> equally passive. (311)

Jupiter Hammon would, of course, agree, but he did not have
the freedom to make his point so overtly. He had to cloak his
definitions of salvation and atonement within a poetic and symbolic framework.

When Hammon wrote "Dear Jesus by thy precious Blood,"
however, he did agree with most eighteenth-century Protestants
that the sacrificial death of Christ was efficacious; that is, that
in his single death Christ was the substitutionary sacrifice for

each individual who believed in him.[13] Thus, "An Evening Thought," as the first offering in Black American literature, had an instant appeal to mainstream Protestantism while simultaneously making a statement which Black slaves could understand and find hope in—without wading through a quagmire of theological debate.

Throughout his writing, Hammon makes a distinction between individual and corporate sins. He implies that Christ's death on the Cross enables all men to obtain forgiveness for those sins for which they bear a personal responsibility as well as for those sins which they inherit. However, concomitant with his mention of Christ's atonement for man's sins, in this poem (and in his essays *A Winter Piece* and *An Evening's Improvement*) is the underlying suggestion that slaveholders cannot use racial selectivity in calling themselves elect and Blacks condemned. Whites, on the one hand, accept atonement for their personal and inherited (or corporate racial) sins and, on the other hand, cite the Cain/Ham curse, which Blacks supposedly inherited, as justification for enslaving Africans. Either Christ's sacrifice was sufficient to erase all individual or corporate sins for all races or it was insufficient for any.

Additionally, in this poem, Hammon describes man as triune: that is, as having soul, spirit, and body. Thus, he presents man as an ethereal being: "unto thee we fly." Here he makes clear distinction among the three. Scripturally, man's "heart" is seen as his "spirit." Likewise, in Heb. 4:12, the Apostle Paul states, "For the word of God is quick, . . . piercing even to the dividing asunder of soul and spirit." In the process of a typical conversion, which is chronicled in the poem, it is the heart or spirit that is born again. But it is the soul—man's mind, will, and emotion—which seeks for that salvation. Hammon may have derived his ideas regarding a tripartite man and even a tripartite conversion (change, as when he speaks of man's bodily change at Christ's Second Coming) from traditional Protestant views. According to A. Leland Jamison, colonial Christians usually demanded that a convert achieve "vastly more than a change of intellectual conviction." He or she had to demonstrate "a metamorphosis of the whole personality, a judgement change in a different dimension, and the absence of any control by the mighty forces of evil" (Jamison and Smith 203). For instance, well-known eighteenth-century minister Thomas Shepard divided "hearts" and "souls" in his *Parable of the Ten Virgins Unfolded*: "That the Hearts and Souls of Believers are Made as Vessels only for the Reception of Christ, His Spirit, and the Graces Thereof" (*Works,* 2:261–68). The body, of course, would be the third part of man's indivisible being. Again, however, the issue is race. While Hammon may admit that the African's body is black and that in eighteenth-century society color may have connotations of evil, he never admits that the soul and spirit within that body are black also.

Once departing the body, the soul and spirit would presumably "fly" to God for judgment. Hammon's concepts of a tribunal were multiplicit and derived from his understanding of Scripture that men would stand before God—both as individuals and as members of a group—to answer for life's deeds. In this poem, as in all of his works, Hammon reveals that he saw eschatological judgment as twofold—separate judgments for the unsaved world and for the children of God. His interpretation of Scripture in both of these judgments is that whites will have to answer for their enslavement of Africans and that, because of this corporate sin, white colonists could take part in only the judgment of the wicked, not that of the saints. At this judgment of the wicked, Hammon believed Blacks would be truly vindicated. Other than this indication, he saw no end to slavery. Later he would write that the Revolutionary War represented early punishment for the practice of slavery and was a warning from God of the ultimate judgment which slaveholders faced if they would not end the institution.

Not until the emergence of the Reverend Nat Turner (*Confessions*) and the Reverend David Walker (in Stuckey) in the 1830's did any other contributor to the canon of Black American literature express a vision of violence as an alternative method to end slavery. Just as those early Black American writers who followed him, Hammon hoped that moral persua-

sion based on Christian principles, such as that in his poetry and
essays, would be effective for the eventual eradication of slavery. For instance, in his *Address to the Negroes in the State of
New York,* he did not urge Blacks to foment insurrection. He
chose instead to express an antislavery statement chiding patriots for their hypocritical bonding of men while they engaged in
a war for their own freedom. He tells his Black audience:

> That liberty is a great thing we may know from our own feelings,
> and we may likewise judge so from the conduct of the white
> people in the late war. How much money had been spent, and
> how many lives have been lost to defend their liberty! I must say
> that I have hoped that God would open their eyes, when they
> were so much engaged for liberty, to think of the state of the poor
> blacks, and to pity us.

Other civil rights leaders expressed the same thoughts throughout the Revolutionary era.[14]

In the old-time camp meetings among Blacks in agrarian
culture, prayer was not consummated unless the supplicant was
assured that he had gotten his prayer through. An understood
phrase was, "My prayers didn't reach no higher than the ceil-
ing." When one had reached that perfect place of meeting with
God, he was said to know emotional assurance within his heart.
Thus when Hammon writes "Ye Shall Not Cry in Vain," he
wants the prayers of his congregation to reach beyond the ceil-
ing. Once the persona priest leading the praying congregation
within the poem believes that this goal has been accomplished,
he concludes with the line "We felt thy Salvation," thus indicating that the supplicants had touched the heart of God and had
received his emotional assurance. The line echoes assumptions
of the revivalist era—that true salvation must be felt in order to
be real. This phenomenon was especially true in private revival
services among slaves.[15]

This emotional response is part of what Hammon means
when he speaks of "a true Motion." While modern literary
critics disparage the terminology as "trite," Hammon is in fact
calling for what was well-known in eighteenth-century revivals

as true repentance. Christian conversion had to be accompanied by sufficient evidence of the sinner's change of heart. This proof could include such great emotional displays as yelling, crying on the mourner's bench, or falling down in consternation—common occurrences with the advent of such great revivalists as Jonathan Edwards, George Whitefield, "Black" Harry Hoosier, and the Tennent brothers.

Reports of supernatural phenomena occurring during the Great Awakening are astounding. Whitefield, preaching in the open air, could be heard clearly four hundred feet away:

> Never did the people show so great a willingness to attend sermons, nor the preachers greater zeal. . . . Religion is become the subject of most conversations. No books are in request but those of piety and devotion; and instead of idle songs and ballads, the people are everywhere entertaining themselves with psalms and hymns and spiritual songs. (Tracy 52)

Hammon was a typical product of this milieu. He was a part-time preacher (when his masters freed him to be) who had not been appointed or ordained by the established church because he was Black and in their eyes not sufficiently educated. Preaching without official sanction was the same charge which the orthodox clergy leveled upon Whitefield, Gilbert Tennent, and other revivalists of the era (Tracy 60–75). Further, orthodox churches especially resisted any preachers who believed in and taught their own brand of doctrine, such as that which Hammon had developed. Thus, Hammon could say in *An Evening's Improvement* that his objectors labeled him "an unlearned Ethiopian," one even unqualified to preach to his fellow slaves. Tracy likewise speaks of an eighteenth-century churchman as saying:

> Private persons of no education and but low attainments in knowledge and in the great doctrine of the gospel, without any regular call, under a pretense of exhorting, taking upon themselves to be preachers of the Word of God, we judge to be a heinous invasion of the ministerial office, offensive to God, and destructive to these churches. (287)

Hammon knew that he surely fit into these definitions of those "rejected of men but called of God." Regardless of attempts to thwart a religious movement among those who were unwelcome in the institutional church, the same exuberant responses which Hammon demanded were burning within burgeoning, underground slave congregations.[16]

Once the congregation attains "true repentance," Hammon, as a faithful and confident priest and shepherd, offers his flock, his audience, to God. As he had asked them to "turn your hearts, accept the Word"—a reference to Christ himself as in John 1:1—and as they had shown true repentance, there is no other step or additive to the spiritual process. The poem moves to the heavenly descent of the Holy Spirit and man's worshipful entrance before God's throne. The pastor-priest has completed his task. His flock has been reconciled to God.

Notes

1.   See entries for "Savior" in Brown 513–14; Covel, n.p.; Grimke 96–100; related exegeses by Poole of Acts 5:31, Phil. 3:20, Titus 2:13 and 3:4, and John 4:14, 42.

2.   See the entire chapter of Ruth 4 as well for more discussion of "redeem" in the sense of buying a kinsman out of slavery.

3.   For more on the colonial redemptioneer system, see Jernegan, *Laboring;* McKee; A. E. Smith, and W. B. Smith. For more on biblical interpretations of the redemption plan, see Beveridge, *Works* 1:56, 214–15; 4:153–54: 6:153–54, 8:184–87; J. Edwards, *Works* 5:360–61; J. Edwards, *History* 12–13, 45–51, 75–83. For biblical studies of ransom and redemption, see Cheever 165–69, 191–93, 201–6; Gillette, *Discourse* 6–9; S. Hopkins, *Works* 1:252–55; J. H. Hopkins 244–49; and Poole, Col. 1:14, Titus 2:14, Lev. 25, and Eph. 1:14.

4.   One other point is important in this context. Does the scriptural word "servant" mean simply a worker or can it be interpreted to mean "slave"? The question was utmost in the slavery controversy. Both proponents and opponents of the American slave institution hinged their arguments on the definition of "servant." Howell Cobb, an advocate for slavery, articulates the view that slavery was both biblical and sanctioned by God:

The term slave occurs but seldom in the Bible, perhaps not more than twice, and in no place in the sense in which it is generally used by us. The terms used which denote slavery are servant, bondman, bondwoman, maid, handmaid, etc. As these are other servants besides slaves frequently spoken of, we must refer to the circumstances of each particular case, for the purpose of ascertaining the condition that is meant. Martindale says: "The word [servant] generally signifies a slave. The Hebrews had two sorts of servants or slaves."—See Lev. xxc. 44, 45. (10)

On the other hand, a modern entry by Leonard D. Agate in Hastings' *Encyclopaedia* summarizes the view of those opposed to Americans making slaves of men for any reason: "Man is a spiritual being akin to his Maker. St. Paul says: 'In Christ is neither bond nor free' " (Hastings 11:611).

5.   The importance of names in colonial society is discussed in Beveridge, *Works,* 7:7, 22–32; Frost, 89–91; Greene, *The Negro,* 268–69; Jordan, *White Man's,* 92–97; Scherer, 58–61, 64–69, 92–97.

6.   Undoubtedly the slaveholders were trying to imitate the importance of naming in the Old Testament where it is also sometimes indicated to establish a curse: see for example 1 Sam. 4:10–21. But a change of name could also be a blessing as in Gen. 17:5.

7.   This vision of racial equality was shared by few colonial clergymen. Exceptions were John Eliot (*Petition of John Eliot* in the *Plymouth Colonial Records* [1675] in Ruchames), Samuel Hopkins, *A Dialogue,* and David Brainerd, *An Account.*

8.   The literature indicates that colonists were in general baffled by the matter of Christian love. Popular colonial minister Joseph Bellamy, *Works* 1:119, 188, speaks of the obligation of the Christian to "esteem" his neighbor and that which the neighbor possesses. Yet Bellamy doubted that the saved man could love God enough, much less his fellowman. For more about Bellamy's theology of love, see "Joseph Bellamy" in Frank Hugh Foster's *Genetic History,* 108–11. See Weimer 67–78 for additional information on the colonial view of Christian love.

9.   Higginbotham cites a further example:

[Virginia statute: 1677] Act III. Whereas some doubts have arisen whether children that are slaves by birth, and by the charity and pity of their owners made partakers of the blessed sacrament of baptism, should by virtue of their baptism be made free, it is enacted that *baptism does not alter the condition of the person as to his bondage or freedom; masters freed from this doubt may*

> *more carefully propagate Christianity by permitting slaves to be
> admitted to that sacrament.* (Higginbotham 37)

For additional discussion of the laws pertaining to baptism and manumission in these and other colonies, refer to Greene, *The Negro* 259–
75; Greene, "Slave-Holding" 527–33; Ovington 151–69; Shea 39–84;
and Worrall.

10.   Robert Barclay and William Penn based their theology on the
Gospel of John: "The Inward Light which the Quakers look to as their
means of 'salvation' is also the Inward Life" (Brinton 1). However,
Quaker biographer Howard Brinton admitted that sole dependence
upon that "Inward Light" could be interpreted as a form of deism. For
instance, George Fox, founder of the Quakers, held that the "Light"
was universal, that it was already set within every man—a theorem
that would obviate the necessity for atonement and redemption. Pro-
viding a qualification, Fox said:

> The Lord God opened to me by his invisible power, how "every
> man was enlightened by the Divine Light of Christ." I saw it shine
> through all, and they that believe in it come out of condemnation to
> the light of life, and became the children of it; but they that hated
> it, and did not believe in it, were condemned by it, tho' they make
> a profession of Christ. (Fox, *Doctrines and Ministry* 9–10)

For more on the relationship between the Quakers and colonial slaves,
see Aptheker, "The Quakers" 331–62; Cadbury; Greene, "Slave-
Holding" 527–33; Ovington, 151–69; Shea 39–84; and Worrall.

11.   Both of these sentiments came to the fore in the debate over
the Halfway Covenant. See P. Miller, *Mind: From Colony* 93–104;
and Pope, particularly 3–74, for details on this covenant.

12.   Poole mentions the more general concept of "atonement" in
his remarks on Rom. 5:11; and Brown defines it in his *Dictionary* 60.

13.   Cotton Mather's grandfather, Samuel Mather, categorized
Christ's sacrifice as a culmination of Old Testament foreshadowing
types: "A type is some outward or sensible thing ordained of God
under the Old Testament, to represent and hold forth something of
Christ in the new" (52). His *Figures or Types of the Old Testament* was
widely read in the eighteenth century and would have influenced
Hammon or at least those preachers whom he heard. Mather concluded that the Old Testament blood rites were "legal sacrifices" in
the same way that Christ's blood was payment for man's sin: "But as
the typical Blood might not be eaten, but was sacred to the Lord: Let
the Blood of Christ be sacred and precious to you" (243). Another

contemporary correlation is *A Review of the Rev. Horace Bushnell's Discourse on the Slavery Question* by Francis Gillette, which correlates Christ's sacrifice with the bane of slavery: "What! Man made after the image of God and ransomed by a Savior's blood . . . to be bought and sold in shambles, to be made a beast of burden, to rank in the creation with cattle, and horses, and swine!" (6).

14. Similarly, throughout her letters to various missionaries and abolitionists, Phillis Wheatley expresses hopes that Christianity, not the deaths of slaves and slaveholders in bloody conflict, would be the impetus that would bring down the slavery institution. See particularly her letter to the Reverend Samuel Hopkins (Wheatley, 109–10).

15. For more on the Black church, particularly its hymnody, read Floyd's article, Southern's text, and the preface to Johnson's work on spirituals. For discussions on the conversion experience of slaves, see Genovese 238–39; Raboteau 266–71; and the entire first section of Rawick's *American Slave,* particularly the narratives "My Jaws Became Unlocked" 11–13, and "God Struck Me Dead" 19–21.

16. For more on revival phenomena among Black and white Christians, see Bacon 155–80; Bragg 71–74; T. M. Cooley 88–95; L. L. Haynes 57–58; R. M. Jones, *The Quakers,* entire work; MacLeod; Raboteau 128–50; Rosenberg; Rutman, *Great Awakening* 1–51, 89–100, 198–200; Whitefield; Whitney, *John Woolman;* Woodson, *The History,* 56–58, 61–65, 71–85.

"An Evening Thought: Salvation by Christ, with Penitential Cries"

1

Salvation[1] comes by Jesus Christ alone,
    The only Son of God;
Redemption now to every one,[2]
    That loves his holy Word.

2

Dear Jesus we would fly to Thee,
    And leave off every Sin,
Thy tender Mercy well agree;
    Salvation from our King.

3

Salvation comes now from the Lord,
    Our victorious King;[3]

His holy Name be well ador'd,
   Salvation surely bring.

4

Dear Jesus give thy Spirit now,
   Thy Grace to every Nation,[4]
That hasn't the Lord to whom we bow,
   The Author of Salvation.[5]

5

Dear Jesus unto Thee we cry,
   Give us thy Preparation;[6]
Turn not away thy tender Eye;
   We seek thy true Salvation.

6

Salvation comes from God we know,
   The true and only One;
It's well agreed and certain true,
   He gave his only Son.[7]

7

Lord hear our penitential Cry:
   Salvation from above;
It is the Lord that doth supply,
   With his Redeeming Love.

8

Dear Jesus by thy precious Blood,
   The World Redemption have:
Salvation comes now from the Lord,
   He being thy captive Slave.

9

Dear Jesus let the Nations cry,
   And all the People say,
Salvation comes from Christ on high,
   Haste on Tribunal Day.

10

We cry as Sinners to the Lord,
   Salvation to obtain;
It is firmly fixed his holy Word,
   Ye shall not cry in vain.[8]

11

Dear Jesus unto Thee we cry,
    And make our Lamentation:[9]
O let our Prayers ascend on high;
    We felt thy Salvation.

12

Lord turn our dark benighted Souls;
    Give us a true Motion,[10]
And let the hearts of all the World,
    Make Christ their Salvation.

13

Ten Thousand Angels cry to Thee,
    Yea louder than the Ocean.
Thou art the Lord, we plainly see;
    Thou art the true Salvation.

14

Now is the Day, accepted Time;
    The Day of Salvation;[11]
Increase your Faith, do not repine:
    Awake ye every Nation.

15

Lord unto whom now shall we go,[12]
    Or seek a safe Abode;
Thou hast the Word Salvation too
    The only Son of God.

16

Ho! every one that hunger hath,[13]
    Or pineth after me,
Salvation be thy leading Staff,[14]
    To set the Sinner free.

17

Dear Jesus unto Thee we fly;
    Depart, depart from Sin,
Salvation doth at length supply,
    The Glory of our King.

18

Come ye Blessed of the Lord,

Salvation gently given;
O turn your Hearts, accept the Word,
Your Souls are fit for Heaven.

19

Dear Jesus we now turn to Thee,
Salvation to obtain;
Our Hearts and Souls do meet again,
To magnify thy Name.

20

Come holy Spirit, Heavenly Dove,[15]
The Object of our Care;
Salvation doth increase our Love;
Our hearts hath felt thy fear.

21

Now Glory be to God on High,
Salvation high and low;
And thus the Soul on Christ rely,
To heaven surely go.

22

Come Blessed Jesus, Heavenly Dove,
Accept Repentance here;
Salvation give, with tender Love;
Let us with Angels share.

FINIS

Emendations

Title		Penitential]	Penetential] R	Penetential] H
Stanza	*Line*			
1	4:	loves]	love] R	
4	1:	thy]	they] R	thy] H
4	3:	hasn't]	han't] R	han't] H
5	2:	thy]	the] R	thy] H
7	1:	penitential]	penetential] R	
8	3:	comes now]	now comes] R	comes now] H
8	4:	Slave]	slave] R	Slave.] H
10	3:	is]	if] R	
10	3:	fixed]	fixt] R	
14	1:	accepted]	excepted] R	
18	2:	gently]	greatly] R	gently] H

Notes

1. The term "salvation" is related to the title of Christ as Savior and to that act of redemption whereby a person is "saved" from sin and Satan. "Savior" is a title for the Old Testament Jehovah who delivered the Israelites from bondage in Egypt. Eighteenth-century readers would have been familiar with the term in this context and as seen in the following Scriptures: "They forgot God their saviour, which had done great things in Egypt" (Ps. 106:21); "For I am the Lord thy God, the Holy One of Israel, thy Saviour" (Isa. 43:3); and "Verily thou art a God that hidest thyself, O God of Israel, the Saviour" (Isa. 45:15).

2. This line—"redemption now to every one"—is the central refrain of the poem because it expresses the interrelatedness of errant theology to the social practice of slavery. Redemption is related to the enslavement of Old Testament Jews who called Jehovah "the great Redeemer" because he "bought" them back from slavery. Examples from the Bible of the use of the term in this way include Exod. 6:6 "I am the Lord, and I will bring you out from under the burdens of the Egyptians . . . and I will redeem you"; Exod. 15:13: "[Jehovah] in thy mercy hast redeemed"; and Ps. 106:10: "And [Jehovah] saved them from the hand of him that hated them, and redeemed them from the hand of the enemy."

3. As can be seen in one of Hammon's later poems, "A Dialogue, Entitled, The Kind Master and Dutiful Servant," the colonial slave's concept of God as King was quite different from that of the slaveholder. Based on the medieval English politicizing of societal classes and in synthesis with the doctrine of Calvinism, British slaveholders, such as the Lloyds who owned Hammon, considered themselves to be God's ordained leaders set apart as a special ruling class inferior only to the British monarchy. But to the slaves, Christ alone was King, and through his redemption they themselves were "A royal priesthood, an holy nation" (1 Pet. 2:9). For more on the slaveholder's perspective, see Jordan, *White Man's* 99–105.

4. With the continual refrain, "every nation," Hammon's emphasis is to detract from the idea that God has selected a favorite nation or race of people. The theology that God had so preordained such a group or race, known as the elect, was pervasive in England and the colonies because Whites felt that they were the ones so favored.

5. Here Hammon has in mind a scriptural verse, quite familiar to eighteenth-century evangelists, where Christ is called "the author and finisher of our fath" (Heb. 12:2).

6. Critics now conclude that the whole notion of the "heart prepared" was really a mild form of Arminianism that had crept into Covenant Congregationalist practice. See Goodwin 214.

7. Hammon's allusion is to that famous Bible verse, John 3:16: "For God so loved the world that he gave his only begotten Son, that whosoever believeth in him should not perish, but have everlasting life." This was the best-known verse of the Great Awakening. For an example of a sermon based on this biblical passage, see Samuel Davies' "Nature of Salvation through Jesus Christ Explained and Recommended" (1:31–54).

8. Although Hammon gave this line unusual punctuational emphasis, it is not verbatim wording from the Bible. Usually in biblical reference "vain" refers to emptiness or to going through spiritual ritual without sincere deific acknowledgment, as in the Old Testament when Isaiah the prophet quotes God as saying, "I said not unto the seed of Jacob 'Seek ye me in vain' " (Isa. 45:19).

9. "Lamentation" of course not only means mournful cry, it also is the title of an Old Testament book by the prophet Jeremiah. To understand Hammon's use of the term, one should note that Jeremiah wrote the brief book to lament Israel's enslavement under Babylon.

10. Modern critics might say that this line is bad poetry, and that perhaps Hammon intended his words to be "true emotion" instead. However, Hammon is concerned here with genuine repentance rather than simply a veneer of church attendance and societal recognition that could result in pseudoassumptions of authentic Christian experience.

11. This is a paraphrase of 2 Cor. 6:2: "Behold, now is the accepted time; behold, now is the day of salvation."

12. Hammon could have in mind here a particular time in Jesus' ministry when many disciples defected because of his insistence on a spiritual Eucharist. After they left, Jesus asked his disciples, "Will you also go away?" to which Peter replied, "Lord, to whom shall we go? Thou hast the words of eternal life" (John 6:68).

13. Here Hammon has possibly one of two scriptural allusions in mind—or perhaps both. Isa. 55 begins: "Ho, every one that thirsteth come ye to the waters." Similarly, Ps. 42 opens: "As the hart panteth after the water brooks, so panteth my soul after thee, O God."

14. Again "staff" is compatible with other biblical images in the poem that refer to slavery. During his confrontation with Pharaoh, the archetypal oppressor of the Israelites, Moses used his staff as a mystical symbol of his power to bring plagues upon the Egyptians. He parted the Red Sea with the same staff and used it to smite a rock to provide water for the tribes as they were exiting from Egypt. For more

background see, Barnes 81–159; Beveridge, *Works* 1:56, 214–15; Cheever 164–68; 191–95; Covel 130–33, 164–69; Dunston 28–33; and J. Edwards, *History* 75–81 and *Works,* 5:355.

15.   The Dove is a New Testament image of the Holy Spirit, the third member of the Godhead who descended from heaven when John the Baptist, in recognition of him as the Messiah, was baptizing Christ. This incident is recorded in all four of the Gospels: for example, Matt. 3:16: "And Jesus, when he was baptized went up straightway out of the water: and, lo, the heavens were opened unto him, and he saw the Spirit of God descending like a dove, and lighting upon him." Hammon alludes to this passage several times within this poem and, as in the scriptural citation, the poet's attitude is one of prayerful reference.

2. An Address to Miss Phillis Wheatley

Introduction: A Literary Heritage
and a Prophetic Call

As indicated in the title, this poem is dedicated to Phillis Wheatley, who by its publication in 1778 was the most famous African living in America. Its formality indicates that, while he may have traveled with the Lloyds to Boston, where Phillis lived, and to Newport, where she accompanied her masters to their vacation home, Hammon had never met the young poetess, although he obviously admired her greatly. The poem's rhetoric makes it clear that Hammon saw himself as the elder statesman of Black American poets and that, as such, he bequeathed a heritage and a charge to this next-generation writer.

Hammon establishes quite early in the missive that they are both outcast Africans living in America by God's predestined allowance and that He permitted this arduous circumstance so that they might hear and receive the Gospel. The poet enjoins Wheatley to the highest moral behavior befitting her status as America's first Black female spokesperson. The times call for such decorum, he reminds her, because God will hold them accountable as among those who have been called to lead a defenseless people for whom there is little other temporal "light." (Wheatley resided in Boston with her owners, John and Susanna Wheatley, and their two children. They had purchased her from a slave sale on the Boston docks when she was about seven years old. Phillis's fame and artistic and political support came from prominent evangelical and political leaders in the Boston area.)[1] He also wants her to resist the seduction of temporal fame, which is a dangerous illusion for one trapped by the same society that lauds her as an eminent poet.

The subscription of stanza 1, taken from Ecclesiastes 12, sets the fatherly tone and theme for this entire poem. After the injunction to youth in the first verse of this famous chapter— "Remember now thy Creator in the days of thy youth"—King Solomon identifies himself as the narrator of Ecclesiastes and continues the chapter with admonitions to the young that life is fleeting and that life's most important charge is to remember one's commitment to God. Hammon patterns his poem with the same injunctions and thematic imagery with which Solomon completes his poetic didactics. The king-poet continues the Ecclesiastes chapter with a symbolic description of the disintegration of the physical body in aging and in death. However, rather than dwelling on bodily degeneration in the grave, Hammon looks forward in hope to the "translation" of Christian saints at the Second Coming of Christ.

Like Solomon, Hammon is concerned that Christian young people, especially Black ones, know the meaning of life, death, and resurrection. His "Poem for Children with Thoughts on Death" reflects that concern, but only in this address does he stretch his eschatology to include God's judgment and rewards. Thus, Hammon advises Wheatley of her special calling to serve God as a writer, as an intellectual who has survived not only the Middle Passage but also the continuing dangers of eighteenth-century slavery, and as one whose responsibility is to leave a record of Black existence, no matter how surreptitious that record may have to be. The senior poet indicates his awareness of the painful realities of slavery which he and Wheatley observe and endure on a daily basis. However, he tells her, she must not despair about her own enslavement or about the miserable conditions of their people in America. She is to keep Christ and his ultimate purposes utmost in mind. Thus, he instructs her—in stanzas 2, 4, 11, and 21—that, in order to develop a character of joy in the midst of this tribulation, she must appropriate a power which is beyond the reach of their captors. That power, he surmises, would come from God and from faith in his word.

Stanza 5 represents the vortex of two of the poem's main themes. First, like all eighteenth-century Christians, Hammon wrestled with the sovereignty of God in the affairs of men. The haunting theme of the deaths of millions of Africans during the Atlantic passage is introduced early in the work. He reminds the young poetess that this holocaust left few Blacks who were schooled enough in the language and iconography of the Western world to use literary talent in order to raise a cry against slavery and the slave trade. When Hammon wrote this poem, as far as he knew, he and Wheatley were the only ones with public accessibility to do so. In the lines "While thousands tossed by the sea, / And others settled down, / God's tender mercy set thee free, / From dangers that come down," Hammon expressed as much anguish over African genocide as the eighteenth-century fourth estate would allow.

For Hammon, as well as for Wheatley, the words "that thou a pattern still might be / to youth of Boston town," does not address the issue of predestination, but does speak of the burden to report the truth while in throes of constraining circumstances. Like those Africans who did not survive the passage, Hammon is reminding Wheatley that they too must die. However, considering the Christian context of death and judgment, he insists that they must answer to God for their unique mission to disclose the evils of slavery.

Hammon was not unconcerned with slavery, as his critics have charged. In his view of eighteenth-century political realities and in his studied eschatology, he simply had no hope that the slave institution would end through the voluntary and merciful intentions of the slaveholding society. In all of his essays, particularly in *An Address to the Negroes in the State of New York,* Hammon presents the same plan to his African-American audience that he presents to Wheatley in this poem. They are to endure slavery and to trust God to judge the slaveholders with both temporal (that is, the Revolutionary War) and eternal judgment.

In "An Address to Miss Phillis Wheatley" Hammon seems to

posit that God placed him and Wheatley in America and that he ordained them to be both writers and slaves:

> O come you pious youth! adore
>   The wisdom of thy God,
> In bringing thee from distant shore,
>   To learn his holy word.
> Thou mightst been left behind,
>   Amidst a dark abode;
> God's tender mercy still combin'd,
>   Thou hast the holy word.
>   . . .
> Thou hast left the heathen shore,
>   Thro' mercy of the Lord;
> Among the heathen live no more,
>   Come magnify thy God.

But elsewhere in his writing, Hammon is ambivalent about whether God sanctions slavery, or if the institution is simply in his "permitted" will. The elder poet wrestles with the Calvinist doctrines of predestination, election, and prevenient grace and replaces them with his own doctrinal understanding that men and women are liable for their own actions and decisions and that they will be held fully accountable for what they do to their fellowmen.[2] In the Calvinist view, although all people are seen as totally depraved sinners with no hope of self-deliverance, God, in his own will and purpose, directs certain chosen sinners into pathways of salvation. And slavery itself could be seen as part of that direction. Wheatley seems to agree that she came to America through God's intervention. In her poem "On Being Brought from Africa to America" she writes:

> 'T'was mercy brought me from my *Pagan* land,
> Taught my benighted soul to understand
> That there's a God, that there's a Saviour too. (Wheatley 7)

Dathorne is quite critical of early Black American writers because they refer to Africans as heathens. However, Hammon and Wheatley considered any persons outside of Christ to be heathens, as evidenced in her attack against the atheistic students at Cambridge and his repeated referrals to white slaveholders as being unsaved. In both cases the heathens were white, but in this instance the poets speak through spiritual perspectives, without considerations of race or color.

Hammon's poem to Wheatley was published in 1778, at which time he may have read Wheatley's earlier work "On Messrs. Hussey and Coffin," which first appeared in 1767, and her more famous elegy "On the Death of the Rev. Mr. George Whitefield," which was published in 1770 with the announcement that Wheatley was a "Servant Girl, of 17 years of age . . . but nine years in this country from Africa." Wheatley's volume of poetry appeared in 1773, giving her an international reputation. But to Hammon she was a vulnerable young African who needed his fatherly advice. The shepherd-pastor symbolism of stanza 12 and its subscript follows the theme of Psalm 23. Christ is the Shepherd and believers are his sheep. Hammon cautions Wheatley that she is to depend on God alone for all the affairs of life, but he also speaks of the slaves' insecurities. Slaves in eighteenth-century America, despite any intellectual accomplishments that they may have achieved, were still on the margins of national, social, and religious life. Thus, as early as Black American literature indicates, Blacks maintained their own loose religious and social structures. Just as the early literature transfers information through coded inferences, those community structures likewise existed in spasmodic, underground, and unannounced relationship to the white world. But they existed nevertheless. As third-class members of white congregations—often denied baptism and communion and always denied a role in church leadership—Black Christians could not go to white pastors for consolation about slavery because most of those pastors supported the slave system. Therefore, these pastors would report any rumors of resistance—topics which began quite naturally in church or any other of the few social settings where servants could congregate—to owners as well as to the state. Just as illegal in the eighteenth-century North as in the nineteenth-century South, such resistance resulted in the death

penalty. Thus, even the church was not a relief from the aliena-
tions of slave life.

Hammon uses the narrative of the woman of Samaria from
John 4 as his best illustration of that alienation. For him, the
parable of this Samaritan, along with stories about publicans
and the poor in Christ's day, served as a very necessary biblical
text for a slave audience because it showed Christ's love for the
utmost of community pariahs. Samaritans were hated by the
Jews, who considered them as less than mongrel dogs (refer to
Brown's entry, 506–7). By edict, Jews could not speak to Samaritans; they walked miles out of their way to avoid going
through the Samaritan region. Additionally, the women of Pal-
estine were denied political or historical inclusion. Jewish men
were particularly forbidden to converse publicly with Samaritan
women—the ultimate symbols of heathen untouchables. To
compound this already lowly status, the woman who talked to
Jesus beside Jacob's well that day had been married several
times and was presently living with a man to whom she was not
married. Yet Christ revealed himself to her as the Messiah, an
admission he seldom made to the Jews. After her conversion,
she led all the townspeople to meet him. Jewish religious leaders condemned this activity. But Christ ignored societal rules
instituted by men and instead set about to establish the love of
God. In most of his seven extant works, Hammon sets the text
of the Samaritan woman before his slave audience to identify
the African with the Samaritan and to illustrate Christ's primary
concern for those rejected and oppressed by a hypocritical society. Hammon implies here and in his other works that, for
slaves, a true pastor—one who devotedly serves his people as
Christ's undershepherd—can only be one who understands and
commiserates with the sufferings of his sheep. While scholarship proves that Hammon was a preacher of considerable experience whom slaveholders invited to preach among Blacks on
their plantations, I also suspect that he was an early pastor of an
underground Black church, although the first open Black congregation did not emerge until the end of the eighteenth century, some twenty years after this poem was written.

The theme of judgment with which Hammon completes the poem is not only personal but he envisions adjudication on multiple and corporate levels: "When God shall send his summons down, / And number saints together." In addition to the individual—in this poem, a "A Poem for Children with Thoughts on Death," and in his essay-sermons—both church and society will be judged. The poet often uses the word "summons" in this poem to indicate God's call to men to face the highest court in the universe. But the Bible (Matt. 25:31–46) speaks of nations' being judged as a body for their oppressive treatment of those who were "hungry," "naked," "a stranger," "sick," or "in prison." The poet implies condemnation of a slaveholding society which sees Africans as "the poor" who are hungry, naked, estranged, ill, and imprisoned but which refuses to minister to their needs. Both Jonathan Edwards (*Works* 284) and William Burkitt (1:130–32) give clear discussions of Christian society's responsibility to "the poor" so that on a corporate level, colonial society stood in jeopardy. In addition, Hammon believed that the church, as the smaller but more moral body within the society, must with even more severity answer for its deeds.

After these summonses, judgment remained for families, for separate church congregations, and for individuals. According to biblical texts, the last three entities will stand in what is prophetically known as the Judgment Seat of Christ. This time of accountability for Christians is diametrical to the judgment of the unsaved, which is known as the "Great White Throne Judgment." Hammon conveys the imagery of this Christian judgment from stanza 19 to the end of the poem. His phraseology "number saints together" also refers to the tribulation period, a future time in the earth, which most contemporary theologians believed will be simultaneous with the Judgment Seat of Christ in Heaven (Rev. 7:1–15).[3]

Also in the poem's last stanza, Hammon merges other images of prophecy with the idea of death and judgment. The "triumphant sound" and "blest angels chant" of stanza 18 refer to scriptural predictions of the Second Coming of Christ found in 1

Thess. 4:16—"For the Lord himself shall descend from heaven with a shout . . . with the trump of God." The poet also alludes to passages in Rev. 4:1–11, 5:9–14, and 19:1–7, all of which are anthems celebrating the return of Christ.[4] With "the humble soul shall fly to God," Hammon suggests both bodily translation at death and the rapture of believers who are alive at the time of Christ's return when, according to Scripture, both the dead and the living shall be transformed into wholly spiritual beings as they travel through the air to meet him.[5]

Thus, the tone of this poem is one of urgency. Hammon urges that Wheatley must conform her art to the needs of Africans confined in a Christian land, and that she must do so while conducting her life with a moral standard which their professing Christian society itself ignores. Her writing should always include both a sense of African history (particularly the immediacy of the Atlantic passage and the century and a half that the race had been enslaved on America's shores) and the knowledge that they must answer for their art in death and judgment. He renders this crucial testament because of his own age ("Blest angels chant, [triumphant sound] / Come live with me forever")—that is, his time to herald the unique message of a Black American writer to his people is almost over—and because opportunity to end the slave institution in a peaceful manner is almost over. He also writes because, as far as he knew, Wheatley was the only one who could perpetuate the witness of Black American Christian intellect.

With his ending anthem, the poet moves the work beyond race or any other temporal consideration. God, who alone shall rescue Wheatley and the rest of Hammon's literary congregation from the evils of their present circumstance, must finally and forevermore be praised:

> Now glory be to the Most High,
>   United praises given,
> By all on earth, incessantly,
>   And all the host of heav'n.

In this last stanza, the poem celebrates the triumphal entry of the entire Body of Christ, in which each individual has a reconstituted physiology, a matured spirit, and a redeemed soul. The "united praises" are taken from intermittent background scenes in such end-time prophecies as shown in Revelation chapters 19–22, all of which are noted in Poole's *Annotations* and Beveridge's *Works* (texts which Hammon read and quoted extensively). All of these prophecies were normal sermon fodder in eighteenth-century pulpits. Not only Phillis Wheatley, but others in Hammon's audience—downtrodden Africans as well as self-esteemed white churchmen—faced that moment when, as equals leveled before God, they would be ushered into glorious eternity.

Notes

1.   For recent articles on Wheatley's life and times, see Robinson's *Critical Essays* and Phillis Wheatley.

2.   More on the doctrines for comparison to Hammon's restructuring of them are included in the works of Burr, *New England's Place* 14–27; McNeil; Newlin 2–4; and Steele and Thomas. Thorough and impartial discussions are also available in Cross, *Dictionary* 10; Hastings, *Encyclopedia* 1:807–16, 3:146–55; and Jackson, *Schaff-Herzog Encyclopedia* 1:296–97, 2:359–64.

3.   This eschatology is in line with eighteenth-century doctrine. See selected passages from Donne's *Sermons* in Jamison and Smith 208–11. For additional information on Hammon's scheme of judgment, especially the Great White Throne Judgment, note Richard Baxter's "Saints' Everlasting Rest" in More and Cross 324–33; Jonathan Edwards' sermons—"The Justice of God and the Damnation of Sinners" and "Sinners in the Hands of an Angry God"—in his *Collected Writings* 273–75, 365–78; and John Pearson's "Exposition of the Creed" in More and Cross.

4.   See J. Edwards, *Apocalyptic Writings* 5:439–43; and his *History* 408–44.

5.   George Bull explains the concept of metempsychosis, or the transmigration of souls, in a section of his *Harmonia Apostalica* 317–21; see also More and Cross. On this reunion of the soul and body, Beveridge affirmed, "I believe, that after a short separation, my soul and body shall be united together again, in order to appear before the

judgement seat of Christ, and be finally sentenced according to my
deserts" (*Works* 1:202–9). Beveridge is speaking of his individual
death, but the biblical prophecy concerning group translation to which
Hammon alludes is a somewhat different occasion. At the time of the
rapture those alive will reportedly be translated through metempsychosis and those bodies in graves will be resurrected, reinhabited, and
translated also.

"An Address to Miss Phillis Wheatley"

Ethiopian Poetess, in Boston, who came from Africa
at eight years of age, and soon became acquainted
with the gospel of Jesus Christ

1

O come you pious youth! adore
The wisdom of thy God,
In bringing thee from distant shore,
To learn his holy word.
Eccles. 12:1[1]

2

Thou mightst been left behind,
Amidst a dark abode;[2]
God's tender mercy still combin'd,
Thou hast the holy word.
Ps. 136:1–3[3]

3

Fair wisdom's ways are paths of peace,
And they that walk therein,
Shall reap the joys that never cease,
And Christ shall be their king.
Ps. 1:1–2; Prov. 3:7[4]

4

God's tender mercy brought thee here,
Tost o'er the raging main;
In Christian faith thou hast a share,
Worth all the gold of Spain.[5]
Ps. 103:1–4[6]

5

While thousands tossed by the sea,
    And others settled down,
God's tender mercy set thee free,
    From dangers still unknown.
                   Death

6

That thou a pattern still might be,
    To youth of Boston town,
The blessed Jesus set thee free,
    From every sinful wound.
              2 Cor. 5:10[7]

7

The blessed Jesus, who came down,
    Unveil'd his sacred face,[8]
To cleanse the soul of every wound,
    And give repenting grace.
              Rom. 5:21[9]

8

That we poor sinners may obtain
    The pardon of our sin;
Dear blessed Jesus now constrain,
    And bring us flocking in.
            Ps. 34:6–8[10]

9

Come you, Phillis, now aspire,
    And seek the living God,
So step by step thou mayst go higher,
    Till perfect in the word.
           Matt. 7:7–8[11]

10

While thousands mov'd to distant shore,
    And others left behind,
The blessed Jesus still adore,
    Implant this in thy mind.
            Ps. 89:1[12]

11

Thou hast left the heathen shore,
    Thro' mercy of the Lord;
Among the heathen live no more,
    Come magnify thy God.

Ps. 34:1–3[13]

12

I pray the living God may be,
    The shepherd of thy soul;
His tender mercies still are free,
    His mysteries to unfold.

Ps. 80:1–3[14]

13

Thou, Phillis, when thou hunger hast,
    Or pantest for thy God;[15]
Jesus Christ is thy relief,
    Thou hast the holy word.

Ps. 13:1–3[16]

14

The bounteous mercies of the Lord,
    Are hid beyond the sky,
And holy souls that love his word,
    Shall taste them when they die.

Ps. 16:10–11[17]

15

These bounteous mercies are from God,
    The merits of his Son;
The humble soul that loves his word
    He chooses for his own.

Ps. 34:15[18]

16

Come, dear Phillis, be advis'd,
    To drink Samaria's flood;
There nothing is that shall suffice,
    But Christ's redeeming blood.[19]

John 4:13–14[20]

17

While thousands muse with earthly toys,
    And range about the street,
Dear Phillis, seek for heaven's joys,
    Where we do hope to meet.

Matt. 6:33[21]

18

When God shall send his summons down,
    and number saints together,
Blest angels chant, (triumphant sound)
    Come live with me forever.

Ps. 116:15[22]

19

The humble soul shall fly to God,
    And leave the things of time,
Start forth as 'twere at the first word,
    To taste things more divine.

Matt. 5:3, 8[23]

20

Behold! the soul shall waft away,
    Whene'er we come to die,
And leave its cottage made of clay,
    In twinkling of an eye.

1 Cor. 15:51–53[24]

21

Now glory be to the Most High,
    United praises given,
By all on earth, incessantly,
    And all the host of heav'n.

Ps. 150:6[25]

Emendations

Stanza	Line			
1	4:	his]	his] R	his] H
	5:	Eccles. 12:1]	Eccles. xii] R	Eccles. xii. i] H
2	1:	behind,]	behind] R	behind,] H
	5:	Ps. 136:1–3]	Psal.cxxxv,2,3.]R	Psal.cxxxvi. 1,2,3] H

3	5:	Ps. 1:1–2; Prov. 3:7]	Psal.i.1,2; Prov. iii. 7] R	Psal. i. 1,2,3 Prov. iii.7.] H
4	1:	here,]	here;] R	here,] H
	5:	Ps. 103:1–4]	Psal. ciii,1,3,4.]R	Psal. ciii. 1,2,3,4]H
5	4:	still unknown]	that come down] R	still unknown] H
	5:	unknown. Death]	down. Death] R	unknown. Death]H
6	5:	2 Cor. 5:10]	2 Cor. v, 10.] R	
7	2:	Unveil'd]	Unvail'd] R	
	5:	Rom. 5:21]	Rom. v, 21.] R	
8	1:	obtain]	obtain,] R	obtain] H
	5:	Ps. 34:6–8]	Psal. xxxiv, 6,7,8] R	
9	5:	Matt. 7:7–8]	Matth. vii, 7,8.]R	
10	5:	Ps. 89:1]	Psal. lxxxix, 1.]R	
11	1:	shore,]	shore;] R	shore,] H
	2:	Lord;]	Lord,] R	Lord;] H
	5:	Ps. 34:1–3]	Psal. xxxiv. 1,2,3] R	
12	5:	Ps. 80: 1–3]	Psal. lxxx. 1,2,3.] R	
13	5:	Ps. 13: 1–3]	Psal. xiii, 1,2,3.]R	
14	3:	his]	His] R	his] H
	5:	Ps. 16:10,11]	Psal. xvi, 10,11.] R	
15	2:	his]	His] R	his] H
	3:	his]	His] R	his] H
	4:	his]	His] R	his] H
	5:	Ps. 34:15]	Psal. xxxiv, 15]R	
16	3:	is that]	that] R	is that] H
		suffice,]	suffice$_e$] R	suffice.] H
	5:	John 4:13–14]	John iv, 13, 14.]R	John iv. 13$_e$ 14] H
17	1:	toys,]	toys;] R	toys,] H
	5:	Matt. 6:33]	Matth. vi, 33.]R	Matth. vi. 33.] H
18	3:	sound)]	sound),] R	sound)] H
	4:	forever.]	forever] R	for ever] H
	5:	Ps. 116:15]	Psal cxvi, 15.] R	Psal. cxvi. 15.] H
19	5:	Matt. 5:3,8]	Matth. v, 3,8.]R	Mat. v. 3$_e$ 8.] H
20	5:	1 Cor. 15:51–53]	Cor. xv, 51,52,53] R	Cor. xv. 51:52,53.] H
21	5:	Ps. 150:6]	Psal. cl, 6.] R	Psal. cl. 6] H

Notes

1. Eccles. 12:1: "Remember now thy Creator in the days of thy youth, while the evil days come not, nor the years draw nigh, when thou shalt say, I have no pleasure in them."

2. Both Wheatley and Hammon experienced the difficulty of a Black writer who is attempting to use the English language for artistic expression without indicating themselves or other Blacks. Both poets refer to Africa as a land of "dark abode." By the time he wrote this poem, Hammon may or may not have even seen the term in her poem

"To the University of Cambridge in New-England." Yet, interestingly both use the same linguistic imagery. However, for them, words like "dark" and "black" indicated sin rather than skin color. For instance, when discussing sin, Wheatley speaks of her presalvation days as "my benighted soul." Similarly, when addressing the sins of white slaveholders in terms of color, Hammon was not speaking of how they looked. Both Wheatley and Hammon had high regard for their African lineage and used the biblical term "Ethiopian" to identify their race as among those included in both the Old and New Testament chronology—a statement that the Indo-Europeans could not make. Read the preface to Johnson's work, 42–46, for more on how Blacks sought to shape English in their art (in this case, spirituals) and the repercussions of their attempts.

3. Ps. 136:1–3: "O Give thanks unto the Lord; for he is good: for his mercy endureth for ever. O give thanks unto the God of gods: for his mercy endureth for ever. O give thanks to the Lord of lords: for his mercy endureth for ever."

4. Ps. 1:1–2: "Blessed is the man that walketh not in the counsel of the ungodly, nor standeth in the way of sinners, nor sitteth in the seat of the scornful. But his delight is in the law of the Lord; and in his law doth he meditate day and night." Prov. 3:7: "Be not wise in thine own eyes: fear the Lord, and depart from evil."

5. Vernon Loggins was critical of Hammon because of his use of the word "Spain" in this stanza, inferring that the poet only used the term for the sake of a rhyme scheme. However, in the eighteenth-century Spain was in the forefront of the slave controversy. That nation introduced slavery into the Western Hemisphere in the late sixteenth century and maintained the leadership of the international slave trade among the British, Dutch, and American colonies throughout the next century. (Note Degler 49, 53; Dunston 78–82; Klein 4–14; and Scherer 19–20, 29–30.) Spain's responsibility was common knowledge in the eighteenth century. Thus, Hammon is saying to Wheatley that salvation is of greater worth than the monetary returns that Spain may have received from making slaves of men.

6. Ps. 103:1–4: "Bless the Lord, O my soul: and all that is within me, bless his holy name. Bless the Lord, O my soul, and forget not all his benefits: Who forgiveth all thine iniquities; who healeth all thy diseases; Who redeemeth thy life from destruction; who crowneth thee with loving kindness and tender mercies."

7. 2 Cor. 5:10: "For we must all appear before the judgment seat of Christ; that every one may receive the things done in his body, according to that he hath done, whether it be good or bad."

8. The poet is speaking here of the incarnation of Christ as God in the flesh (1 Tim. 3:16), but the language is also an allusion to Moses in Exod. 34:30 and 2 Cor. 3:14–15. After he had been in communion with God for several weeks, Moses had to hide his face behind a veil because its brightness was frightening to many people. Read more on the deity of Christ in Bayne, chap. 2.

9. Rom. 5:21: "That as sin hath reigned unto death, even so might grace reign through righteousness unto eternal life by Jesus Christ our Lord."

10. Ps. 34:6–8: "This poor man cried, and the Lord heard him, and saved him out of all his troubles. The angel of the Lord encampeth round about them that fear him, and delivereth them. O taste and see that the Lord is good: blessed is the man that trusteth in him."

11. Matt. 7:7–8: "Ask, and it shall be given you; seek, and ye shall find; knock, and it shall be opened unto you: For every one that asketh receiveth; and he that seeketh findeth; and to him that knocketh it shall be opened."

12. Ps. 89:1: "I will sing of the mercies of the Lord for ever: with my mouth will I make known thy faithfulness to all generations."

13. Ps. 34:1–3: "I will bless the Lord at all times: his praise shall continually be in my mouth. My soul shall make her boast in the Lord: the humble shall hear thereof, and be glad. O magnify the Lord with me, and let us exalt his name together."

14. Ps. 80:1–3: "Give ear, O Shepherd of Israel, thou that leadest Joseph like a flock; thou that dwellest between the cherubims, shine forth. Before Ephraim and Benjamin and Manasseh stir up thy strength, and come and save us. Turn us again, O God, and cause thy face to shine; and we shall be saved."

15. The line "When thou hunger hast," is adapted from a text which Hammon often uses, Isa. 55:1: "Ho, every one that thirsteth, come ye to the waters, and he that hath no money; come ye, buy, and eat." And the next line is a reference to Ps. 42:1: "As the hart panteth after the water brooks, so panteth my soul after thee, O God."

16. Ps. 13:1–3: "How long wilt thou forget me, O Lord? for ever? How long wilt thou hide thy face from me? How long shall I take counsel in my soul, having sorrow in my heart daily? How long shall mine enemies be exalted over me? Consider and hear me, O Lord my God: lighten mine eyes, lest I sleep the sleep of death."

17. Ps. 16:10–11: "For thou wilt not leave my soul in hell; neither wilt thou suffer thine Holy One to see corruption. Thou wilt show me the path of life. In thy presence is fullness of joy; at thy right hand there are pleasures for evermore."

18. Ps. 34:15: "The eyes of the Lord are upon the righteous, and his ears are open unto their cry."

19. Along with the Samaritans and publicans as groups in the New Testament that were ostracized by their communities, Hammon uses the terms "redeem," "redemption," and "Redeemer" as a method of protest that would be somewhat acceptable to white society. Scripturally, "redeem" means "to buy back," as from slavery where one is sold because of his crimes or debts. The blood of Christ is considered a payment for the debt of sin and because of it the believer was supposedly set free from all bondage. While contemporary whites took the stand that this was freedom from spiritual rather than physical bondage, Hammon used the concept interchangeably.

20. John 4:13–14: "Jesus answered and said unto her, Whosoever drinketh of this water shall thirst again: But whosoever drinketh of the water that I shall give him shall never thirst; but the water that I shall give him shall be in him a well of water springing up into everlasting life."

21. Matt. 6:33: "But seek ye first the kingdom of God, and his righteousness; and all these things shall be added unto you."

22. Ps. 116:15: "Precious in the sight of the Lord is the death of his saints."

23. Matt. 5:3, 8: "Blessed are the poor in spirit: for theirs is the kingdom of heaven. . . . Blessed are the pure in heart: for they shall see God."

24. 1 Cor. 15:51–53: "Behold, I show you a mystery; We shall not all sleep, but we shall all be changed, In a moment, in the twinkling of an eye, at the last trump: for the trumpet shall sound, and the dead shall be raised incorruptible, and we shall be changed. For this corruptible must put on incorruption, and this mortal must put on immortality."

25. Ps. 150:6: "Let everything that hath breath praise the Lord. Praise ye the Lord."

3. A Winter Piece

Introduction: Black Consciousness
and the Colonial Spirit

Just as he wrote his first published poem as an a cappella hymn, skeins of sermon themes can be seen in Hammon's essays. While all were printed texts, Hammon probably gave *An Evening's Improvement* and *An Address to the Negroes in the State of New York* first as public exhortations. But he presented *A Winter Piece* originally as a written essay. In *An Evening's Improvement* he states, "I have had an invitation to give a public exhortation; but did not think it my duty at the time; but now, my brethren, by divine assistance, I shall endeavor to show . . . " and then continues as if he were fulfilling that invitation. Schomburg and Wegelin think that Hammon was an indigenous preacher among the slaves and that his essays were extensions of his sermons (Ransom 24). Jacqueline Overton says that Hammon was a folk poet who was well known to Long Island citizens and that, in addition to those selections included in this edition, he wrote several works, including a poem celebrating the visit of Prince William Henry to Oyster Bay (147). That poem and *An Essay on the Ten Virgins,* which was advertised in the *Connecticut Courant* in December of 1779, are but two of several Hammon poems and essays which have so far not been found.

Hammon may have borrowed the title of *A Winter Piece* from a seventeenth-century devotional in the second volume of Hervey's *Meditations,* a work listed among the books in the Lloyds' library (*Lloyd Papers* 2:910). However, Hervey's topic covers God's role in creation and the changing of natural seasons. His rhetoric is very prosaic with little emphasis on salvation or evangelism, whereas Hammon's use of the wording is very symbolic: that is, "winter" as the sign of aging and death, and "piece" as a pun on the "peace" he had attained through faith and experience. Hammon was in his early seventies when he published this essay and by then he considered himself to be a knowledgeable, patriarchal slave who could subtly comment on the slave institution through biblical hermeneutics.

He begins this work with a verse of Scripture—Matt. 11:28: "Come unto me, all ye that labor and are heavy-laden"—which was the basis for traditional Christian song lyrics and which had become a major refrain of many Negro spirituals. In this former instance, Christ's invitation certainly seems to be to those who are utterly overworked and oppressed. Many slaves took the language and sentiment in this verse as applying directly to their forced labor.[1]

Clearly, as in all of his writing, Jupiter Hammon intends his prose to be a coded message to Black American slaves. In this essay he separates his readers racially by referring to his white readers—many of whom objected to his "forwardness"—as "Sirs." In *An Evening's Improvement* he complains of whites' speaking of him as "an unlearned Ethiopian," and further that they view Blacks as incapable of understanding the word of God. Thus, when Hammon writes "my brethren" repeatedly in his essays, he is, first, being ironic toward whites in his audience and, second, addressing his remarks more to his "brethren" racially than to his "brethren" in Christ. He insists that he writes "to enlighten the minds of my brethren . . . we are a poor despised nation" and he refers to "my brethren, for whom this discourse is designed." He also clearly defines his audience with "my brethren it is not we servants only that are unworthy."

He not only delineates his audience; he makes no attempt to merge them under a joint Christian banner. Although he does chide whites for their lack of concern for slave children, nowhere does he challenge whites to love Blacks or encourage slaves to love their masters. But he tells the slaves that "if we love God, Black as we be and despised as we are, God will love us." While he was aware of the New Testament instruction to "let brotherly love continue" (Heb. 13:1; see also James 2:8, 1 Pet. 1:22, etc.), like his contemporaries—Richard Allen, Absalom Jones, Phillis Wheatley, and Samson Occom—Hammon was too affected by the rejection of most white churchmen to pretend further their brotherhood or their love.[2] Thus the aging minister is being ironic when he speaks of slaves brought to "a Christian land" to be reared by "what are called Christian families." Throughout his work he implies that as God had commanded "real" Christians to help the poor—and slaves were foremost in the ranks of poverty in the colonies—white slaveholders were directly disobeying that commandment, which obviated their profession of Christianity.[3]

Hammon introduces the main body of this essay with a popular theme of early Black American literature. He alludes to Moses' deliverance of the Children of Israel from Egypt:

> My brethren, many of us are seeking a temporal freedom and I wish you may obtain it; remember that all power in heaven and on earth belongs to God. If we are slaves, it is by the permission of God; if we are free, it must be by the power of the Most High God. Stand still and see the salvation of God. Cannot that same power that divided the waters from the waters for the children of Israel to pass through make way for your freedom?

The language is part of Moses' speech to the Israelites when he raised his staff to part the water of the Red Sea: "Fear ye not, stand still, and see the salvation of the Lord, which he will show to you to day: for the Egyptians who ye have seen to day, ye shall see them again no more for ever" (Exod. 14:13). In as obvious a public statement against slavery that a slave can make, Hammon says that the same God who freed Israel can free the African from American tyranny. He was the first Black believer of Christian persuasion to relate Israel's bondage to the African slaves in writing, but the theme is continuous in Black American literature and theology.[4] Hammon concludes his allusion to the Israel passage with another text that other Black preachers, singers, and writers employed until the Civil War era: "If the Son therefore shall make you free, ye shall be free indeed" (John 8:36). While contemporary white theologians preferred to limit biblical intent to spiritual, not physical, freedom, the hope that this essay provides for oppressed slaves was, Hammon knew, undeniable.

In addition to "my brethren," Hammon calls his fellow slaves "Africans by nation" or "Ethiopians." Although born in America, Hammon was the first African to leave printed evidence that slaves recognized the treachery of cultural alienation. He refers to his brethren as "ancient" in order to uplift his fellow servants with a sense of inclusion in a history older than that of their British masters. Whether Hammon acquired this vision of his ethnic past through parental training or biblical exposure, that view of ancient history has been a continuing source of pride and identity for Black Americans to the present day. It has also been the impetus for a recurring quest for authentic African history and culture. His knowledge of an African presence in ancient times—along with his eschatological hope of ultimate and everlasting victory for Africans—provided a view of time past and time future that ameliorated somewhat his suffering. His immediate literary descendant, Phillis Wheatley, also saw the ambiguous relationship that Blacks had with America. In her poem "On the Death of the Reverend Mr. George Whitefield," Wheatley pens, "Take him my dear *Americans*" and then "Take him, ye *Africans,*" making a distinction in both race and nationality. Apparently the tensions between African Americans and European Americans loomed as irreconcilable in the eighteenth century as they do today.

Black, white, slave, free. These—like life, death, judgment, and eternity—were, for Hammon, always dichotomous. He reduced life to the slave's struggle to be free, at least spiritually, from his oppression, even if physical freedom seemed impossible. Hammon espoused no apocalyptic vision of the end of physical bondage during his lifetime. He believed that only through death could the slave, or even the free Black, escape the imponderable effects of racism. Within his dual parameters those slaves who did not accept Christ succumbed to oppressive attempts to put them into a state of spiritual and moral lethargy from which Hammon felt only interior faith could awaken them. Those who discovered this faith awakened to a new experience, one continuing after death through a physical transformation eventually erasing the separating veils of color and race.

Hammon, therefore, looked for biblical examples to complement and explain these opposites in order to give Blacks in his audience an idea of how God viewed them. One biblical character helpful in this regard was the woman of Samaria from John 4, a text which Hammon used often precisely because it proves Christ's concern for those whom dominant society ostracizes. As with "Redeemer," Hammon's audience would have clearly recognized his association of Samaritans with the oppressed.[5]

Hammon also draws upon the publican, another outcast in Hebrew society at the time of Christ. The Greek term for publican means "tax gatherer" (Cruden 520). These men, considered traitors to their native Israel, not only collected taxes for the Roman Empire, but levied additional surcharges which they pocketed themselves. The religious Pharisees, who composed the aristocratic class of the Jewish nation, constantly condemned Jesus because he often dined with publicans and had many friends among them. To the Pharisees, publicans remained anathema. They branded these tax collectors as among the worst of sinners (Matt. 11:19, Luke 5:29). Repeatedly throughout his essays, Hammon relates Africans with those publicans so hated by the power brokers of their day. He cites an occasion when Christ lauded a penitent publican as more acceptable to God than a self-righteous Pharisee. Thus, Hammon equated churchgoing slaveholders with those Pharisees. He also indicates that African slaves can find more acceptance with God than religionists using all of their political machinations.

When Hammon quotes Acts 10:34–35—"Then Peter opened his mouth, and said, Of a truth I perceive that God is no respecter of persons: But in every nation he that feareth him, and worketh righteousness, is accepted with him"—he wants his audience to know that the Apostle Peter, leader of Christian believers in Acts, included Africans in the invitation for salvation. Peter, as an orthodox, circumspect Jew and a diligent keeper of the Laws of Moses, had very little contact with Gentiles. Before God called him to take the Gospel to an Italian military officer named Cornelius, Peter has a vision in which he saw a sheet filled with various forbidden animals. When a voice commanded him to eat these animals, Peter refused, saying that as a circumspect Israelite he had "never eaten anything . . . common or unclean." To which the voice in the vision replied, "What God hath cleansed that call not thou common."

During his meeting with Cornelius, the first European to whom the Apostles took the Gospel, Peter voices a subsequently oft-repeated phrase: "God is no respecter of persons." Again Hammon's eighteenth-century readers would have been quite comfortable with the text and the phrase. The Apostle James repeats the admonition in explaining the obligations that the rich have to care for the poor (James 2:8–16). Abolitionists used the "respecter of persons" text often in the battle against slavery. Hammon also drew upon it as a favorite text source. Donald G. Mathews in his article, "Religion and Slavery: The American South," agrees that abolitionists employed the "God is no respecter of persons" verse quite prevalently in antislavery arguments in both the eighteenth and nineteenth centuries. Hammon intended white colonists to concede that just as Peter had to forsake his traditional cultural moorings in order to obey the Gospel of Christian love, they must do the same.

Hammon's discourses were biblically based for both spiritual and civil reasons. Often during, and even before, the Great Awakening, evangelists used the concepts of "faith" and "repentance" as necessary facets of personal soul-searching preceding salvation.[6] He demonstrated to Blacks in his audience that he expected true repentance from them, that God accepted only faith and conversion, without hypocrisy.[7] But he is urging that slaves not only accept Christ but also try to enter the church mainstream through baptism and Communion. What twentieth-century critics (who claim that Hammon was so concerned with religion that he ignored slavery) do not realize is that with this "religious" advice, Hammon was once again directly challenging societal slave laws and the conscience of the church. In seventeenth-and eighteenth-century New England, baptism meant political enfranchisement and economic empowerment for whites. But when a minute number of Blacks experienced conversion and sought the same privileges, the baffled colonists changed the laws. Edwin V. Morgan, in his "Slavery in New York," cites legislation in 1706 that prohibited freedom as a result of baptism: "The Baptizing of any Negro, Indian or Mulatto Slave, shall not be any cause or reason for the setting them or any of them at Liberty"(8).[8]

For the Puritan Congregationalists (members of the church that the Lloyds attended for several years until an Anglican church was built in their hamlet), not even baptism guaranteed slaves the same assurances as those guaranteed the children of the Puritans. Norman Pettit makes the colonists' prejudiced perspective plain. No amount of baptism, conversion, or Communion could make a non-white communicant equal to the Puritan's child:

> If any "black Moors," people of "other nations," or "men out of the East Indies" will submit to the covenant, they must be baptized. But those who have been "consecrated to God" from birth have an "inward right to glory." They have received "more helps from the Almighty" than those who have not been God's children and so must "return more." (92)

After baptism, Communion, as the visible union of God and man in the earth, became the central act in Christian fellowship. Stoddardism was the acknowledged theory of Communion in the middle colonies by the time of Hammon's adulthood. He often quotes its namesake, Solomon Stoddard of Massachusetts, an important seventeenth-century evangelical theologian and pastor who had a propensity for preaching colorful hellfire sermons. Stoddardism, a concept that enraged other clergymen (like Increase Mather and Jonathan Edwards) provided that persons of good moral character could share in Communion although they had not exhibited what more conservative Calvinists could authenticate as outward evidences of grace. This more liberal access to the Communion table broadened the church door for Blacks throughout the colonies, thus giving them more contact with the larger community (Malone 59–60). Just as with baptism, conservative colonists resisted "integrated" Communion service with Africans. Following Mather's advice, they preferred that slaves would commune in a separate fellowship. But before the burgeoning of Black churches and clergy leadership throughout the colonies in the nineteenth century, all-Black congregating, even for Communion, was illegal. Thus, every time Hammon encourages his fellow Africans to seek full participation in the sacred rituals, he is testing the sincerity of white evangelical commitment to Christ's commandments for love and brotherhood, especially around the Communion table (as explained in Luke 22:1–20, Matt. 26:20–29, etc.). Not in line with expectations of Christian piety in early New England, such testing put a strain on white churchmen to allow slaves the social privileges offered to other communicants.[9]

The presence of Native Americans and Africans provided the ultimate test of Christian experience for white Christians. Even many of those who sincerely wanted to end slavery did not envision brotherhood and equality for the African within the Body of Christ. For instance, Samuel Sewall, one of the earliest antislavery advocates, says in his tract, *The Selling of Joseph,* "And there is such a disparity in their conditions, colour and hair, that they can never embody with us, and grow up into orderly families, to the peopling of the Land." Yet, in his text, Sewall uses brotherhood itself as a basis for the sin of the patriarch Joseph's enslavement and what he saw as the comparable crime of American slavery. Such ambiguity was contrary to the way that colonial Blacks interpreted biblical requirements for Christian love, but it was the stance of some of the most liberal eighteenth-century white Christians. Even some of the very antislavery activist Quakers, who, like Sewall, adamantly denounced slavery, nonetheless showed reticence to include Blacks wholly in church worship and even less in church leadership.

After their conversions, African slaves had very different perspectives of God and of Christ than those of whites. They believed that God created all men equally and that he called them (as Hammon says "of every nation") without a schema of superiority for some, inferiority for others. Not only did slaves see Christ as particularly reaching out to pariahs like the Samaritans and publicans, they saw him as their own unique Deliverer. Aware of this reality, Hammon, in his writing and public speaking, always presented Christ as liberating the outcast, the ill, the condemned. An avid Bible reader, he also knew that the term "Savior" is usually found in the Old Testament in conjunction with God's deliverance of Israel from slavery in Egypt. Most colonists would have heard sermons illustrating this usage of a major title for Jesus Christ. A contemporary reference, Covel's *Dictionary* lists a particularly pertinent definition of "Savior" as "a deliverer, preserver, who saves from danger or destruction, and brings into a state of prosperity and happiness" (427). As Covel purports, "Savior" was known in the eighteenth century as an omnipotent deliverer, a protector from any evil, whether the trouble be of a temporal, earthly nature or of an ethereal, other-worldly origin.[10]

Literate Christians would also have read the term often in Scripture—again usually dealing with Israel's deliverance from slavery in Egypt: "My saviour, thou savest me from violence" (2 Sam. 22:3); "They forgat God their saviour, which had done great things in Egypt" (Ps. 106:21); "And it shall be for a sign and for witness unto the Lord of hosts in the land of Egypt: for they shall cry unto the Lord because of oppressors, and he shall send them a saviour and a great one, and he shall deliver them" (Isa. 19:20).

A theologian widely read in England and the colonies, William Burkitt (whose work was in the Lloyd library), wrote of Christ as "that Saviour not a particular Saviour to the Jews only, but an universal Saviour, whose *salvation is to the ends of the earth*" (1:266). Hammon and his fellow Africans saw the benevolence of such a Savior as being as racially applicable to them as to Jews or Caucasians.

Similarly, in his essay "Christ the Only Saviour," the seventeenth-century Anglican bishop William Beveridge equates "Savior" with the actor and "salvation" with the act:

> For salvation is a word that has various significations in Holy Scripture; sometimes it is used for deliverance from temporal troubles; sometimes for safety and protection from them; sometimes for grace to eschew evil and do good; sometimes for the remission of sins and reconciliation unto God; sometimes for eternal life and happiness in the other world. Now the question is, in what sense the word is to be understood in my text? I answer, in all senses: all sorts of salvation are here signified by it; for the apostle here speaks indefinitely. There is no salvation in any other but in Christ; no name whereby we can be any way saved but this; he is the only Saviour of mankind in all respects. (*Works* 3:5)

As the leading Anglican theologian in print in England and the colonies, Beveridge (whose volumes were also included in the Lloyd library) wanted evangelicals to apply "Savior" to all aspects of human experience. When any oppressed people accept this theology, obviously they would seek Christ as the Deliverer from their most immediate oppressions; and for the African in America the paramount oppression was slavery.

The slaves' self-formulated concepts about God and his relationship to them also included assumptions about the essence of God's identity and "physical" appearance, subjects of great interest to evangelical revivalism. Though usually unspoken, the underlying assumption made by white colonists—based on the symbolic spiritualization of blackness and whiteness—was that God is light skinned or white. Certainly, Western iconography, through Anglicized images of Christ, had made him so by the eighteenth-century. In institutionalized Christianity, Satan was seen as black and God as white. Testimony during seventeenth- and eighteenth-century witchcraft trials reinforced this thinking and helped to increase walls of suspicion and hatred between the races.

Light and dark imagery as a supposed continuation of spiritual realities can be seen in Poole's treatment of a verse from Eph. 5:8 ("For ye were sometimes darkness, but now are ye light in the Lord: walk as children of light"):

> And because the night is the time of darkness, and the day of light, he therefore hereby describes their present state positively, "ye are all the children of the light, and the children of the day," which is an Hebraisme: Ye are darker Light of Nature, or the Light of Prophecy which the Jews had, compared to a Lamp, 2 Peter 1:19. but ye are Children of the day, as the time of the Gospel is called day, Romans, 13:12, 2 Cor. 6:2. Negatively, "Ye are not of the night nor of darkness," your state is exceeding different from other Gentiles, and from what it once was, as the light is from the darkness, and day from night, not as if there was no ignorance remaining in them, for the best men see but through a glass darkly, 1 Cor. 13:12. but the Apostle compares them with their former estate when they were Gentiles, and with the Jews, under the Law, and with respect to their state is Christ, they were not Children of night, or as to their state of the night, but children of the Light, and of the Day. (Poole, n.p.)

Another example of the translation from spiritual to material reality through the medium of color is articulated in Cotton Mather's discussion of witchcraft:

> Go tell mankind, that there are Devils and witches; and that those nightbirds least appear where the Day-light of the Gospel comes, yet New-Engl. has had examples of their Existence and Operation; and that not only the Wigwams of Indians, where the pagan Powers often raise their masters, in the shapes of Bears and Snakes and Fires, but the Houses of Christians, where our God has His constant Worship, have undergone the Anoyance of Evil spirits. (Burr, *Narratives* 99)

Within the contexts of these conclusions are implicit theories that material appearances merely reflect spiritual realities.[11]

The church easily incorporated such theology in the society through the power of language. In *A Winter Piece* Hammon writes of the potency of language to demarcate the status of the African as a quasi beast and a slave. In effect, slaveholders turned their own definitions of Black identity into a curse by permeating every aspect of the victim's life with a slave mentality, thus making the African contemptible among his countrymen. Hammon's observations confirm the incompatibility of a professing Christian who would bless God as his Father (that is, image maker) on the one hand and on the other hand curse his fellowman. With the mere force of language, white colonists exalted themselves as chosen above other men—as elect, pure, and "white"—and condemned their slaves as beneath other men—as rejected, evil, and "black." Thus, they devised rather self-serving interpretations of the Bible, renderings which Hammon and most other Blacks in the colonies rejected.[12]

Whites based conclusions about innate evil in Africans on hypotheses of inherited racial sin. In his discussions of sin, Hammon has in mind several separate but interdependent definitions to counter such postulates. When he says to his African audience, "It is not we only that are unworthy," he speaks of the curse of Ham (Genesis 9), the curse's connection to African racial identity, and its implications of God's preordination of slavery. Certain revelation could thwart white theologians attempts to laden Africans with abnormal guilt. While Hammon's masters probably gave him a name to identify him with the biblical Ham,[13] nowhere does the poet ever accept the Anglo-European theory that Africans descended from Ham or were included in Ham's curse. Conversely, he attempts to inauthenticate colonial philosophy that Blacks as descendants of Ham inherited a peculiar depravity predisposing them to be slaves. Hammon insists that—as stated in Gal. 3:13—Christ's blood absolves this and all other curses to which mankind is heir. The aged preacher wants Blacks to know that even if true, Christ's death erased the Ham curse. Moreover, he argues that all mankind, not just Africans, fell through Adam's sin, and all can be saved only through true and absolute belief in Christ.

When Hammon speaks to Blacks in his audience about sin, he is concerned with their individual natures and moral acts, behavior which cannot be directly attributed to the fault of their oppressors. He believed that they would answer for these acts after death; thus, he asked his African readers to repent. He does not offer repentance of individual sins as an avenue to his white readers because he concludes that they have heard the Gospel and have, through their lack of love for men of other races, individually and corporately, rejected Christ.[14]

Thus for his fellow Africans, this preacher, who was very typically an eighteenth-century hellfire evangelist in many ways, would not use the rhetoric of fear endemic to his age. He knew that fear served as the cudgel of slavery and that his people had been hammered far too much with this emotion. When he ends the essay with an appendage, "Contemplation on the Death of Christ," he carefully tells his readers, "I shall not attempt to drive you to Christ by the terrors of the law, but I shall endeavor to allure you by the invitation of the gospel." Surely this tenderness is one of the characteristics which made Hammon so popular among slaves and even ingratiated him to some slave masters, who nonetheless had to endure antithetical attention— his veiled, but nonetheless harsh, condemnation.

Notes

1.   For example, see such slave hymns as "O Brothers, Don't Get Weary"; "Sweet Music"; and "Cheer the Weary Traveler"; and slave narratives by William and Ellen Craft (in Bontemps); Frederick Douglass; Olaudah Equiano; and others. For additional information on the themes and rhythms of slave spirituals, see Fisher; Floyd; Katz; and Thurman.

Patricia Caldwell notes that "all ye" of Matt. 11:28, according to the Geneva Bible (a sixteenth-century translation that may have been available to Hammon), refers to all who "fele the waight, & grief of your sinnes and miseries" (28). Blacks in Hammon's time understandably took this phrase as appropriately applying to physical tiredness as well as to spiritual need.

2.   For similar Black evangelical experiences, see Allen, *Life Experience,* which also includes Jones' testimony; Wheatley's letter to the Native American preacher Samson Occom written after her freedom [Lay, *Am I Not* 306].

3.   Two other noted churchmen writing about the slavery question, S. Hopkins (*Timely Articles*) and J. C. Lovejoy (*Memoir*), castigated

whites and identified Blacks as the nation's poor who should have been receiving solace from Christians and not enslavement.

4.   Eugene D. Genovese remarks that the American slave particularly merged the persons of Moses and Christ into one figure (251–55). See also Coleman 84; Thurman 12–15; and Gustavas Vassa's *Life* in Bontemps 79–80.

5.   For instance, see Burkitt's entry for Luke 17:11–15 in *Notes* 1:372–73; and Poole's entries for John 4, Matt. 10:5, and Luke 9:52–53.

6.   For instance, Bishop Beveridge in his *Thesaurus* has a sermon outline on preparation for Communion. The communicant was first to know Christ. Then he was to repent of "original, actual, and habitual" sin. Beveridge said, "No repentance, no faith . . . without repentance, no pardon."

7.   The irony of slave conversion is a fascinating topic in American history; see Andrews; Beveridge, "Faith and Repentence"in *Works,* vol. 8; Cherry 100, 117, 128; Ernst; Greene, *The Negro* 259–75; Jernegan, "Slavery" 504–27; McKee, 24–40; and Scherer 15–18, 114–49.

8.   In addition, see Ernst; Greene, *The Negro* 259–275; C. Mather's *Negro Christianized,* in Ruchames 66–68; Greene, "Slave-Holding" 505–10; and E. J. McManus, *History* 19–21.

9.   See Baird Tipson's discussion, "Invisible Saints" 460–71, as well as the Apostle John's direction that love of the brethren is the test of true Christianity in 1 John 3–4. For further discussion of the slaves' baptism, conversion, and church membership as instruments of freedom, see studies by Greene, *The Negro* 257–89; Jernegan, "Slavery" 504–27; Scherer 89–91; and Weatherford 31–35. For other texts that describe and assess Stoddard's inclusion of all men in the sacraments and church membership, refer to Carr 274–78; Coffman 69–82; and Walsh 97–114.

10.   See also Brown's *Dictionary* 513–14.

11.   For further reading, see Baltazar 149–65; Berwanger 266–75; Cantor; Clarkson 213–20; Devisse and Mollat, vol. 2; Dunston 3–13; Jordan, *White over Black;* Littlejohn; Ovington; and Snowden, *The Image,* vol. 1. The color symbolism quickly led to the conclusion that the African was soulless. See Jordan, *White Man's* 3–25. Regarding the Black man's need for a God who is Spirit and who is not imaged as either black or white, see the portion of Countee Cullen's poem "Heritage" and Benjamin Mays' accompanying discussion in *The Negro's God,* 218–20.

12.   For more discussion on Black perceptions of white Christians and of codifications of their own Christian experience, see Agate,

"Slavery and Christian Theology," in Hastings 611–12; P. M. Jones; Litwack; Mays; Tipson 460–71; and both of Kelly Miller's texts. For remarks by slaves who believed that their theology was superior to that of white Christians see the letter from Nathaniel Paul of Bristol, England, to William L. Garrison, in Woodson, *The Mind* 166; and Pennington, in Bontemps 10–11, 71.

13.   Refer to Branston; Cobb 25–30, 47–49; Dunston 51–53; S. Hopkins, *Timely Articles* 263–65; Remy 24–25; Ruchames 89–99; 212–16; and Sewall's *Selling of Joseph*.

14.   Hammon's basic conception of sin and incomplete or shallow conversion is no different from the Anglican-Calvinist view, shown for example in Beveridge, *Works* 7:7, 240–42. As Thomas A. Schafer writes, "According to covenant theology, Adam and Christ are federal heads and the sin of one and the righteousness of the other are imputed to those represented by them" (54). Also see Hindson; and Steele and Thomas 24–30.

A Winter Piece

As I have been desired to write[1] something more than poetry, I shall endeavor to write from these words: "Come unto me, all ye that labor and are heavy-laden" (Matt. 11:28). My brethren, I shall endeavor by divine assistance to show what is meant by coming to the Lord Jesus Christ laboring and heavy-laden, and to conclude, I shall contemplate the death of Jesus Christ.

My brethren, in the first place I am to show what is meant by coming to Christ laboring and heavy-laden. We are to come with a sense of our own unworthiness to confess our sins before the Most High God, to come by prayer and meditation, and we are to confess Christ to be our Savior and Mighty Redeemer. "Whosoever therefore shall confess me before men, him will I confess also before my Father which is in heaven" (Matt. 10:32). Here, my brethren, we have great encouragement to come to the Lord and to ask for the influence of his Holy Spirit and that he would give us the water of eternal life. "But whosoever drinketh of the water [as the woman of Samaria did] that I shall give him shall never thirst; but the water that I shall give him shall be in him a well of water springing up into everlasting life" (John 4:14). Then we shall believe in the merits of Christ for our eternal salvation and come laboring and heavy-laden with a sense of our lost and undone state without an interest in the merits of Christ. It should be our greatest care to trust in the Lord, as David did, "In thee, O Lord, I put my trust" (Ps. 31:1).

My brethren, we must come to the divine fountain to turn us from sin to holiness and to give us grace to repent of our sins; this none can do but God. We must come laboring and heavy-laden, not trusting to our own righteousness, but we are to be clothed with the righteousness of Christ. Then we may apply this text: "Blessed is he whose transgression is forgiven, whose sin is covered" (Ps. 32:1). This we must seek by prayer and meditation, and we are to pray without ceasing, as set forth by David in Ps. 51:1: "Have mercy upon me, O God, according to thy loving kindness: according unto the multitude of thy tender mercies blot out my transgressions." My brethren, we are to come poor in spirit.

In the second place, in order to come to the divine fountain laboring and heavy-laden, we are to avoid all bad company and to keep ourselves pure in heart. "Blessed are the pure in heart: for they shall see God" (Matt. 5:8). Now, in order to see God, we must have a saving change wrought in our hearts, which is the work of God's Holy Spirit, which we are to ask for. "Ask, and it shall be given you; seek, and ye shall find" (Matt. 7:7). It may be asked, what shall we find? Ye will find the mercies of God to allure you, the influence of his Holy Spirit to guide you in the right way to eternal life. "For every one that asketh receiveth" (Matt. 7:8). But then my brethren, we are to ask in a right manner, with faith and repentance, for except we repent, we shall surely die.[2] That is, we must suffer the wrath of the Most High God, who will turn you away with this pronunciation: " . . . depart from me, ye that work iniquity" (Matt. 7:23). Therefore you see how dangerous a thing it is to live in any known sin, either of commission or omission, for if we commit any willful sin, we become the servants of sin. " . . . Whosoever committeth sin is the servant of sin" (John 8:34).

My dear brethren, have we not rendered ourselves too much the servants of sin by a breach of God's holy commandments, by breaking his holy Sabbath when we should have been preparing for our great and last change? Have we not been amusing ourselves with the pleasures of this life? Or if we have attended divine service, have we been sincere? For God will not be mocked,[3] for he knows our thoughts. "God is a Spirit: and they that worship him must worship him in spirit and in truth" (John 4:24). Therefore, my brethren, we see how necessary it is that we should be sincere when we attempt to come to the Lord, whether in public service or private devotion, for it is not the outward appearance, but the sincerity of the heart. This we must manifest by a holy life. For it is "not everyone that saith unto me, Lord, Lord, shall enter into the kingdom of heaven; but he that doeth the will of my Father which is in heaven" (Matt. 7:21).

Therefore we ought to come laboring and heavy-laden to the throne of grace and pray that God may be pleased to transform us anew in Christ Jesus. But it may be objected by those who have had the advantage of studying that everyone is not calculated for teaching others. To those I answer, "Sirs I do not attempt to teach those who I know are able to teach me, but I shall endeavor by divine assistance to enlighten the minds of my brethren. For we are a poor despised nation whom God in his wise providence has permitted to be brought from their native place to a Christian land, where many thousands have been born in what are called Christian families and brought up to years of understanding."

In answer to the objectors, "Sirs, pray give me leave to inquire into the state of those children that are born in those Christian families. Have they been baptized, taught to read, and taught their catechism? Surely this is a duty incumbent on masters or heads of families. Sirs, if you had a sick child, would you not send for a doctor? If your house were on fire, would you not strive to put it out to save your interest? Surely then, you ought to use the means appointed to save the souls that God has committed to your charge and not forget the words of Joshua: 'As for me and my house we will serve the Lord' (Josh. 24:15). Children should be taught the fear of God. See what Solomon says: 'The fear of the Lord is to hate evil' (Prov. 8:13);

'The fear of the Lord is the beginning of wisdom' (Prov. 9:10); 'The fear of the Lord is a fountain of life' (Prov. 14:27). Here we see that children should fear the Lord.''

But I turn to my brethren, for whom this discourse is designed. My brethren, if you are desirous of being saved by the merits of Jesus Christ, you must forsake all your sins and come to the Lord; by prayer and repentance of all your former sins, come laboring and heavy-laden. For we are invited to come and rely on the blessed Jesus for eternal salvation. "Whosoever therefore shall confess me before men, him will I confess also before my Father which is in heaven" (Matt. 10:32). Here we have our Savior's words for our encouragement. See to it, my brethren, that you live a holy life and that you walk more circumspectly, or holy, than you have done heretofore. I now assure you that "God is a Spirit: and they that worship him must worship him in spirit and in truth" (John 4:24). Therefore, if you would come unto him, come as the poor publican did and say: "God be merciful to me, a sinner." "And the publican, standing afar off, would not lift up so much as his eyes unto heaven, but smote upon his breast, saying, God be merciful to me a sinner" (Luke 18:13). For if we hope to be saved by the merits of Jesus Christ, we cast off all self-dependence as our own righteousness. "For by grace are ye saved through faith; and that not of yourselves: it is the gift of God" (Eph. 2:8).

Here we see that the imperfection of human nature is such that we cannot be saved by any other way but the name of Jesus Christ and that there must be a principle of love and fear of God implanted in our hearts if we desire to come to the divine fountain laboring and heavy-laden with our sins. But the inquirer may inquire, "How do you prove this doctrine? Are you not imposing on your brethren, as you know that many of them cannot read?" To this I answer, "Sir, I do not mean to impose on my brethren but to show them that there must be a principle of fear and love to God." And now I am to prove this doctrine that we ought to fear God. "For as the heaven is high above the earth, so great is his mercy toward them that fear him. . . . Like as a father pitieth his children, so the Lord pitieth them that fear him" (Ps. 103:11, 13). "O fear the Lord, ye his saints: for there is no want to them that fear him. . . . Come, ye children, hearken unto me: I will teach you the fear of the Lord" (Ps. 34:9, 11). This may suffice to prove the doctrine that we ought to fear the Lord. Here, my brethren, we see how much our salvation depends on our being transformed anew in Christ Jesus, for we are sinners by nature and are adding thereunto every day of our lives. For man is prone to evil, as the sparks to fly upward.[4] This thought should put us on our guard against all manner of evil, especially of bad company. This leads me to say that we should endeavor to glorify God in all our actions, whether spiritual or temporal, for the apostle hath told us that whatever we do, do all to the glory of God (1 Cor. 10:31).

Let us now labor for that food which tendeth unto eternal life. This none can give but God only. My brethren, it is your duty to strive to make your calling and election sure by a holy life, working out your salvation with fear and trembling, for we are invited to come without money and without price: "Ho, every one that thirsteth, come ye to the waters, and he that hath no money; come ye, buy, and eat; yea, come, buy wine and milk without money and without price" (Isa. 55:1). This leads me to say that if we suffer as sinners, under the light of the gospel as sinners, the fault is in us, for our Savior hath told us that if he had not come, we should not have had sin, but now we have no cloak for our sins. Let us now improve our talents by coming laboring and burdened with a sense of our sins. This certainly is a necessary duty of all mankind: to come to the divine fountain for mercy and for the influence of God's Holy Spirit to guide us through this wilderness to the mansions of eternal glory.[5]

My brethren, have we not great encouragement to come unto the Lord Jesus Christ? "Ask, and it shall be given you; seek, and ye shall find; knock, and it shall be opened unto you" (Matt. 7:7). Therefore, if you desire to be saved by the merits of Christ, you must come as the prodigal son did: "And the son said unto him, Father, I have sinned against heaven, and in thy sight, and am no more worthy to be called thy son" (Luke 15:21). This is the language of the true penitent, for he is made sensible that there is no other name given by which he can be saved but by the name of Jesus. Therefore we should put our trust in him and strive to make our calling and election sure by prayer and meditation. "Give ear to my prayer, O God; and hide not thyself from my supplication" (Ps. 55:1).

But, my brethren, are we not too apt to put off the thoughts of death till we are sick or some misfortune happens to us, forgetting the bountiful hand that gives us every good gift? Doth not the tokens of mortality call aloud to us all to prepare for death, our great and last change, not flattering ourselves with the hopes of a long life, for we know not what a day may bring forth? Therefore, my brethren, let it be your greatest care to prepare for death, that great and irresistible king of terrors. We are, many of us, advanced in years and we know not how soon God may be pleased to call us out of this life to an endless eternity. For this is the lot of all men, once to die, and after that the judgement. Let us now come to the Lord Jesus Christ with a sense of our own impotence to do any good thing of ourselves and with a thankful remembrance of the death of Christ, who died to save lost man and hath invited us to come to him laboring and heavy-laden. My ancient brethren, let us examine ourselves now to see whether we have had a saving change wrought in our hearts and have repented of our sins. Have we made it our greatest care to honor God's Holy Word and to keep his holy Sabbaths and to obey his commandments? God says that he shows "mercy unto thousands of them that love me, and keep my commandments" (Exod. 20:6). Have we been brought to bow to the divine sovereignty of the Most High God and to fly to the arms of the crucified Jesus, at whose crucifixion the mountains trembled, and the rocks rent, and the graves were opened, and many bodies of saints that slept arose?

Come, my dear fellow servants and brothers, Africans by nation, we are all invited to come: "Then Peter opened his mouth, and said, Of a truth I perceive that God is no respecter of persons: But in every nation he that feareth him, and worketh righteousness, is accepted with him" (Acts 10:34–35). My brethren, many of us are seeking a temporal freedom and I wish you may obtain it; remember that all power in heaven and on earth belongs to God. If we are slaves, it is by the permission of God; if we are free, it must be by the power of the Most High God.[6] Stand still and see the salvation of God. Cannot that same power that divided the waters from the waters for the children of Israel to pass through make way for your freedom? I pray that God would grant your desire and that he may give you grace to seek that freedom which tendeth to eternal life. "And ye shall know the truth and the truth shall make you free. . . . If the Son therefore shall make you free, ye shall be free indeed" (John 8:32, 36).[7] This we know, my brethren: " . . . that all things work together for good to them that love God . . . " (Rom. 8:28). Let us manifest this love to God by a holy life.

My dear brethren, as it hath been reported that I had petitioned to the court of Hartford against freedom, I now solemnly declare that I have never said nor done anything, neither directly nor indirectly, to promote or to prevent freedom. But my answer hath always been: "I am a stranger here and I do not care to be concerned or to meddle with public affairs." By this declaration I hope my friend will be satisfied and all prejudice removed. Let us all strive to be united together in love and to become new creatures, for " . . . if any man be in Christ, he is a new creature: old things are passed away; behold, all things are become new" (2 Cor. 5:17). Now, to be a new creature is to have our minds turned from darkness to light, from sin to holiness, and to have a desire to serve God with our whole hearts and to follow his precepts. "More to be desired are they than gold, yea, than much fine gold: sweeter also than honey and the honeycomb. Moreover by them is thy servant warned: and in keeping of them there is great reward" (Ps. 19:10–11).

Let me now, my brethren, persuade you to prepare for death by prayer and meditation. That is the way of Matt. 6:6: " . . . when thou prayest, enter into thy closet, and when thou hast shut thy door, pray to thy Father which is in secret; and thy Father which seeth in secret shall reward thee openly."

My brethren, while we continue in sin, we are enemies to Christ, ruining ourselves and harming the commonwealth. Let us now, my brethren, come laboring and heavy-laden, with a sense of our sins; and let us pray that God may in his mercy be pleased to lift up the gates of our hearts and open the doors of our souls, that the King of Glory may come in and set these things home on our hearts. "Lift up your heads, O ye gates; and be ye lift up ye everlasting doors; and the King of glory shall come in" (Ps. 24:7). Then may we rely on the merits of Christ and say as David did: "In the Lord put I my trust" (Ps. 11:1); and again, "whom have I in heaven but thee? and there is none upon earth that I desire beside thee" (Ps. 73:25).

And now my brethren, I shall endeavor to prove that we are not only ruining ourselves by sin, but many others. If men in general were more humble and more holy, we should not hear the little children in the street taking God's holy name in vain. Surely our conversation should be yea, yea and nay, nay or to that purpose. "But let your communication be, Yea, yea; Nay, nay: for whatsoever is more than these cometh of evil" (Matt. 5:37). Therefore, my brethren, we should endeavor to walk humbly and holy, to avoid the appearance of evil, to live a life "void of offense toward God and toward man" (Acts 24:16). Hear what David saith: "Blessed is the man that walketh not in the counsel of the ungodly, nor standeth in the way of sinners" (Ps. 1:1). Here we see how much it becomes us to live as Christians, not in rioting and drunkenness, uncleanness, Sabbath breaking, swearing, taking God's holy name in vain; but our delight should be in the law of the Lord.

The righteous man is compared to a tree that bringeth forth fruit in season: "And he shall be like a tree planted by the rivers of water, that bringeth forth his fruit in his season; his leaf also shall not wither; and whatsoever he doeth shall prosper" (Ps. 1:3). Let us not forget the words of holy David: "man is but the dust, like the flower of the field" (Ps. 103:15).

Let us remember the uncertainty of human life and that we are many of us within a step of the grave, hanging only by the single thread of life, and we know not how soon God may send the cold hand of death and cut the thread of life. Then will our souls either ascend to the eternal mansions of glory or descend to eternal misery, our bodies lodged in the cold, silent grave, numbered with the dead. Then shall the Scripture be fulfilled: "In the sweat of thy face shalt thou eat bread, till thou return unto the ground; for out of it wast thou taken: for dust thou art, and unto dust shalt thou return" (Gen. 3:19).

Now I am to call to the unconverted, my brethren. If we desire to become true converts, we must be born again; we must have a spiritual regeneration. "Verily, verily, I say unto thee, Except a man be born again, he cannot see the kingdom of God" (John 3:3). My brethren, are we not, many of us, ignorant of this spiritual regeneration? Have we seen our lost and undone condition when we have no interest in the merits of Jesus Christ? Have we come weary and heavy-laden with our sins and to say with holy David, "O Lord, rebuke me not in thine anger, neither chasten me in thy hot displeasure" (Ps. 6:1). Hath it been our great care to prepare for death, our great and last change, by prayer and meditation?

My dear brethren, though we are servants and have not so much time as we could wish for, yet we must improve the little time we have. Mr. Burkitt, a great divine of our church,[8] says that a man's hand may be on his plow and his heart in heaven, by putting forth such prayers and ejaculations as these: "Hear my cry, O God; attend unto my prayer," and "whom have I in heaven but thee? and there is none upon earth that I desire beside thee" (Ps. 61:1; 73:25).

We should pray that God would give us his Holy Spirit so that we may not be led into temptation and that we may be delivered from evil, especially the evil of sin. "But now being made free from sin, and become servants to God, ye have your fruit unto holiness, and the end everlasting life. For the wages of sin is death; but the gift of God is eternal life through Jesus Christ our Lord" (Rom. 6:22, 23).

My brethren, seeing I am desired by my friends to write something more than poetry, give me leave to speak plainly to you. Except you repent and forsake your sins, you must surely die. Now we see how much it becomes us to break our alliance with sin and Satan, to fly to a crucified Savior, and to enlist under Christ's banner so that he may give us grace to become his faithful subjects—this should be our constant prayer. We should guard against every sin, especially against bad language.

Therefore, my brethren, we should always guard against every evil word, for we are told that the tongue is an evil member because with the tongue we bless God and with the tongue we curse men.[9] "For he that will love life, and see good days, let him refrain his tongue from evil, and his lips that they speak no guile" (1 Pet. 3:10). But the thoughtless and unconverted sinner is going on in open rebellion against that divine power which can in one minute cut the thread of life and cast sinners away with this pronunciation: Depart from me, you workers of iniquity. "Then shall he say also unto them on the left hand, Depart from me, ye cursed, into everlasting fire, prepared for the devil and his angels" (Matt. 25:41).

And now my brethren, shall we abuse the divine sovereignty of a holy God, who hath created us rational creatures, capable of serving him under the light of the gospel? For he hath told us that if he had not come unto us we had not had sin but now we have no cloak for our sin.[10] Come now, my dear brethren, accept Jesus Christ on the terms of the gospel, which is by faith and repentance. Come laboring and heavy-laden with your sins and a sense of your unworthiness.

My brethren, it is not we servants only that are unworthy; but all mankind by the fall of Adam became guilty in the sight of God (Gen. 2:17). Surely then, we are sinners by nature and are daily adding thereto by evil practices, and it is only by the merits of Jesus Christ that we can be saved. We are told that he is a Jew who is a Jew in his heart, so he is a Christian who is a Christian in his heart. And not everyone who says "Lord, Lord," shall enter into the kingdom of God but he that doeth the will of God.[11] Let our superiors act as they shall think best; we must resolve to walk in the steps our Savior hath set before us, which were a holy life and a humble submission to the will of God. "And he was withdrawn from them about a stone's cast, and kneeled down, and prayed, Saying, Father, if thou be willing, remove this cup from me: nevertheless not my will, but thine, be done" (Luke 22:41–42).

Here we have the example of our Savior, who came down from heaven to save men who were lost and undone without an interest in the merits of Jesus Christ. The blessed Jesus then gave his life, a ransom for all that come unto him by faith and repentance. And shall not "he that spared not his own Son, but delivered him up for us all, how shall he not with him also freely give us all things" (Rom. 8:32)? Come, let us seek first Christ, "the kingdom of God, and his righteousness; and all these things shall be added unto you" (Matt. 6:33). Here we have great encouragement to come to the divine fountain.

Bishop Beveridge says in his third resolution that the eyes of the Lord are intent upon us; he seeth our actions. If our sins are not washed out with our tears and crossed with the blood of Christ, we cannot be saved.[12] Come, my brethren, "O taste and see that the Lord is good: blessed is the man that trusteth in him" (Ps. 34:8). Let us not stand as Felix did and say, "Almost thou persuadest me to be a Christian."[13] But let us strive to be altogether so. If you desire to become converts, you must have a saving change wrought in your hearts that shall bring forth good works meet for repentance: "Repent ye therefore, and be converted" (Acts 3:19). We are not to trust in our own strength but to trust in the Lord. "Trust in the Lord with all thine heart; and lean not unto thine own understanding" (Prov. 3:5).

My brethren, are we not encircled with many temptations: the flesh, the world and the devil? These must be resisted at all times. We must see to it that we do not grieve the Holy Spirit of God. Come, let us, my dear brethren, draw near to the Lord by faith and repentance, for "faith without works is dead" (James 2:20); and "for with the heart men believeth unto righteousness; and with the mouth confession is made unto salvation" (Rom. 10:10). Here we see that there is something to be done by us as Christians. Therefore we should walk worthy of our profession, not forgetting that there is a divine power which takes a just survey of all our actions and will reward everyone according to his works. "Also unto thee, O Lord, belongeth mercy: for thou renderest to every man according to his work" (Ps. 62:12). Therefore it is our indispensable duty to improve all opportunities to serve God, who gave us his only Son to save all that come unto him by faith and repentance.

Let me, my brethren, persuade you to a serious consideration of your danger while you continue in an unconverted state. Did you feel the operations of God's Holy Spirit? You then would leave all for an interest in the merits of Christ: For " . . . the kingdom of heaven is like unto treasure hid in a field; that which when a man hath found, . . . he selleth all that he hath, and buyeth that field" (Matt. 13:44). So will every true penitent part with all for the sake of Christ. I shall not attempt to drive you to Christ by the terrors of the law, but I shall endeavor to allure you by the invitation of the gospel to come laboring and heavy-laden.

Man at his best estate is like a shadow of the field.[14] We should always be preparing for death, not having our hearts set on the things of this life. For what profit will it be to us to gain the whole world and lose our own souls? (Matt. 16:26). We should be always preparing for the will of God, working out our salvation with fear and trembling. O may we abound in the works of the Lord. Let us not stand as fruitless trees or encumberers of the ground, for by your works you shall be justified and by your works you shall be condemned: for every man shall be rewarded "according to his works" (Matt. 16:27). Let us then be pressing forward to the mark, for the prize of the high calling of God is Christ Jesus. Let our hearts be fixed where true joys are to be found. Let us lay up "treasures in heaven, where neither moth nor rust doth corrupt, and where thieves do not break through nor steal" (Matt. 6:20).[15]

Contemplation on the Death of Christ

Now I am come to contemplate the death of Christ; it remains that I make a short contemplation. The death of Christ who died! Died to save lost man. "For since by man came death, by man came also the resurrection of the dead. For as in Adam all

die, even so in Christ shall all be made alive" (1 Cor. 15:21–22).
Let us turn to the Scriptures, and there we shall see how our
Savior was denied by one and betrayed by another:

> Judas . . . went unto the chief priests, And said unto them, What
> will you give me . . . ? And they covenanted with him for thirty
> pieces of silver. And from that time he sought opportunity to
> betray him (Matt. 26:14–16). For this is my blood of the new
> testament, which is shed for many for the remission of sins (Matt.
> 26:28). Peter answered and said unto him, Though all men shall
> be offended because of thee, yet will I never be offended (Matt.
> 26:33). Jesus said unto him, Verily I say unto thee, That this
> night, before the cock crow, thou shalt deny me thrice (Matt.
> 26:34). Then saith he unto them, My soul is exceeding sorrowful,
> even unto death: tarry ye here, and watch with me (Matt. 26:38).
> And he went a little farther and fell on his face, and prayed,
> saying, O my Father, if it be possible, let this cup pass from me:
> nevertheless not as I will, but as thou wilt. (Matt. 26:39)

My brethren, here we see the love of God plainly set before
us: that while we were yet sinners, he sent his Son to die for all
those that come unto him, laboring and heavy-laden with a
sense of their sins. Let us come with a thankful remembrance of
his death, whose blood was shed for us guilty worms of the dust:

> But Jesus held his peace. And the high priest answered and said
> unto him, I adjure thee by the living God, that thou tell us
> whether thou be the Christ, the Son of God (Matt. 26:63). Jesus
> saith unto him, Thou hast said: nevertheless I say unto you,
> Hereafter shall ye see the Son of man sitting on the right hand of
> power, and coming in the clouds of heaven (Matt. 26:64). Then
> the high priest rent his clothes, saying, He hath spoken blas-
> phemy; what further need have we of witnesses? behold, now ye
> have heard his blasphemy. (Matt. 26:65)

Here the high priest charged the blessed Jesus with blasphemy.
But we must believe that he is able to save all that come unto
him, by faith and repentance. "And Jesus came and spake unto
them, saying, All power is given unto me in heaven and in
earth" (Matt. 28:18). This should excite us to love and fear God
and to strive to keep his holy commandments, which are the

only rule of life. But how apt are we to forget that "God spake all these words, saying, I am the Lord thy God, which have brought thee out of the land of Egypt, out of the house of bondage" (Exod. 20:1–2)? Thus we see how the children of Israel were delivered from Egyptian service.

But my brethren, we are invited to the blessed Jesus, who was betrayed by one and denied by another:

> The Son of man goeth as it is written of him: but woe unto that man by whom the Son of man is betrayed! it had been good for that man if he had not been born. Then Judas, which betrayed him, answered and said, Master, is it I? He said unto him, Thou hast said. (Matt. 20:24–25)

Thus we see, my brethren, that there is a woe pronounced against everyone who sins by omission or commission. Are we not going on in our sins and disobeying these words of God? "If ye love me, ye will keep my commandments" (John 14:15). Are we not denying the Lord Jesus, as Peter did?

> Then began he to curse and to swear, saying, I know not the man. And immediately the cock crew (Matt. 26:74). And Peter remembered the word of Jesus, which said unto him, Before the cock crow, thou shalt deny me thrice. And he went out, and wept bitterly. (Matt. 26:75)

Surely then, we ought to come to the Divine Sovereign, the blessed Jesus, who was crucified for us sinners. Oh! we ought to come on the bended knees of our souls, and say, "Lord, we believe; help thou our unbelief." Come, my brethren, let us cry to the life-giving Jesus and say, "Son of God, have mercy on us! Lamb of God, that taketh away the sins of the world, have mercy on us!" Let us cast off all self-dependence and rely on a crucified Savior. "Pilate therefore, willing to release Jesus, spake again to them" (Luke 23:20). "But they cried, saying, Crucify him, crucify him" (Luke 23:21). Here we may see the love of God, in giving his Son to save all that come unto him by faith and repentance. Let us trace the sufferings of our Savior a little further: "He went away again the second time, and prayed, saying, O my Father, if this cup may not pass away from me, except I drink it, thy will be done" (Matt. 26:42). Here we trace our Savior's example set before us so that we should not murmur at the hand of Divine Providence; for God hath a right to deal with his creatures as he pleaseth.

Come, let us contemplate the death of the blessed Jesus and the fearful judgement that the Lord passes on the guilty sinner.

> Then shall they begin to say to the mountains, Fall on us; and to the hills, Cover us (Luke 23:30). And there were also two other, malefactors, led with him to be put to death. And when they were come to the place, which is called Calvary, there they crucified him, and the malefactors, one on the right hand, and the other on the left. (Luke 23:32–33)

And thus was the Scripture fulfilled: " . . . and he was numbered with the transgressors" (Isa. 53:12).

> And when they had platted a crown of thorns, they put it upon his head, and a reed in his right hand. . . . (Matt. 27:29). Likewise also the chief priests mocking him, with the scribes and elders, said, He saved others; himself he cannot save. If he be the King of Israel, let him now come down from the cross, and we will believe him (Matt. 27:41–42). Now from the sixth hour there was darkness over all the land unto the ninth hour (Matt. 27:45). And about the ninth hour Jesus cried with a loud voice, saying, Eli, Eli, lama sabachthani? that is to say, My God, my God, why hast thou forsaken me? (Matt. 27:46)

My brethren, should not a sense of these things on our minds implant in us a spirit of love to God, who hath provided a Savior who is able to save to the uttermost all that come unto him by faith and repentance? "For godly sorrow worketh repentance to salvation not to be repented of: but the sorrow of the world worketh death" (2 Cor. 7:10). My brethren, see what sin hath done: it hath made all flesh guilty in the sight of God.[16]

May we now adopt the language of David: "O remember not against us former iniquities: Let thy tender mercies speedily prevent us" (Ps. 79:8). "Turn us again, O Lord God of hosts, cause thy face to shine; and we shall be saved" (Ps. 80:19).

Let us contemplate a little further on the death of Christ.

> Jesus, when he had cried again with a loud voice, yielded up the
> ghost (Matt. 27:50). And, behold, the veil of the temple was rent
> in twain from the top to the bottom; and the earth did quake, and
> the rocks rent. (Matt. 27:51)

Here we see that the death of Christ caused all nature to trem-
ble and the power of heaven to shake. Here we may see not
only the evil of sin but also the unmerited mercy of God, in
giving his only Son. Should not our hearts be filled with fear
and love for God? We must believe that Jesus is the Son of
God.

> Now when the centurion, and they that were with him, watching
> Jesus, saw the earth quake, and those things that were done, they
> feared greatly, saying, Truly this was the Son of God. (Matt. 27:54)

Now this was done for the remission of our sins, for "without
shedding of blood [there] is no remission" (Heb. 9:22) of sin.
This we have confirmed in the Holy Sacrament. "For this is my
blood of the new testament, which is shed for many" (Matt.
26:28). But the unbelieving Jews still persisted in their unbelief
and would have prevented the resurrection of our Savior if it
had been in their power:

> . . . the chief priests and Pharisees came together unto Pilate,
> Saying, Sir, we remember that that deceiver said, while he was
> yet alive, After three days I will rise again (Matt. 27:62–63). So
> they went, and made the sepulchre sure, sealing the stone, and
> setting a watch. (Matt. 27:66)

Here we see the spirit of unbelief in Nathaniel:

> Philip findeth Nathaniel, and saith unto him, We have found him,
> of whom Moses in the law, and the prophets, did write, Jesus of
> Nazareth, the son of Joseph. And Nathaniel said unto him, Can
> there any good thing come out of Nazareth? Philip saith unto
> him, Come and see. (John 1:45–46)

Thus we are to come and see the mercy of God in sending his
Son to save lost men.

Let us contemplate the manner of Christ's resurrection. "Behold, there was a great earthquake: for the angel of the Lord descended from heaven, and came and rolled back the stone from the door, and sat upon it" (Matt. 28:2). Here we see that our Savior was attended by an angel, one of those holy spirits we read of in Revelation:

> . . . they rest not day and night, saying, Holy, holy, holy, Lord God Almighty, which was, and is, and is to come (Rev. 4:8). Saying with a loud voice, Worthy is the Lamb that was slain to receive power, and riches, and wisdom, and strength, and honour, and glory, and blessing. (Rev. 5:12)

And our Savior himself tells us he hath received his power: "And Jesus came and spake unto them, saying, All power is given unto me in heaven and in earth" (Matt. 28:18). Then he gives his disciples their charge: "Go ye therefore, and teach all nations, baptizing them in the name of the Father, and of the Son, and of the Holy Ghost" (Matt. 28:19).

But I must conclude in a few words and say: my dear brethren, should we not admire the free grace of God, which he is inviting us to come and accept of Jesus Christ, on the terms of the gospel? And he is calling us to repent of all our sins. This we cannot do of ourselves, but we must be saved in the use of means, not to neglect those two great articles of the Christian religion—baptism and the Sacrament. We ought, all of us, to seek by prayers, but the Scripture hath told us that we must not depend on the use of means alone. The apostle says, "I have planted, Apollos watered; but God gave the increase" (1 Cor. 3:6). Here we see that if we are saved, it must be by the power of God's Holy Spirit. But, my dear brethren, the time is hastening when we must appear.[17]

Emendations

Page	Line		
97	1:	poetry]	Poetry] R
	2:	words:]	words, Mathew xi, 28 [11:28],] R
		me,]	me.] R
	3:	-laden (Matt. 11:28). My]	laden.] R
		brethren]	Brethren] R
	5:	heavy-laden]	heavy laden] R
	6:	contemplate the]	contemplate on the] R
	7:	place.]	place,] R
	8:	heavy-laden]	heavy laden] R
	9:	unworthiness, to]	unworthiness, and to] R
	10:	Most High]	most high] R
		God, to]	God, and to] R
	11:	Mighty Redeemer.]	mighty redeemer, Matthew x, 33 [10:33].] R
	11–12:	Whosoever therefore shall]	Whosoever shall] R
	13:	my Father which is in heaven]	my heavenly father] R
	14–15:	Lord, and to ask]	Lord, and ask] R
		Holy Spirit]	holy spirit] R
	16:	life.]	life, John iv. 14 [4:14]] R
	19:	life]	life, then] R
	20:	Christ.]	Christ,] R
98	1:	salvation.]	salvation,] R
		heavy-laden]	heavy laden] R
	3–4:	did, In]	did, Psalm xxxi, 1 [31:1] R
	4:	thee, O Lord,]	thee, O Lord.] R
		I put]	put I] R
	5:	brethren]	Brethren] R
	6:	holiness.]	holiness,] R
	7–8:	heavy-laden,]	heavy laden.] R
	9:	clothed]	cloathed] R
	10:	text: Blessed]	text, Psalm xxxiii, 7 [33:7].] R
		sin]	sins] R
	11:	seek by]	seek for by] R
	12:	ceasing, as set]	ceasing, and the word is set] R
	12–13:	Ps. 51:1]	Psalm lxi, 1] R
	13:	upon me,]	on me.] R
	13–14:	lovingkindness:]	loving kindness,] R
	15:	brethren,]	Brethren.] R
	17:	place,]	place.] R
	18:	heavy-laden]	heavy laden] R
		company and.]	company,] R
	19:	heart. Blessed]	heart. Matthew v. 8 [5:8]] R
		pure]	poor] R
		heart:]	heart.] R
	20:	God (Matt. 5:8).]	God.] R
		God,]	God.] R

22:	Holy Spirit,]	holy spirit,] R
	for.]	for, Matthew vii, 7 [7:7]] R
	Ask,]	Ask,] R
23:	you;]	you,] R
	seek,]	seek,] R
	find (Matt. 7:7).]	find.] R
24:	asked,]	asked,] R
25:	his Holy Spirit]	his holy spirit] R
26:	life.]	life, Matt. vii, 8 [7:8]] R
26–27:	receiveth (Matt. 7:8).]	receiveth,] R
27:	brethren,]	brethren,] R
28:	repent,]	repent,] R
29:	die. That]	die, that] R
29–30:	Most High]	most high] R
30:	pronunciation:]	pronunciation,] R
31:	me,]	me,] R
	ye that work]	ye workers of] R
	iniquity (Matt. 7:23)]	iniquity, Matthew vii, 23 [7:23].] R
33:	willful]	willful] R
34:	sin. Whosoever]	sin John viii, 34 [8:34].] R
	committeth]	committeth] R
35:	sin (John 8:34).]	sin. My] R
37:	sin.]	sin,] R
1:	Sabbath.]	Sabbath,] R
	preparing]	fitting] R
3:	life? Or.]	life, or,] R
5:	thoughts. God]	thoughts. John iv, 24 [4:24],] R
	Spirit:]	spirit,] R
6–7:	truth (John 4:24)]	truth. Therefore] R
7:	brethren,]	Brethren] R
8:	Lord,]	Lord,] R
10:	appearance,]	appearance,] R
	but the sincerity]	but sincerity] R
11:	life. For]	life; for] R
11–12:	saith unto me,]	says Lord,] R
12:	heaven]	Heaven] R
13:	doeth]	doth] R
	my Father, which is in heaven (Matt. 7:21).]	my heavenly Father, Matt. vii, 21 [7:21].] R
14:	Therefore.]	Therefore,] R
	heavy-laden]	heavy laden] R
15:	grace.]	grace,] R
17:	studying that everyone]	studying, every one] R
18:	teaching others]	teaching of others] R
	Sirs.]	Sirs,] R
21:	brethren. For]	brethren; for] R
	nation.]	nation,] R
23:	Christian]	christian] R
	, where]	, and] R
	have been born]	born] R
24:	Christian families.]	christian families,] R

99

25:	understanding.]	understanding. In] R
26:	give]	given] R
	inquire]	enquire] R
27–28:	Christian families. Have]	christian families, have] R
28:	baptized]	baptised] R
28–29:	taught their]	learnt their] R
31:	were]	was] R
	fire,]	fire.] R
32:	then,]	then.] R
33:	that]	which] R
34:	charge.]	charge,] R
	Joshua: As]	Joshua
35:	Lord (Josh. 24:15).]	Lord.] R
36:	God.]	God:] R
	says: The]	says, Prov. viii, 18 [8:18]. The] R
37:	evil (Prov. 8:13);]	evil; chapter ix, 10, [9:10].] R
100 1:	wisdom (Prov. 9:10);]	wisdom; chapter xiv, 17 [14:17].] R
2:	life (Prov. 14:27).]	life.] R
4:	brethren,]	Brethren.] R
5:	brethren]	Brethren] R
	you]	ye] R
	of being saved]	to be saved] R
6:	you]	ye] R
	sins.]	sins,] R
7:	Lord;]	Lord.] R
8:	heavy-laden. For]	heavy laden; for] R
9–10:	salvation. Whosoever therefore shall]	salvation. Mathew x, 32 [10:32]. Whosoever shall] R
10:	confess also before]	confess before] R
11:	my Father which is in heaven (Matt. 10:32).]	my heavenly father.] R
12:	it,]	it.] R
13:	you live]	ye live] R
	life.]	life,] R
	you walk]	ye walk] R
	circumspectly,]	circumspect.] R
14:	holy,]	holy.] R
	than you]	than ye] R
15:	Spirit:]	spirit,] R
16:	truth (John 4:24). Therefore,]	truth; therefore.] R
	you]	ye] R
17:	did.]	did,] R
	say: God]	say.] R
18:	me,]	me.] R
	sinner. And]	sinner; Luke xv, 11 [15:11]. And] R
	publican,]	publican.] R
	off,]	off.] R
20:	breast,]	breast.] R
20–21:	sinner (Luke 18:13).]	sinner.] R

22:	dependence.]	dependence,] R
	righteousness. For]	righteousness; for] R
23:	are ye]	ye are] R
	faith;]	faith,] R
	yourselves:]	yourselves,] R
24:	God (Eph. 2:8).]	God.] R
25:	imperfection]	imperfections] R
	such.]	such,] R
27:	Christ.]	Christ,] R
28:	hearts.]	hearts,] R
29:	heavy-laden]	heavy laden] R
29–30:	inquirer]	enquirer] R
30:	inquire, How]	enquire. how] R
	doctrine?]	doctrine,] R
	Are]	are] R
31:	know that many]	know many] R
32:	read?]	read.] R
33:	brethren.]	brethren,] R
	them that there]	them there] R
34:	God. And]	God, and] R
35:	God.]	God, Psalm ciii, 11
		[103:11].] R
	heaven]	heavens] R
36:	toward]	towards] R
	him. . . .]	him. Verse 13] R
1:	him (Ps. 103:11, 13).]	him. Psalm xxxiv, 9 [34:9].] R
	Lord,]	Lord.] R
	saints:]	saints,] R
2:	him. . . .]	him. Verse 11.] R
	Come,]	Come.] R
	children,]	children.] R
3:	me:]	me,] R
	Lord (Ps. 34:9, 11).]	Lord.] R
5:	Lord. Here, my brethren,]	Lord, here. by brethren] R
8:	lives. For]	life, for] R
	evil,]	evil.] R
	upward. This]	upward, this] R
10:	say. that]	say,] R
11:	actions,]	actions.] R
12:	us that]	us] R
13:	God (1 Cor. 10:31).]	God. 1 Cor. x, 30 [10:30].] R
15:	life. This]	life, this] R
	only.]	only:] R
	brethren]	Brethren] R
18:	price: Ho,]	price. Isaiah lv, 1.
		[55:1]Ho] R
19:	thirsteth,]	thirsteth.] R
	waters,]	waters;] R
20:	money;]	money,] R
	ye,]	ye.] R
	buy,]	buy.] R
	yea,]	yea.] R
	come, buy]	come. and buy] R

101 (margin, at line 1)

22:	say that if]	say if] R
23:	us that if]	us if] R
24:	come,]	come.] R
	we have]	they have] R
25:	our sins]	their sins] R
26:	burdened]	burthened] R
27:	mankind:]	mankind,] R
28:	Holy Spirit]	holy spirit] R
30:	brethren]	Brethren] R
30–31:	unto the]	untothe]H
31:	Christ?]	Christ, Matthew vii, 7 [7:7].] R
	Ask,]	Ask.] R
	you; seek,]	you, knock.] R
31–32:	and ye shall find; knock,]	you, knock.] R
33:	Therefore,]	Therefore.] R
	you]	ye] R
	you]	ye] R
34:	did:]	did, Luke xv, 21 [15:21].] R
	him,]	him.] R
35:	Father,]	father.] R
	heaven,]	Heaven.] R
36:	son (Luke 15:21).]	son.] R
37:	penitent]	penetent] R
102 1:	saved.]	saved,] R
3:	sure.]	sure,] R
	meditation.]	meditation. Psalm lv, 1 [55:1].] R
4:	prayer,]	prayer.] R
	God;]	God,] R
5:	supplication (Ps. 55:1).]	supplication.] R
6:	brethren]	Brethren] R
7:	sick.]	sick,] R
8:	the]	that] R
	that gives]	who gives] R
	gift?]	gift:] R
10:	death,]	death.] R
12:	forth? Therefore, my	forth, therefore, my
	brethren,]	Brethren.] R
13:	irresistible]	irresistable] R
13–14:	We are, many of us,]	Are we, many of us,] R
16:	eternity. For]	eternity, for] R
17:	Christ.]	Christ,] R
18:	impotence]	impotency] R
	ourselves.]	ourselves,] R
19:	Christ,]	Christ.] R
20:	man.]	man,] R
21:	heavy-laden]	heavy laden] R
	brethren]	Brethren] R
21–22:	ourselves now to see whether]	ourselves now wither] R
23:	hearts.]	hearts,] R
	sins. Have]	sins, have] R

	24:	Holy Word]	holy word] R
	25:	Sabbaths]	Sabbath's.]
		commandments?]	commandment.] R
	25–26:	God says that he shows]	Exodus xx
	26:	unto]	to] R
		me,]	me.] R
	27:	commandments (Exod. 20:6). Have]	commandments, Have] R
	29:	crucifixion]	crucification] R
	31:	opened,]	opened.] R
		arose,]	arose. Come] R
	32:	Come,]	Come.] R
	33:	come:]	come, Acts x, 34 [10:34].] R
	34:	mouth,]	mouth.] R
		Of]	of] R
	35:	persons:]	persons, verse 35,] R
	35–36:	him, and worketh righteousness]	him.] R
	36:	with him (Acts 10:34, 35).	of him. My Brethren] R
	36–37:	My brethren]	
	37:	freedom.]	freedom,] R
103	2:	God. If]	God; if] R
		slaves,]	slaves.] R
		God;]	God,] R
	3:	free,]	free.] R
		Most High]	most high] R
	4:	God. Cannot]	God, cannot] R
	6:	through.]	through,] R
		freedom? I]	freedom, and] R
	7:	desire.]	desire,] R
	8:	life.]	life, John viii, 32 [8:32],] R
	9:	free. . . .]	free. Verse 36,] R
	10:	therefore shall make]	shall make] R
		free, ye]	free. you] R
	10–11:	indeed (John 8:32, 36).	indeed.] R
	11:	This]	
		know,]	know.] R
		brethren: . . . that]	brethren
	12:	God . . . (Rom. 8:28).]	God.] R
	14:	brethren]	Brethren] R
	16:	have never said.]	never have said,] R
		anything]	any thing] R
	17:	freedom. But]	freedom; but] R
	18:	been:]	been.] R
	19:	affairs. By]	affairs, and] R
	20:	satisfied.]	staisfied,] R
	21:	love.]	love,] R
	22:	for . . . if]	for if] R
		Christ,]	Christ Jesus.] R
	22–23:	creature: old]	creature, 2 Cor. v. 17 [2 Cor. 5:17]. Therefore if any may be in Christ he is a new creature. Old] R

23:	away;]	away.] R
	behold,]	behold.] R
23–24:	new (2 Cor. 5:17). Now,]	new, now.] R
25:	holiness,]	holiness.] R
26:	hearts.]	hearts,] R
27:	precepts.]	precepts. Psalm xix, 10 [19:10].] R
	desired are they]	desired] R
	yea,]	yea.] R
28:	gold:]	gold,] R
	sweeter]	sweeter also] R
	honeycomb.]	honeycomb. Verse 11] R
29:	warned:]	warned,] R
	in keeping of]	by keeping] R
30:	reward (Ps. 19:10, 11).]	reward.] R
32:	meditation. That]	meditation, that] R
	way of Matt. 6:6:]	way Mat. vi. (6:6) But] R
32–33:	. . . when thou prayest,]	But when thou prayest.] R
33:	and.]	and,] R
33–34:	thy door]	the door] R
34:	Father which is]	father] R
	secret;]	secret,] R
	Father]	father] R
36:	in sin,]	to sin.]
37:	ourselves.]	ourselves,] R
	harming]	a hurt to] R
	commonwealth. Let]	commonwealth.] R
104 1:	heavy-laden,]	heavy laden.] R
2:	sins;]	sins,] R
3:	lift]	life] R
	hearts.]	hearts,] R
4:	in.]	in,] R
5:	hearts.]	hearts. Psalm xxiv. 7 [24:7].] R
	heads,]	heads.] R
	gates;]	gates,] R
6:	lift up,]	lifted us,] R
	doors;]	doors,] R
	glory]	Glory] R
7:	in (Ps. 24:7). Then]	in; then] R
	Christ.]	Christ,] R
8:	say.]	say,] R
	did:]	did,] R
	(Ps. 11:1); and]	trust, Psalm xi 4 [11:4]. And] R
9:	thee?]	thee,] R
	upon]	on] R
10:	earth that I]	earth I] R
	beside thee (Ps. 73:25).]	besides thee.] R
11:	now.]	now,] R
12–13:	men in general]	the generality of men] R
15:	yea.]	yea,] R
	nay, or]	nay, or] R

16:	purpose.]	purpose. Matt. v. 7 [5:7].] R
	be,]	be,] R
	Yea, yea;]	yea, yea,] R
16–17:	Nay, nay:]	nay, nay,] R
17–18:	evil (Matt. 5:37).]	evil. Therefore] R
18:	Therefore,]	Therefore.] R
	brethren]	Brethren] R
19:	humbly]	humble] R
	evil,]	evil;] R
20:	offense]	offence] R
	toward God]	toward God] R
	toward man] (Acts 24:16).]	towards man.] R
21:	saith:]	saith, Psalm i, 1 [1:1].] R
22:	ungodly,]	ungodly.] R
	sinners (Ps. 1:1).]	sinners.] R
24:	Christians]	christians] R
28:	season:]	season. Psalm 1,3 [1:3].] R
29:	forth his fruit]	forth fruit] R
	season; his]	season: His] R
30:	wither;]	wither,] R
30–31:	prosper (Ps. 1:3)	prosper.] R
31:	David:]	David,] R
31–32:	but the dust,]	but dust.] R
32:	field (Ps. 103:15).]	field
33:	life,]	life,] R
36:	life.]	life;] R
37:	ascend]	ascend up] R
	descend]	descend down] R
105 1:	cold,]	cold.] R
2:	dead. Then]	dead, then] R
	Scripture]	scripture] R
	fulfilled:]	fulfilled,Gen. iii. 19 [3:19].] R
4:	unto]	to] R
	ground;]	ground,] R
	taken:] R	taken,] R
	art,]	art.] R
5:	shalt thou return (Gen. 3:19).] R	thou shalt return.] R
6:	brethren. If]	brethren, if] R
7:	converts,]	converts.] R
	again;]	again,] R
8:	regeneration. Verily]	regeneration. John iii, 3 [3:3]. Verily] R
	verily,]	verily.] R
	thee]	you] R
	Except]	except] R
9:	again,]	again.] R
9–10:	God (John 3:3). My]	God.] R
12:	when we have no]	without an] R
13:	Christ? Have]	Christ; have] R
	heavy-laden]	heavy laden] R
	sins,]	sins,] R

	14:	David,]
		O Lord,]
	15:	displeasure (Ps. 6:1).]
	16:	death,]
	17:	meditation?]
	20:	have. Mr.]
		Burkitt]
	20–21:	says that]
	22:	forth]
		these:]
	23:	cry, O God;]
		attend unto]
		and whom]
	24:	thee? and]
		upon]
		that I]
	25:	beside]
		thee (Ps. 61:1; 73:25).]
	26:	Holy Spirit.]
		so that]
	27:	led]
		temptation.]
	28:	sin. But]
		now.]
	29:	to God]
	31:	death;]
	32:	Lord (Rom. 6:22, 23)]
	35:	sins, you]
	37:	to]
106	1:	banner.]
		so that]
	2:	subjects—this should]
		prayer.]
	4:	brethren]
		guard]
	5:	member.]
	6:	because]
		God.]
	7:	men. For]
		will love life]
		see]
	8:	evil,]
		that they speak no]
	8–9:	guile (1 Pet. 3:10).]
	10:	rebellion.]
	11:	life.]
		sinners]
	12:	pronunciation:]
		me, you]
	12–13:	iniquity. Then]

David, Psalm vi. 10 [6:10].] R
Lord.] R
displeasure.] R
death.] R
meditation.] R
have] R
Burket] R
says,] R
up] R
these
cry, O God,] R
attend to] R
and again, Whom] R
thee, and] R
on] R
I] R
besides] R
thee.] R
holy spirit,] R
that] R
lead] R
temptation,] R
sin. Rom vi. 22, 23 [6:22,23].] R
now,] R
of God] R
death,] R
Lord.] R
sins, ye] R
and to] R
banner,] R
, and that] R
subjects, should] R
prayers.] R
Brethren] R
be guarding] R
member,] R
for] R
God,] R
men. 1 Peter iii. 10 [3:10.] R
loves life,] R
would see] R
evil.] R
from speaking] R
guile.] R
rebellion,] R
life,] R
them] R
pronunciation,] R
me, ye] R
iniquity. Matt. xxv. 41 [25:41]. Then] R

14:	, ye cursed,]	‚ye cursed‸] R
	fire,]	fire‸] R
15:	angels (Matt. 25:41).]	angels.] R
16:	now‸]	now,] R
	my]	by] R
18:	gospel? For]	Gospel, for] R
19:	that if]	if] R
	sin‸]	sin,] R
20:	sin. Come]	sin.] R
	now,]	now‸] R
21:	accept]	accept of] R
22:	heavy-laden]	heavy laden] R
	sins‸]	sins,] R
24:	brethren]	Brethren] R
	unworthy;]	unworthy,] R
25:	Adam‸ became]	Adam, became] R
26:	God (Gen. 2:17). Surely]	God. Gen. ii. 17 [2:17].
		Surely] R
	then,]	then‸] R
	nature‸]	nature,] R
28:	that we]	we] R
	saved. We]	saved, we] R
29:	Jew who]	Jew that] R
	Christian who]	Christian that] R
30:	heart. And]	heart, and] R
	not]	it is not] R
	everyone]	every one] R
	who]	that] R
31:	God‸]	God,] R
	doeth]	doth] R
32:	best;]	it best,] R
34:	were]	was] R
	life‸ and a]	life, a] R
34–35:	God. And]	God. Luke xxii. 41, 42
		]22:41, 42]. And] R
35:	stone's]	stones] R
	and]	and he] R
36:	down,]	down‸] R
	prayed,]	prayed‸] R
	Saying, Father,]	saying, father‸] R
	willing,]	willing‸] R
107	1:	me:]	me,] R
4:	men who were]	mankind,] R
5:	Christ. The]	Christ, the] R
6:	life,]	life‸] R
7:	repentance. And]	repentance; and] R
	Son]	son] R
8:	also freely]	him freely] R
9:	things (Rom. 8:32). Come]	things.] R
	Come,]	Come‸] R
10:	God,]	God;] R
	righteousness;]	righteousness,] R
	these]	other] R

11:    you (Matt 6:33).]   you. Matt. vi. 33 [6:33]. Here] R

13:    Beveridge]   Beverage] R
    says.]   says,] R
    resolution, that the]   resolution, the] R

14:    are]   is] R
    us;]   us,] R
    actions. If]   actions; if] R

15:    tears.]   tears,] R
    crossed]   crost] R

16:    , my]   , my] R

17:    good: blessed]   good, and blessed] R

18:    him (Ps. 34:8).]   him. Psalm xxxiv. 8 [34:8].] R
    did.]   did,] R

19:    Christian. But]   christian, but] R
    , let]   , let] R

20:    you]   ye] R
    converts,]   converts.] R

22:    repentance: Repent]   repentance: Acts iii. 19 [3:19]. Repent] R

22–23:   , and be converted (Acts 3:19)]   , be converted:] R

24:    Lord. Trust]   Lord; Proverbs iii, 4 [3:4]. Trust] R

24:    heart;]   heart,] R

26:    encircled]   incircled] R
    temptations:]   temptations,] R

27:    devil? These]   devil; these] R

28:    Holy Spirit]   holy spirit] R

29:    Come,]   Come,] R
    us,]   us,] R

30–31:   dead (James 2:20); and for]   dead. James ii. 20 [2:20]. and Rom., x, 10 [10:10]. For] R

31:    believeth unto righteousness;]   believeth,] R

33:    that there]   there] R

34:    Christians. Therefore]   Christians; therefore] R

36:    actions.]   actions] R
    everyone]   every one.] R

37:    his works. Also]   their works. Psalm lxii, 2 [62:2]. Also] R
    unto thee,]   unto the] R
    O Lord,]   the Lord.] R
    mercy:]   mercy,] R

108

1:    renderest to]   rememberest] R
    his work (Ps. 62:12)]   his works] R

2:    Therefore.]   Therefore,] R

3:    Son]   son] R

7:    Holy Spirit? You]   holy spirit, you] R

8:    Christ:]   Christ;] R

9:    like unto]   like a] R

9–10:   that which when]   for which] R

10:    hath found, he . . . selleth]   will sell] R

10–11:	hath, and buyeth that field (Matt. 13:44)]	hath, to purchace, Matt. x. 44 [10:44].] R
14:	gospel.]	gospel,] R
14–15:	heavy-laden]	heavy laden] R
16:	Man]	Matt. xi. 27 [11:27]. Man] R
18:	life.]	life:] R
	us.]	us,] R
19:	lose our own souls? (Matt. 16:26).]	loose his own soul. Matt. xvi. 26 [16:26].] R
22:	encumberers]	cumberers] R
23:	justified.]	justified,] R
24:	condemned:]	condemned;] R
25:	works (Matt. 16:27).]	works
28:	heaven]	Heaven]
29:	and where thieves do not]	nor theives] R
31:	Contemplation on the Death of Christ]	no subtitle] R
32:	Christ;]	Christ,] R
32–33:	remains that]	remains I] R
34:	man.]	man
35:	of the]	from the] R
	dead.]	dead:] R

109

1:	die,]	died.] R
	Christ.]	Christ,] R
	alive (1 Cor. 15:21–22).]	alive."] R
2:	Scriptures]	scriptures] R
3:	another:]	another. Matt. xxvi, 14 [26:14].] R
4:	Judas . . .]	Judas went] R
	chief priests, And]	Chief Priest, and] R
	said unto them]	said] R
	What]	what] R
5:	me . . . ? And they covenanted with him]	me, and they agreed] R
6:	silver. And from that time he]	silver, then they] R
7:	him (Matt. 26:14–16).	him. Verse 28.] R
7–8:	new testament]	New Testament] R
8–9:	sins (Matt. 26:28).]	sins. Vers. 33] R
9:	Though]	though] R
	shall]	should] R
10–11:	offended (Matt. 26:33).]	offended. Ver. 34.] R
11:	Verily]	verily] R
11–12:	That this night]	this night] R
12–13:	thrice (Matt. 26:34).]	thrice. Ver. 38,] R
13:	My]	my] R
14:	here,]	here.] R
	me (Matt. 26:38).]	me. Ver. 39.] R
15:	farther]	further] R
	face,]	face.] R
16:	O my Father]	O Father] R
17:	nevertheless]	Nevertheless] R
	wilt. (Matt. 26:39)]	wilt.] R

18:	brethren]	Brethren] R
19:	us:]	us;] R
	Son]	son] R
20:	heavy-laden]	heavy laden] R
21:	sins. Let]	sins; let] R
22:	dust:]	dust. Matt xxvi. 63.] R
23:	peace.]	peace,] R
	high priest]	High Priest] R
24:	living]	Living] R
	us.]	us,] R
25:	Christ,]	Christ.] R
	Son]	son] R
	God (Matt. 26:63).]	God. And ver.64] R
26:	Thou]	thou] R
27:	Hereafter]	hereafter] R
	man]	Man] R
28:	heaven (Matt. 26:64).]	heaven. Ver. 64] R
29:	high priest]	High Priest] R
	He]	he] R
30:	witnesses?]	witness:] R
	behold]	Behold] R
31:	blasphemy. (Matt. 26:65)]	blasphemy. Here] R
32:	high priest]	High Priest] R
	blasphemy.]	blasphemy:] R
34:	repentance.]	repentance. Matt. xxviii.18 [28:18].] R
	spake]	spoke] R
35:	All]	all] R
35–36:	in earth (Matt 28:18). This]	on earth. As this] R
36:	God.]	God,] R
37:	are]	is] R
110 1:	life.]	life:] R
	God spake all]	God spoke] R
2:	have brought]	brought] R
3:	, out]	,and out] R
3–4:	bondage (Exod. 20:1–2)?]	bondage, Exod. xx. I [20:1].] R
5:	from]	from the] R
6:	brethren]	Brethren] R
7:	another:]	another. Matt. xx. 24 [20:24].] R
8:	man]	Man] R
	him:]	him;] R
9:	of man]	of Man] R
10:	had not]	had never] R
	born.]	born. Ver. 24.] R
	Judas,]	Judas.] R
11:	him,]	him] R
	Master,]	Master.] R
	Thou]	thou] R
12:	said. (Matt. 20:24–25)]	said.] R
13:	brethren]	Brethren] R
14:	everyone who]	every one that] R

	commission. Are]	commission, are] R
15:	sins.]	sins,] R
	these words]	the word] R
	God?]	God:] R
17:	did?]	did. Matt. xxvi. 14 [26:24].] R
18:	to swear]	swear] R
18–19:	man. And]	man; and] R
19:	crew (Matt. 26:74).]	crew. And ver. 74] R
20:	word]	words] R
	which said]	which he said] R
	Before]	before] R
21:	crow,]	crow.] R
	thrice.]	thrice:] R
	out,]	out.] R
22:	bitterly. (Matt. 26:75)]	bitterly.] R
23:	then,]	then.] R
24:	Jesus,]	Jesus,] R
26:	believe;]	believe,] R
	Come,]	Come.] R
	brethren]	Brethren] R
27:	life-giving]	life giving] R
	Jesus.]	Jesus,] R
29:	self-dependence.]	self-dependence,] R
30:	Savior.]	Savior. Luke xxiii. 20 [23:20].] R
	spake]	spoke] R
31:	them (Luke 23:20).]	them. Ver 21.] R
	saying, Crucify]	saying, crucify] R
32:	him (Luke 23:21).]	him.] R
35:	further:]	further: Matt. xxvi. 42 [26:42].] R
111 2:	done (Matt. 26:42)]	done.] R
3:	us.]	us;] R
6:	Come,]	Come.] R
	the]	on the] R
	Jesus.]	Jesus;] R
7:	the]	on the] R
	that the Lord passes]	of the Lord passing] R
	sinner.]	sinner. Luke xxii. 30 [23:30].] R
8:	Fall]	fall] R
	us;]	us,] R
9:	Cover us (Luke 23:30)]	cover. us. Ver. 32,33.] R
9–10:	two other, malefactors,]	two. malefactors,] R
10:	death.]	death;] R
12:	him,]	him.] R
13–14:	left (Luke 23:32–33). And]	left; and] R
14:	Scripture]	scripture] R
	fulfilled: . . .]	fulfuilled: For] R
15:	the transgressors (Isa. 53:12).]	transgressors. Matt. xxvii. 29 [27:29].] R
16:	platted]	plated] R
17:	hand. . . . (Matt. 27:29)]	hand. Ver. 42, 42.] R

17–18:	Likewise also the]	Likewise the] R
18:	chief priests]	Chief Priests] R
18:	scribes and elders]	Scribes and Elders] R
19:	He]	he] R
	others;]	other,] R
	save.]	save:] R
	King]	king] R
20:	now come]	come] R
21:	him (Matt. 27:41–42).]	him. Ver. 44.] R
22:	hour (Matt. 27:45).]	hour. Ver. 46] R
24:	lama sabachthani? that]	Lama Sabachthani! That] R
	say, My]	say, my] R
25:	me? (Matt. 27:46)]	me? My] R
26:	minds]	mind] R
27:	who]	which] R
	Savior.]	Saviour,] R
29:	repentance?]	repentance. 2 Cor. vii. 10 [7:10].] R
	godly]	Godly] R
30:	salvation.]	salvation,] R
	of:]	of,] R
31:	death (2 Cor. 7:10).]	death.] R
32:	done:]	done;] R
33:	now]	not] R
	David:]	David. Psal. lxxix 8 [79:8].] R
34:	iniquities:]	iniquities.] R
	thy]	they] R
35:	us (Ps. 79:8).]	us. Psal. lxxx 19 [80:19].] R
	Lord.]	Lord,] R
	hosts]	Hosts] R
36:	shine;]	shine,] R
	saved (Ps. 80:19).]	saved.] R
112 1:	Christ.]	Christ. Matt. xxvii. 40 [27:40].] R
2:	cried again with]	cried with] R
3:	ghost (Matt. 27:50).]	ghost. Ver.4,] R
	And, behold,]	And, behold,] R
	veil]	vail] R
4:	twain.]	twain,] R
5:	rent. (Matt. 27:51)]	rent.] R
6:	tremble.]	tremble,] R
7:	to shake.]	shaken:] R
8:	sin.]	sin,] R
	unmerited]	unmeritted] R
9:	for]	to] R
10:	God? We]	God; and we] R
	God.]	God. Matt. xxvii. 54 [27:54].] R
11:	centurion,]	Centurion] R
12:	Jesus,]	Jesus,] R
13:	Truly]	truly] R
13–14:	God. (Matt. 27:54)]	God.] R
15:	remission (Heb. 9:22)]	remission] R

17:	Holy Sacrament.]	holy sacrament. Matt. xxvi. 27 [26:27].] R
18:	new testament]	New Testament] R
	is]	was] R
18–19:	many (Matt. 26:28).]	many:] R
19:	unbelief.]	unbelief,] R
20:	Savior]	Saviour,] R
21:	power:]	power. Matt. xxvii. 62 [27:62].] R
22:	. . . the chief priests]	The Chief Priests] R
	came]	come] R
	Pilate,]	Pilate. Ver. 63,] R
24:	After]	after] R
	again (Matt. 27:62–63).]	again. Ver. 66.] R
25:	went,]	went.] R
	stone,]	stone.] R
27:	Nathaniel:]	Nathaniel. John i. 45 and 46.] R
28:	We]	we] R
29:	law, and the prophets,]	law. of the prophets.] R
30:	Joseph.]	Joseph:] R
31:	Can]	can] R
32:	Come]	come] R
	see. (John 1:45–46)]	see.] R
113 1:	God.]	God,] R
2:	men.]	men. Let] R
3:	the]	on the] R
	resurrection]	resurrection. Matt. xxv. 2 [25:2].] R
4:	Behold,]	Behold.] R
	earthquake:]	earthquake;] R
5:	came]	come] R
	rolled back the]	rolled the] R
6:	it (Matt. 28:2).]	it.] R
7:	angel,]	angel;] R
8:	Revelation:]	the Revelations, vi. 8 [6:8].] R
9:	. . . they]	They] R
	Holy]	holy] R
	holy, Lord]	holy. Lord] R
10:	was,]	was.] R
	come (Rev. 4:8).]	come. Ver. 4,12.] R
11:	Saying.]	Saying,] R
	Worthy]	worthy] R
	Lamb.]	Lamb,] R
	slain.]	slain,] R
12:	power,]	power.] R
	honour]	honor] R
13:	blessing. (Rev. 5:12)]	blessing.] R
14:	power:]	power. Matt. xxviii 19 [28:19].] R
15:	spake]	spoke] R
	All]	all] R

16:	earth (Matt. 28:18).]	earth.] R
17:	charge:]	charge. Ver. 19.] R
	ye.]	ye,] R
18:	them]	then] R
	Father, and of]	Father, of] R
19:	Ghost (Matt. 28:19).]	Ghost. But] R
20:	words.]	words,] R
	say:]	say,] R
	my]	My] R
21:	brethren]	Brethren] R
22:	which]	that] R
	us]	of us] R
23:	gospel? And]	gospel; and] R
24:	sins.]	sins:] R
25:	means,]	means.] R
26:	religion—]	religion,] R
27:	Sacrament.]	sacrament;] R
	We ought,]	and we ought.] R
	us,]	us.] R
27–28:	prayers, but]	prayers: But] R
28:	Scripture]	scripture] R
29:	alone. The]	alone. 1st Cor. iii. 6 [3:6].] R
30:	planted,]	planted.] R
	Apollos watered;]	Apolos watered,] R
30–31:	increase (1 Cor. 3:6).]	increase.] R
31:	that if]	if] R
32:	Holy Spirit]	holy spirit] R
	But,]	But.] R
	brethren,]	Brethren.] R

Notes

1.   Hammon has three extant sermon essays. While all were printed, probably *An Evening's Improvement* and *An Address to the Negroes in the State of New York* were given first as public exhortations, while *A Winter Piece* was created to be a written essay.

2.   When Hammon speaks of death, it is spiritual not physical death. His language reflects familiarity with Jesus' sermon in Luke 13:3–8 in which he told his audience, "Except ye repent, ye shall likewise perish." This issue was not that those who heard Christ would die if they did not repent, as that is the end of all mankind, but that they would suffer both here and hereafter in the quintessence of spiritual death which is life without the Light of God. All the major colonial denominations would have reached consensus on this point, but especially from the Quakers would Hammon have received this sense of God's presence as the Light within the reborn human soul.

3.   Here Hammon is referring to a quotation on judgment that was familiar to most eighteenth-century readers, Gal. 6:7: "Be not de-

ceived; God is not mocked: for whatsoever a man soweth, that shall he also reap."

4. Hammon's metaphor is a paraphrase of Job 5:7: "Yet man is born unto trouble, as the sparks fly upward."

5. This paragraph is filled with paraphrases and allusions to various New Testament passages. The first is a partial quote of 2 Pet. 1:10: "Wherefore the rather, brethren, give diligence to make your calling and election sure: for if you do these things, ye shall never fail." Hammon combines this with a phrase from Phil. 2:12: "Wherefore, my beloved, as ye have always obeyed, not as in my presence only, but now much more in my absence, work out your own salvation with fear and trembling." Finally Hammon puts some of his readers in the position of the Pharisees of whom Jesus said in John 15:22: "If I had not come and spoken unto them, they had not had sin: But now they have no cloke for their sin."

6. Hammon often wrestled with the dilemma of whether slavery was the direct or permitted will of God. This was a prevalent theological question in his day. See S. Hopkins, *Timely Articles;* Sewall; and Slater.

7. This entire section, particularly following a discussion of the Apostle Peter's disavowal of racial prejudice, alludes to Moses' deliverance of the Jewish slaves from Egypt. The language is part of Moses' speech to the Israelites when he raised his staff to part the Red Sea: "Fear ye not, stand still, and see the salvation of the Lord, which he will shew to you to day: for the Egyptians whom ye have seen to day, ye shall see them again no more for ever" (Exod. 14:13).

8. William Burkitt, a seventeenth-century evangelist and Anglican clergyman, marked his career with both charity and charismatic preaching. He took pains to aid French exiles, indigent students, and missionaries bound for the colonies. His popularity stemmed from his ability to preach extemporaneously and vehemently, and many of his exhortations and guides are published (Stephen and Lee 2:3). He published a two-volume expository on the New Testament which was among the books in the Lloyd library that Hammon used as source material.

9. Here Hammon has James 3:8–9 in mind: "But the tongue can no man tame; it is an unruly evil, full of deadly poison. Therewith bless we God, even the Father; and therewith curse we men, which are made after the similitude of God."

10. Just as he had indicated earlier that if his African readers had not heard the Gospel they would not have been held responsible for God's word, the same standard can be implicitly applied to his white readers—i.e., had white colonists not been challenged with the pres-

ence of Blacks and Native Americans, their Christian utopia might have succeeded. But these "heathen," untoward to them, quickly evaporated whatever penchant to Christian love most early colonists possessed. If the presence of other races was the test of that love, the colonists failed that test.

11.   Like the words in the Negro spiritual, "everyone that talks about heaven ain't going there," Hammon's use of Matt. 7:21—"Not every one that saith unto me, 'Lord, Lord,' shall enter into the king-dom of heaven; but he that doeth the will of my Father which is in heaven"—is a direct confrontation with what he considers to be white hypocrisy. Hammon's description of those who had not had this heart-felt conversion but who still call Christ "Lord," is intended to show that, although they have gone through the steps which E. S. Morgan (*Visible Saints*) describes, the slave masters, because of the slave sys-tem, are not fulfilling the requirements for good moral behavior. Therefore, their actions are not to be imitated: "Let our superiors act as they shall think best." See also Agate, in Hastings 611–12; and Tipson 460–71.

12.   Hammon's quote about Beveridge's third resolution is taken from the latter's *Works* 1:222. William Beveridge was a popular seven-teenth-century bishop of the Church of England and a college presi-dent. He was noted for his publications of treatises in various scholarly languages and his preaching of sermons on a range of subjects from prayer to the Great Fire of 1666. Although he held many positions of power within the Anglican church, he consistently opposed attempts to relax its requirements (Stephen and Lee 2:447–48).

13.   To defend his beliefs against the accusations of the Jews, the Apostle Paul had to appear before three Roman governors. Felix, governor of Judea, was one of these governors but Hammon has the three rulers—all of whom are mentioned in the book of Acts—confused. It was King Agrippa, not Felix, who said to the Apostle Paul: "Almost thou persuadest me to be a Christian" (Acts 26:28).

14.   Here Hammon seems to be meshing two Bible verses in order to warn his readers about the elusiveness of earthly life: "For all flesh is as grass, and all the glory of man as the flower of grass. The grass withereth, and the flower thereof falleth away. But the word of the Lord endureth for ever" (1 Pet. 1:24–25); and "For the sun is no sooner risen with a burning heat, but it withereth the grass, and the flower thereof falleth, and the grace of the fashion of it perisheth: so also shall the rich man fade away in his ways" (James 1:11). Another analogous text is Ps. 39:5: "verily every man at his best state is alto-gether vanity."

15.   Hammon's injunction on preparation is taken from Phil. 2:12—"Wherefore, my beloved, as ye have always obeyed, not as in my presence only, but now much more in my absence, work out your own salvation with fear and trembling"—and from 1 Cor. 15:58: "always abounding in the works of the Lord." While the essayist may have had in mind here the barren fig tree which Christ cursed because of its fruitlessness in Mark 11:12–26, the intended word was "encumberers." That God can prepare the sinner for his grace was a common belief in early eighteenth-century theology. See Pettit's book, *The Heart Prepared.*

16.   In the first part of this paragraph, Hammon has in mind Heb. 7:25: "Wherefore he is able also to save them to the uttermost that come unto God by him, seeing he ever liveth to make intercession for them." The term "by faith and repentance" was used often during and even before the Great Awakening as a necessary part of personal soul-searching before salvation. Whites often suspected slaves who professed conversion, thinking that the servants knew nothing of true faith and repentance but were rather only seeking freedom from their duties. Yet slaveholders seemed only to want genuine conversion, because they believed that it would result in more obedient slaves. Hammon differentiated from the slave masters' requirements and wrote instead that they themselves had never fully obeyed God in faith and repentance. The irony of slave conversion is a fascinating topic in America history. See Beveridge, "Faith and Repentence" in *Works* 7; Cherry 100, 117, 128; Greene, *The Negro* 259–75; Jernegan, "Slavery" 504–27; McKee 24–40; Scherer 15–18, 144–49.

17.   Apparently printing space demanded that Hammon's printer end this sentence before the thought was completed. Hammon probably had written here 2 Cor. 5:10: "For we must all appear before the judgement seat of Christ; that everyone may receive the things done in his body, according to that he hath done, whether it be good or bad.'

4. A Poem for Children with Thoughts on Death

Introduction: Hope for *All* of God's Children

Hammon draws the structure, symbolism, and theme of this elegiac poem from the Wisdom Books of the Bible—Ecclesiastes and Proverbs. Like the Old Testament Hebrew monarch, King Solomon, the author of those works, Hammon would have young people live a life of piety because of the imminence of death, resurrection, and judgment. The poet's concern for young Africans becomes particularly evident in this work. In the eighteenth-century psyche, all children, whether Black or white, were theoretically equal in their need for Christian instruction. Everywhere in the colonies, ministers and missionaries pursued the education and evangelization of youth, often with more energy and conviction than they devoted to the catechization and conversion of adults. This zeal for youth was particularly advantageous to slaves because it greatly enhanced their opportunities for education. It also provided those evangelists, rejected by a sometimes indifferent white community, a welcome audience. For instance, David Humphreys, the secretary for the Society for the Propagation of the Gospel in Foreign Parts (SPG), tells of a New York minister who at Sunday night services found himself before a group of "sometimes 200 Children, Servants and Negroes" (244). One gentleman, in praise of the SPG's establishment of a Christian school in Dorchester, South Carolina, exhorted:

> The chief Source of Irreligion and immorality here, is the Want of Schools; and we may justly be apprehensive, that if our Children continue longer to be deprived of Opportunities of being instructed, Christianity will of Course decay insensibly, and we shall have a Generation of our own, as ignorant as the Native Indian. (Humphreys 125)

But SPG officials insisted that, along with educating the children of white colonists, they likewise wanted to educate, and thereby evangelize, the children of slaves.

Because his masters wanted him trained enough to work as a clerk in their local store, Hammon received a minimal, elementary education through the SPG system. He desired that all Black children would receive enough schooling at least to read the Bible, the SPG's major textbook. However, he desired for the African child not just education and evangelization but emancipation as well. Whenever he argued for the freedom of slaves, Hammon primarily pleaded for the manumission of young people. Thus, he contributed to the eventual release of young men and women both in the Lloyd Manor and in New York province. At the turn of the century, one member of the Lloyd family freed his slaves when they reached twenty-one, and in 1799 the State of New York passed a law manumitting all young and unborn slaves when they reached adulthood. Other contemporary abolitionists considered the call for the liberation of children to be at least a first-step compromise for diehard slaveholders. For example, in 1778 Pennsylvania considered a bill, drafted largely through the efforts of abolitionist George Byron, which would free all slave children born after the legislation's passage, on the condition that they work as indentured servants for their mothers' masters for a prescribed number of years. Earlier, another abolitionist in Pennsylvania, Benjamin Rush, author of *An Address to the Inhabitants of the British Settlements in America, upon Slavekeeping* (1773), requested solely that whites free their young slaves because these workers, unlike others, had not been tainted by "the vices of slavery" (Zilversmit, 95, 120–22).

Hammon's concern for young Africans resulted directly from the SPG's zeal to reach enslaved children earlier in the century. Those SPG ministers who came to Oyster Bay to teach not only the Lloyds' sons but also their young slave Jupiter gave America's first African writer a basic understanding of biblical symbolism. On his own, he then acquired enough proficiency to turn the Bible, the most widely read book in the colonies, into both a vehicle and a framework for his artistic protests against slavery. The whole thrust of this poem (and of "An Address to Miss Phillis Wheatley")—that youth must gain wisdom to succeed on earth and to prepare for heaven—is a reflection of the evangelical outreach that touched Hammon's life.

Writers produced much popular poetry in the eighteenth century for children of Christianized parents. Of special interest to most white colonists was the question of children's predetermined state, based on the election or rejection of the parent. The procedure for determining the spiritual state of either was a major theological debate, one especially surrounding a child's eternal destiny, if death occurred before adulthood. Most of those in established traditional denominations believed that the parents' election assured their offsprings' salvation.[1] Similarly, the doctrines of original sin and total depravity condemned the children of the unsaved to perdition with their parents. In the same choiceless manner, this eternal death warrant applied to unsaved lower-caste British colonists, and much more to the African slave. The children of Africans had not been considered seriously in the debate since the early commitment of the SPG to educate and evangelize them in the first quarter of the century (Weatherford 57). Hammon, angered by the oversight, castigated whites in some of his most unsubtle remarks for their sinful neglect of slave children. Attached to *A Winter Piece,* an essay which Hammon directed to his fellow slaves, this poem has slave children as its object.

A guideline based on racial selectivity transformed for social and cultural uses, the very psychology of the doctrine of election embodied a cultural rejection of Africans. Thus, while his more famous contemporary, Michael Wigglesworth, says plainly in *Day of Doom* that innocent infants of non-Christian parents cannot possibly be saved, Hammon, in this treatise on death directed toward children, makes no such reference, primarily because he is speaking to children of African descent whose parents had no opportunity to become Christians. In subscriptional entries for verse 166, Wigglesworth predicts that "reprobate Infants plead for themselves" (68). Then he has his God turn down their pleas: "Hence you were born in a state forlorn, / with Natures so deprav'd" (71). Wigglesworth's well-known epic was published eleven times in the eighteenth century. Undoubtedly Hammon read it, but he refuses to make such a distinction about children of unchurched parents. In the fourth and fifth verses of this poem, the African poet has Jesus call all children to heaven.[2] Slater's study, *Children in the New England Mind in Death and in Life,* gives background to illuminate the gracious, compassionate universality of Hammon's stand. Slater says that the colonial period was an age when the realities of early death, discussions of inescapable sin and of inevitable judgment made a child's life full of unrelenting fears (15–48). Thus the poem's theme would have brought hope to all children, including those of underprivileged whites and enslaved Blacks, not just the offspring of the elect.

Not only did Hammon have difficulty accepting what the church of his masters had to say about the election of children (the Lloyds attended Anglican and Puritan churches, both of which agreed about the preelection of their children), he also approached the Puritan doctrine of prevenient grace with ambiguity. This tenet held that man is powerless to pursue God without God's initiation. Calvinist theologians considered prevenient grace the work of God in the human heart before the candidate's exposure to the Christian message. Such grace allowed the "elected" listener to have "the heart prepared." In "An Evening's Thought: Salvation by Christ, with Penitential Cries," while he does say that God must guide the child's thoughts and teach the willing soul to pray, Hammon likewise urges his readers to implore God for the preparation of the soul. Yet, in that poem and in all of his works, he argues that since Christ's atonement, all men can accept salvation without further work by God.[3]

Midway in "A Poem for Children," Hammon superimposes the theme of Christ's Second Coming over ostensibly simplistic lines apparently intended to remind children of death. At that point in the work, the Second Coming of Christ becomes the poet's salient theme. As a prefiguration of a child's death, Christ's death, resurrection, ascension, and return become the metaphoric example of the fates of all men and women. Here, as in "An Address to Miss Phillis Wheatley," Hammon draws his visual and aural imagery from 1 Cor. 15; 1 Thess. 4–5; Matt. 24–25; and the Apostle John's visions of the seven angels sounding their trumpets and descending with a thunder of ethereal voices in Rev. 8–10. His phraseology "graves give up" is related to Rev. 20:13: "And the sea gave up the dead which were in it."[4]

The imagery of this corporate resurrection continues with the metempsychosis of resurrected bodies into eternal, incorruptible forms, as when the Apostle Paul says, "We shall all be changed, In a moment, in the twinkling of an eye" (1 Cor. 15:51–52). Eighteenth-century revivalists believed that the soul of the saint at death immediately left its body and traveled heavenward to God, rather than sleeping in the grave until the Second Coming. As the Corinthians chapter foretells, Christians still alive at the Second Coming will change into spiritual forms as God lifts them heavenward. Then the corpses of those who had died believing in Christ will rise and join the throng.

Other eighteenth-century elegists drew upon the imagery as well. Richmond limns Wheatley's art as consumed with death and this type of death imagery (48–52). In "On the Death of the Rev. Dr. Sewall, 1769," Wheatley describes "A saint ascending to his native skies"; likewise (when imagining the immediate afterlife experience of another minister), she cries, "Behold the prophet in his tow'ring flight! / He leaves the earth for heav'n's unmeasur'd height, / And worlds unknown receive him from our sight."[5] She taps the imagery of the soul arising from the depths of earth in "On the Death of a Young Lady of Five Years of

Age," which begins: "From dark abodes to fair etherial light / Th'enraptur'd innocent has wing'd her flight" (10–11).

Similarly, in his poem titled "An Elegy Address'd to His Excellency Governour Belcher: On the Death of his Brother-in-Law, the Honorable Daniel Oliver, Esq.," Mather Byles, minister and prominent eighteenth-century elegiac poet, illustrates this spiritual dichotomy of body and soul. He distinctly refers to the soul's flight, when "the spirit of the good governor talks with Angels and beholds his GOD," while the deceased's body is lowered into the grave and "descends to Death" (39–44). Hammon's "Poem for Children" ranks equal in form, imagery, and style to these better-known threnodies. The poem shows his familiarity both with the elegy as an eighteenth-century art form and with the religious eschatology that determined an elegy's purposes.

Hammon uses the imagery of dust and worms to describe the final step in the transformation of the departed children, again reflecting a practice prevalent in eighteenth-century verse and sermons. Preaching his hellfire message, "Sinners in the Hands of an Angry God," Jonathan Edwards constantly describes human beings as worms; also, he warns sinners that to God they remain merely "great heaps of light chaff before the whirlwind; or large quantities of dry stubble before devouring flames" (J. Edwards, *Representative Selections* 155–72). Byles remarks in "To a Friend, on the Death of a Relative": "How soon the Beauties vanish from your forms, / Fall into Dust, and mingle with the Worms!" (44–48). And in "On the Death of the Rev. Mr. George Whitefield. 1770," Wheatley combines the same dust imagery Hammon uses with that of reconstitution of the body at its reunion with the soul:

> But, though arrested by the hand of death,
> *Whitefield* no more exerts his laboring breath,
> Yet let us view him in th' eternal skies,
> Let ev'ry heart to this bright vision rise;
> While the tomb safe retains its sacred trust,
> Till life divine re-animates his dust.
>
> (Wheatley 9–10)

Unlike Byles and Edwards, Wheatley as well as Hammon employs dust in a spirit of hope rather than admonition, punishment, or regret. Both of them buttress that hope with connotations of the Second Coming and the rehabitation of the body at a postmortem remarriage with the soul. To reinforce this suggestion, she also describes Whitefield's soul ascending in triumph heavenward, thus capping this verse with two kinds of after-death images—the soul's flight and the body's decay—both popular in eighteenth-century literature.

Not one to accept establishment theology casually, Hammon experiments with the possibilities of variant stages of metempsychosis. Are both body and soul "asleep" in the grave? Does Christ "preserve" the soul in abeyance until a mass resurrection and judgment? How can that be if souls fly directly to heaven? Is there an ethereal compartment for New Testament saints, like Abraham's bosom in the Old Testament Sheol which Christ empties after his resurrection?[6] Hammon continues exploration of extrabiblical dogma by suggesting that Christ included this soul preservation as one of the bundle of graces purchased with his sacrifice. Or possibly, "preserved" can refer simply to the protected state of the soul after salvation, without any reference to death.

Familiar in colonial church culture, the "angelic train" of verse 15 provides many contemporary Black writers and Christian believers with both religious and racial metaphors. While it does symbolize heaven, eternal glory, and a multiracial stream of Christ's followers who will come from every tribe and every nation (Rev. 7:9), "angelic train" can be construed as pertaining to Black/white relationships. As Western iconography presumes God's angels to be white, their Satanic counterparts logically become the opposite hue. Wheatley gives the irony of the angelic train perhaps the best tension in her poem "On Being Brought from Africa to America" when she states: "Remember, *Christians, Negroes* black as *Cain* / May be refin'd, and join th'angelic train."[7] Hammon quite possibly had the same usage in mind.

In the poem's final verses, Hammon brings his theological thrust back to the orthodox mainstream. He asserts that the soul which inhabited the body of a deceased Christian before the corporate resurrection of the Body of Christ (that is, all Christians who have lived since Christ's resurrection) will at the return of Christ rise from the grave in a reformed physical state. He then meshes all eschatological possibilities in scenes of a final victory celebration in heaven before the throne of God. His similes are drawn from such passages in Revelation as 4:2–11, 5:9–14, and 19:1–6. He also includes the additional resurrection of those who will die during and after the Great Tribulation. This interpretation accommodates his repetition of the trumpets' roar and the bodily resurrections. The vision of angels as Christ's guards possibly alludes to Armageddon, which will end the tribulation, according to canonical prophecy. Thus Hammon is delineating progressive steps in biblical eschatology. Interestingly, most eighteenth-century theologians did not make this clear a distinction between a pre- and postmillennial Second Coming.

In the same fatherly tone, the preacher concludes the poem with the finality of unity on three levels. First, the child's body will be reunited with his soul and spirit at death. Second, the child is assured that he or she will indeed rejoin a Christian family either in heaven or at a corporate resurrection. And third, as depicted in the "angelic train" idiom, the child will then join an extended and authentic Christian community. This ultimate union will obviate the racial, class, and age division existing among professing Christians on earth. Thus, Hammon assures children, death becomes the ultimate victory, the final and eternal glorious life.

Notes

1.   Discussions of election are included in Beveridge, *Works* 2:430; Beveridge, *Private Thoughts* 394–95; Bayne 32–63; Carr 62–67; Foster 112–18; as well as in Hastings' entry on Puritanism 507–15.

2.   Note Poole's discourse on Isa. 45:4, 9, 22; Mark 13:20, 22, 27; and Rom. 8:29, 30.

3.   See 2 Thess. 2:3–10. Pettit has the most recent and the best explanation of the prevenient grace doctrine.

4.   For more on allusions to the Second Coming in eighteenth-century literature, see Stein, "Providence and the Apocalypse" 250–67. See Burkitt's explications of these verses in his *Notes* 2:456, 836.

5.   From "On the Death of the Rev. Mr. George Whitefield, 1770." This and the former poem appear in Wheatley 7–8, 9–10.

6.   See Matt. 27:50–53, Luke 16:19–24, and Eph. 4:8.

7.   See Baltazar; Boyer and Missenbaum; Burr, *Narratives* 308–20, 344–55, Hutchinson; and Weimer 72–74.

"A Poem for Children with Thoughts on Death"

1

O ye young and thoughtless youth,
    Come seek the living God,
The Scriptures are a sacred truth,
    Ye must believe the word.

                                        Eccles. 12:1[1]

2

'Tis God alone can make you wise,
    His wisdom's from above,[2]
He fills the soul with sweet supplies
    By his redeeming love.[3]

                                        Prov. 4:7[4]

3

Remember youth the time is short,
    Improve the present day[5]
And pray that God may guide your thoughts,
    And teach your lips to pray.

                                        Ps. 30:9[6]

4

To pray unto the most high God,
    and beg restraining grace,
Then by the power of his word
    You'll see the Saviour's face.[7]

5

Little children they may die,
　　Turn to their native dust,
Their souls shall leap beyond the skies,
　　and live among the just.

6

Like little worms they turn and crawl,
　　and gasp for every breath,
The blessed Jesus sends his call,
　　and takes them to his rest.

7

Thus the youth are born to die,
　　The time is hastening on,
The Blessed Jesus rends the sky,
　　and makes his power known.

　　　　　　　　　　Ps. 103:15[8]

8

Then ye shall hear the angels sing
　　The trumpet give a sound,
Glory, glory to our King,
　　The Saviour's coming down.

　　　　　　　　　　Matt. 26:64[9]

9

Start ye Saints from dusty beds,
　　and hear a Saviour call,
'Twas Jesus Christ that died and bled,
　　and thus preserv'd thy soul.

10

This the portion of the just,
　　Who lov'd to serve the Lord,
Their bodies starting from the dust,
　　Shall rest upon their God.

11

They shall join that holy word,
　　That angels constant sing,
Glory, glory to the Lord,
　　Hallelujahs to our King.[10]

12

Thus the Saviour will appear,
    With guards of heavenly host,
Those blessed Saints, shall then declare,
    'Tis Father, Son and Holy Ghost.
                                        Rev. 1:7–8[11]

13

Then shall ye hear the trumpet sound,
    The graves give up their dead,
Those blessed saints shall quick awake,
    and leave their dusty beds.[12]
                                        Matt. 27:51–52[13]

14

Then shall you hear the trumpet sound,
    and rend the native sky,
Those bodies starting from the ground,
    In the twinkling of an eye.
                                        1 Cor. 15:51–54[14]

15

There to sing the praise of God,
    and join the angelic train,
And by the power of his word,
    Unite together again.

16

Where angels stand for to admit
    Their souls at the first word,
Cast sceptres down at Jesus' feet
    Crying holy, holy Lord.
                                        Rev. 4:8[15]

17

Now glory be unto our God
    all praise be justly given,
Ye humble souls that love the Lord
    Come seek the joys of Heaven.

Hartford, January 1, 1782

Emendations

Stanza	Line			
1	1:	ye]	Ye] R	
	5:	Eccles. 12:1]	Eccle. xii.1.] R	
2	1:	'Tis]	Tis] R	
	5:	Prov. 4:7]	Prov. iv. 7.] R	
3	5:	Ps. 30:9]	Psalm xxx. 9.] R	
4	4:	You'll]	You'l] R	
6	2:	breath,]	breath.] R	breath,] H
7	5:	Ps. 103:15]	Psalm ciii. 15.] R	
8	5:	Matt. 26:64]	Matth. xxvi. 64.] R	
9	3:	'Twas]	Twas] R	
10	4:	God. They]	God. They] R	God. Their] H
11	3:	Glory,]	Glory,] R	Glory] H
12	4:	'Tis]	Tis] R	
	5:	Rev. 1:7–8]	Rev. i. 7,8] R	
13	5:	Matt. 27:51–52]	Matth. xxvii. 51,52.] R	
14	5:	1 Cor. 15:51–54]	I Cor. xv. 51, 52, 53, 54.] R	
15	1:	praise]	parise] R	
16	3:	Jesus']	Jesus] R	
	4:	holy,]	holy$_e$] R	
	5:	Rev. 4:8]	Ransom has no reference	Matt. 4:8] H
17	1:	17 Now]	xvii Now] R	7. Now] H

Notes

1. Eccles. 12:1: "Remember now thy Creator in the days of thy youth, while the evil days come not, nor the years draw nigh, when thou shalt say, I have no pleasure in them."

2. This image of descending wisdom is taken from James 1:17, the New Testament book of practical instruction: "Every good gift and every perfect gift is from above, and cometh down from the Father of lights, with whom is no variableness, neither shadow of turning."

3. The meaning of "redeem" in the eighteenth century had both sociological and theological implications, yet in either case its essential sense was "to buy back." White indentured servants in the American colonies were called "redemptioneers," for they had someone bank their earnings until they could pay their way out of servitude. In the Bible a Hebrew whose relative was sold into slavery for unpaid debts might assume the task of "redeeming" him, or again buying him out of his bondage. The King James translation of the Bible likewise consistently refers to God's delivery of the Israelites from enslavement to the Egyptians as "redemption."

4. Prov. 4:7: "Wisdom is the principal thing; therefore get wisdom: and with all thy getting get understanding."

5. This admonition is probably based on Eph. 5:16: "Redeeming the time, because the days are evil."

6. Ps. 30:9: "What profit is there in my blood, when I go down to the pit? Shall the dust praise thee? Shall it declare thy truth?"

7. This title "Savior" all inclusively refers to an omnipotent deliverer, unto whom a helpless and penitent victim can look for heroic rescue. Usually when the epithet is seen in the Hagiographa, it refers to the Jews' deliverance from slavery in Egypt. In the New Testament that rescue was seen as one of Christ's preincarnate acts. Thus Hammon's Bible-reading audience should have been well aware of the implications of the term "Savior" for American slavery. For more on the Exodus of the Jews from Egypt, see J. Edwards, *History,* and *Works* 5:355; Barnes 81–159; and a portion of Coleman's "Testimony" in *Friends' Review* 84.

8. From Ps. 103:15: "As for man, his days are as grass: as a flower of the field, so he flourisheth."

9. From Matt. 26:64: "Thou hast said: nevertheless I say unto you, Hereafter shall ye see the Son of man sitting on the right hand of power, and coming in the clouds of heaven."

10. Hammon joins all eschatological possibilities in scenes of a final victory celebration in heaven before the throne of God. His similes are drawn from such passages in Revelation as 4:2–11, 5:9–14, and 19:1–6.

11. Rev. 1:7–8: "Behold, he cometh with clouds; and every eye shall see him, and they also which pierced him: and all kindreds of the earth shall wail because of him. Even so, Amen. I am Alpha and Omega, the beginning and the ending, saith the Lord, which is, and which was, and which is to come, the Almighty."

12. While the affixed Scripture is discussing the appearance of some deceased Israelites at Jesus' crucifixion, basically Hammon's text is based on 1 Thess. 4:16: "For the Lord himself shall descend from heaven . . . with the trump of God: and the dead in Christ shall rise first." Also see Burkitt's discussion, 2:456, 836.

13. From Matt. 27:51–52: "And, behold, the veil of the temple was rent in twain from the top to the bottom; and the earth did quake, and the rocks rent; And the graves were opened; and many bodies of the saints which slept arise."

14. Note 1 Cor. 15:51–54: "Behold, I show you a mystery; We shall not all sleep, but we shall all be changed, In a moment, in the twinkling of an eye, at the last trump: for the trumpet shall sound, and the dead shall be raised incorruptible, and we shall all be changed. For

the corruptible must put on incorruption, and this mortal must put on immortality. So when this corruptible shall have put on incorruption, and this mortal shall have put on immortality, then shall be brought to pass the saying that is written, Death is swallowed up in victory."

15.   From Rev. 4:8: "And the four beasts had each of them six wings about him; and they were full of eyes within: and they rest not day and night, saying, 'Holy, holy, holy, Lord God Almighty, which was, and is, and is to come.' "

5. An Evening's Improvement

Hammon structured *An Evening's Improvement* around a theme taken from the first chapter of John, which sets forth Christ as the Lamb of God. As the epigraph from John 1:29 indicates, Hammon weaves his theme around a quote from the Gospel written by John the Apostle, evangelist and one of the Twelve Disciples. The phrase "Behold, the Lamb of God" is, however, part of the testimony of John the Baptist, Jesus' cousin but not one of his disciples. As one who received public acclaim earlier than Jesus, John the Baptist identified his cousin as the Messiah by telling the Jews that the Lamb of God had come. In the audience hearing this announcement, the Apostle John, when reconstructing the life of Jesus, included the narrative of the Baptist's sermon. In his many references and allusions to that biblical text, Hammon poetically draws upon both Baptist and the Apostle through the use of the common name John.

In Hammon's theological schema, accepting the deity of Christ held axiomatic position before any slave could accept the poet's evangelistic zeal and comprehend his plan for slave re-identification and emancipation. Second, Christ, as God, had the will to do so. Hammon expected the same force of faith that contributed to the settlement of the colonies to deliver Africans to freedom. The Lamb of God theology inculcates the "purchase" of the slave's freedom through Christ's sacrifice.[1] In addition to the Lamb of God theme in this essay, Hammon presents Christ as God's Bondservant (Slave), as the Savior

(Rescuer), and as Redeemer (that is, Payer of Ransom) of the slave.

As in his other two essays, Hammon clearly aims his art at a Black audience: "But, my brethren, for whom this discourse is designed." As his intended audience his "brethren" provide a key for decoding the poet's textual themes. Although sponsored by a few whites, Hammon primarily does not write to a white audience. When he does address them, he carefully sets aside a frame based on responses to a pseudoinquirer such as, "Sir, you may ask why one who is so unlearned would attempt to teach his brethren." But as whites are his sponsors and are in most cases those who read his works to Blacks, Hammon speaks in an intellectually artistic language—with metaphors that require Black readers to trust his intentions and motives and with biblical vehicles that are acceptable enough to whites that they will pass the word along.

Throughout his work, Hammon identifies the slave with Christ—first, because "Servant" is Christ's biblical title and second, because Christ constantly aligned himself with Israel's outcasts. That designation may, however, be dangerously ambiguous for the American slave. "Lamb of God" refers to the Old Testament ritual requiring Hebrews to sacrifice animals in order to atone for sins. Hammon's repetition of the Baptist's admonition to behold the "Lamb" directs Africans to consider Christ's "sacrificial" willingness to give up his life in saving service to others. Nineteenth-century abolitionists later offered such a theorem. For instance, Harriet Beecher Stowe presents stereotypes like Uncle Tom as religious supplicants who willingly give their lives to "redeem" a sinful nation (239–40). Twentieth-century spokesmen James Baldwin (*Notes of a Native Son*) and Richard Wright (*Uncle Tom's Children*) vigorously rejected such a dictum. In this essay, Hammon speaks of Christ as the resurrected—now victorious—Lamb whom he believes will return to earth as King and Conqueror to pass judgment on slave and master alike.[2]

Also in this essay, and as a pivotal point in all of his works, Hammon cites the heart of his argument against slavery: regardless of the Ham curse (Genesis 9), the Cain curse (Genesis 4), or any other supposed act of ancient history that would have incurred such multigenerational guilt and divinely destined punishment like eternal servitude, Christ's sacrifice at Calvary removed the guilt and the punishment of "sin." Christ's atonement would nullify the "sin" of African lineage, thus rendering the basis for the slave master's morality, and the slaveholding society, inauthentic. If, on the other hand, Christ's sacrificial death did eliminate this "sin," the Cain/Ham theology used to justify the slave institution obviously sprang from manipulative motives.

By putting his white readers in this quandary, Hammon begins a tradition of literary logic that would endure in Black American writing until the cultural changes in the 1960's: (1) Christianity itself, which whites held as the world's only true religion, proved slavery to be un-Christian and sinful; (2) Christianity and the Bible provided the Black man his greatest defense and the proof text by which he could plead for legal and moral freedom; (3) if true, the doctrines of Christianity placed the slave master, and the society supporting him, in jeopardy of a fearful judgment from God; and (4) a basic difference existed between the slave's understanding of Christianity and that of the master. Other pre-twentieth-century Black writers who espoused Christianity and generally advocated these themes in their works include Phillis Wheatley, Olaudah Equiano, Linda Brent, George Moses Horton, Richard Allen, and, most prominently, Frederick Douglass.

Only in this essay does Hammon refer directly to the Cain myth. And even then, he does so through mention of Abel, the brother whom Cain murdered. According to the narrative from Genesis 4, God put a mark upon Cain as a punishment for the crime. To make enslavement of Africans more palatable, theologians told slaveholders that the mark was black skin and that, as descendants of Cain, slaves had to fulfill Cain's punishment. Never agreeing with this interpretation, Hammon counters with Isa. 53:12: "[Christ] was numbered with the transgressors." Therefore, Hammon argues, Christ served as the substitutionary sacrifice for Cain's guilt. Thus, neither the African nor any-one else must pay the price for another's sin. Second, Hammon says that, although Abel's murder called for justice, Christ's blood provided full retribution. Thus, only mercy awaits Cain's descendants, if indeed Africans are his descendants.

Phillis Wheatley and George Moses Horton, the only other Americans to publish while in slavery, also used the Cain myth as a theme treating it in much the same way. Most famous are Wheatley's lines: "Remember, *Christians*, *Negroes*, black as *Cain*, / May be refin'd, and join th'angelic train" ("On Being Brought from Africa to America," Wheatley 7). From the time of the first shipment of slaves to the colonies in 1619, whites employed the Cain/Ham myths to explain the African's nation-ality and to justify his enslavement.[3]

Abolitionists knew the effectiveness of the Ham/Cain myths as fodder for slavery. In his *Journal,* John Woolman details the disconsolation he experienced when several Quakers in one meeting tenaciously insisted that these biblical accounts proved God's willingness to make slaves of Black men:

> [A] friend in company began to talk in support of the slavetrade, and said the Negroes were understood to be the offspring of Cain, their blackness being the mark of God set upon him after he murdered Abel his brother; that it was the design of Provi-dence they should be slaves, as a condition proper to the race of so wicked a man as Cain was. . . . One of them said that after the flood Ham went to the Land of Nod and took a wife; that Nod was a land far distant, inhabited by Cain's race, and that the blood did not reach it; and as Ham was sentenced to be a servant of servants to his brethren, these two families, being thus joined, were undoubtedly fit only for slaves.[4]

Woolman could do nothing to dissuade the men from this position.

In correlation with the discussion of "the sin," Hammon points to individual action rather than corporate, historical in-dictment about which the individual can do nothing. Now that Christ has redeemed all men, including the Africans, from any generative or racial curse (Gal. 3:13), the individual can freely go to God about acts for which he feels personally responsible and receive forgiveness. Hammon always includes this twofold message to the slave: Christ's sacrifice obviates the argument for predetermined slavery and offers the slave freedom from personal sin through full and equal salvation in Christ.

Of course, for most colonists, black symbolized the color of sin. Therefore, the first Black writer in American literature looked for biblical images that would free Africans from that negative connotation. He found literary and historical entries about Ethiopians to be most useful tools to convict whites and to encourage Blacks. While England or Europe do not appear in Scripture, Ethiopia—as a cognitive referent for Africa—has repeated and favorable mention. Bible-reading whites knew that an Ethiopian rescued the prophet Jeremiah (Jer. 38:7–12), that King David prophesied that all Ethiopia would come to God (Ps. 68:31), that Moses, an admitted type of Christ, married an Ethiopian woman who would therefore be considered as the bride of Christ (Num. 12:1), and that the first non-Palestinian Gentile who accepted Christ was an Ethiopian eunuch, the treasurer of Candace, the Ethiopian monarch (Acts 8:27). For Blacks, Hammon simply attempted to restore pride in the historical and cultural ethnicity which white power brokers worked so arduously to tear down. Once slaves knew that they descended from a royal nation, whites would have a much harder time convincing them of their supposedly overt sinfulness and sensual, bestial natures.[5]

Hammon perceived that colonists used the characteristic of skin color to assign Africans to perpetual slavery, while allowing other servants and redemptioneers the hope of freedom and the opportunity for economic and political self-determination. Indigenous testimony about so-called witchcraft experience appeared particularly damaging. "Eyewitnesses" claimed that they had seen Satan himself as a tall black man, that evil animals and other emblems showed themselves as black, and that black emanated as the color of ultimate evil. Despite colonial theologians' preachings that prevarication remained the hallmark of satanic membership, the many witchcraft trials in New

England and the middle colonies had as much to do with hatred and fear of the African's skin color and the entrenchment of slavery in the American colonies as any other factor.[6]

Hammon presented another crucial point in the persuasive logic he employed to win his fellow slaves to Christ: that, while to God all men are equal, he particularly offers solace to those whom the dominant society rejects. Thus, in addition to the Samaritan and publican references, Hammon draws upon a passage from Acts 10, which gives an account of the second time that the apostles shared the Gospel with Gentiles. Again, the emphasis is primarily racial. Through a vision God told the Apostle Peter—who, as a rigidly orthodox Jew, avoided all contact with Gentiles even after the formation of the church on the Day of Pentecost—that what God had cleansed Peter must not reject. Later, when Cornelius, a leading Italian military officer, invited Peter to his home, the Apostle interpreted the vision to mean that God no longer made distinctions between Gentiles and Jews but instead called men from every nation into the church. Again, Hammon challenges Bible-reading Christians to proffer Blacks the same equality that Peter promised Cornelius precisely because "God is no respecter of persons" (Acts 10:34). Undoubtedly Hammon read Poole's analysis of this text many times:

> God does not accept of one because he is a Jew, and respect another because he is a gentile; tho. St. Paul being Prejudiced by his Education, had been carryed along with that error of the Jews; against which notwithstanding, God had declared himself even unto them, Deut. 10.17. which is also conformed unto us in the New Testament, Rom 2.11 I Pet. 1.17 for thout our being of any Nation or any condition, rich or poor, honoured or despised; as the one side recommends us not unto God; and on the other side, it will not hinder us from being accepted with the Lord.[7]

Because of this premise concerning God's impartiality and because he freed the Jews from slavery, Hammon insisted that only divine intervention could end American slavery: "If we are slaves, it is by the permission of God. If we are free, it must be

by the power of the most high God." The operative word is
"power." Most slave narrators speak of escape from slavery as
a result of their faith in the power of Christ to free them. They
considered physical freedom as part of the "bundle" of life
apprehended during salvation. If Christ indeed had the power
to free men from unmitigated anguish, then the slave could only
logically assume that this power extended to emancipation.[8]

Particularly apropos is the poet's mention of miraculous resurrection, not just Christ's return from the dead but the principle of resurrection demonstrable in the lives of men. Obviously
whites intended Africans to be "dead" culturally, intellectually,
and spiritually and further sought only to awaken them within a
context of eurocentric reculturalization. They used Christianity
primarily as a tool of that reindoctrination, allowing education
only under church guidance and primarily for biblical consump-
tion. Just as in Southern colonies, Northern whites gave slaves
freedom to congregate only for religious services and only here
could Africans legally recall the ethos of ethnic culture. Why
then should anyone wonder that the heart of the Black abolition and civil rights movements began within that limited freedom of religious expression?

God's permitted will seemed to be a logical explanation to
reconcile the existence of slavery in a universe wherein ostensibly he had absolute control. However, in contrast, faith in his
goodness and power to move against slavery's inhumanity was a
necessary adjunct for a slave's conversion. Hammon drew upon
the supreme acts of Creation and the re-creation or redemption
of the human soul as allegorical proof of God's power to abolish
slavery. As Blacks had few advocates in the white world, as
they were under the strict control of apartheid slave codes, and
as they had no possibility of bringing about a militant end to
slavery, Hammon set forth God's providence as the only possible and effective power for mass manumission. For this man of
faith, then, Christianity could not function as just a system of
platitudes with which to make Blacks in his audience more
submissive to white rule. Conversely, he believed that faith and

the truth of the Christian message were the only forces that could persuade whites to end slavery.

By quoting Gen. 1:16—"And God made two great lights, the greater light to rule the day, and the lesser light to rule the night" . . . Hammon synthesizes several divine attributes: the ability to create life; the ability to set man free internally, through regeneration; and the ability to free a captive group, the Israelites, from physical bondage. This coalescence also exists in his use of John 8:36, which was to become a favorite Scripture of African-American preachers throughout the next century. Olaudah Equiano gives perhaps the best narrative of "new creature" experience in all of American literature. Through several chapters, Equiano first vividly paints the hollow displacement of an African slave's itinerancy in Western experience. He even delineates fruitless attempts to absolve his soul's stirrings through baptism and catechism rituals. The narrative of his soul's search for Christ covers a period of several years until he claims to find a personal relationship with Christ, and attributes to that experience amelioration of the loneliness he suffered as a wandering sailor and ostracized slave. In Equiano's art, one sees the peace and security that he experiences as he settles in England and begins a career as that country's most articulate African (and ex-slave) abolitionist. His life's story represents the possibilities for freedom and change that Hammon—who claimed to have also had the "new creature" experience—envisioned for his readers.

However, Hammon continually implied that many whites who said they were Christians had not had this same new creation experience. Many critics believe that outspoken protest against Christian hypocrisy in this country began in the eighteenth century. However, Jupiter Hammon labeled America as "so-called Christian land" as early as 1787. He warned slaves that too many whites trusted in group identification, by church or nation, as the sole assurance of salvation. He further pointed to the existence of slavery and the mistreatment of slaves as proof that slave owners, as well as the national community which protected them, were not Christians at all.[9]

Because of these inconsistencies, Hammon insisted that white slaveholders faced two judgments, one of a temporal nature—that is, the Revolutionary War—and another at the end of time. He perceived the first judgment to be carried out both in the nation and, more immediately, in the Lloyds' household. During part of the war, Hammon relocated to Hartford with the Lloyd family. Although the stay enhanced the poet's career (several of his first works were published there), this period proved tragic for the Lloyd family. Joseph Lloyd, then head of the estate, committed suicide because he, one of few patriots in a straitlaced Loyalist family, mistakenly believed that the colonies had lost the war. Perhaps for these reasons Hammon viewed the war as tantamount to God's judgment.

One must, however, additionally read Hammon's *Address to the Negroes in the State of New York* to understand his conclusion that judgment resulted because white colonists sought their own freedom without regard for the African's bondage. The war raged as a time of great upheaval for most colonists and their slaves. Richmond's commentary on Phillis Wheatley's displacement during the war illustrates the nation's impoverished condition (43–52). War refugees traveled to various rural areas, while those remaining in or returning to cities often lived in shelled-out houses in greatly reduced economic circumstances. Thus when Hammon wrote of judgment he undoubtedly had much in the Hartford landscape to support his opinion. However, he wants Blacks to see themselves as separate from this judgment in view of their noncitizenship in the revolting colonies. Slaves should use that alienation as a reason to draw closer to God's protectiveness, as they were not the ones being reproved.[10]

In the second judgment that Hammon envisions, slaves and slaveholders will again separate. This separation, he believes, will take place at Christ's second return to earth. A major skein in all his works, the Second Coming captured center stage in eighteenth-century eschatological theology. The return includes two judgments: one for the saved and another for the unsaved. In both instances, Christ and his saints (who, within Hammon's priorities, are the righteous and "freed" slaves) will be the judges. Thus, the positions of power will be reversed. While the white slaveholder may reign on earth, in the earliest development of their own theology, Blacks believed that slaves will reign in heaven, where they will judge former oppressors and demand retribution for violence endured on earth.[11]

Hammon always invites the slave to prepare for the judgment of the righteous by accepting Christ. He likewise implies that the unrepentant slave master's actions render him fit only for the judgment of the wicked. Because of his enslavement, Hammon usually expresses the latter only through aesthetic subtlety. He uses several of Christ's parables to prove that rich men—obviously the slaveholders because of the dichotomous discussion of freedom versus the world's wealth—will not be included in this judgment of rewards for the righteous. Instead, Hammon indicates, the rich will be condemned by Christ because they, possessing money, did not share with the poor, feed the hungry, or care for the naked and homeless (the slaves) as in Matt. 25:33–46. Poole draws a similar conclusion in his commentary on 1 Tim. 6:9–10:

> They who out of a covetous and immoderate desire of being rich in this Worlds Goods, will use any arts, and any unlawful thing without any just regard to the Law of God. Fall into many temptations and snare. Kendling in them many foolish and pernicious desires contrary to the Law to the eternal ruine of their Souls not to be prevented but by the face and powerful Grace of God.

Eighteenth-century Christian readers knew that Scripture specifically instructed the rich to provide for the poor. Some literary theologians, though usually only those who also considered themselves abolitionists, even identified African slaves as the poor in the society who must be cared for.

Samuel Sewall, as well as John Hepburn, another seventeenth-century abolitionist, led other contemporary liberal colonists by stating that the Africans should receive the care for the poor outlined in those verses. While Hammon's coevals read the works of these men, they also read Woolman, S. Hopkins, Coleman, Benezet, Rush, and scores of others who shared the same view.[12] Thus, for Hammon, his Christian "brethren" who would not be judged with the wicked included those whites who had repented of their sins and those Africans who made up the nation's poor.

While Hammon suggests that these two classes must also accept Christ as Savior, he does not stress conversion as a necessity when discussing the distinct judgments of the rich and the poor. Only these "brethren" will inherit an eternal kingdom; those who have not cared for the poor and neglected slaves, as outlined in Matthew 25 from which he quotes extensively at the end of this essay, will be cursed to join the devil and his angels.[13] Although perhaps not the overt antislavery rhetoric that some modern critics might prefer, the use of passages such as Matthew 25 was as close as a captive slave could come to condemning his captors. Moreover, the text provided an appropriate argument for his more biblically minded eighteenth-century audience.

Thus, clearly Hammon's end-time creed included physiological, psychological, and sociological changes that made salvation inextricable from manumission. He ends this essay with a quote from 1 Cor. 15:51–53: "We shall all be changed. For this corruptible must put on incorruption, and this mortal must put on immortality." Slavery's consequences affected the body, but the slave discarded that body with its vulnerability to pain, at death. Further, eighteenth-century Christians held deep hope that any basis for racial hatred would be removed at death when the transcendence of the soul would begin. Thus the yearning for inclusion, prominence, and total acceptance in an authentic Christian community became the ultimate aim of this slave writer's vision. And in all of his works, he offered that hope to his African-American readers and to those whites who would accept it.

Notes

1. The Lamb of God also refers to Rev. 7:14: "These are they which came out of great tribulation, and have washed their robes, and

made them white in the blood of the Lamb." Poole points out that Christ, the Sacrificed Lamb, would also become the Lamb who will judge. His notes on John 1:29 and Isaiah 53 must have also been a guide to Hammon.

2. The image of the Lamb as a returning, conquering hero is consistent with Rev. 6:1–2 and 1 Thess. 4:16. See also Bushnell, vol. 2; and Thomas 97 for a discussion of the terms "servant" and "minister," which are synonymous in the Bible and also analogous to the biblical use of "slave."

3. For example, seventeenth-century theologian Samuel Mather divided the world into three races of men in "Asia, Africa, and Europe" and said that Ham's tribes settled in Africa and that the curse to Ham's posterity befitted the sin (20–29).

4. Additionally see S. Hopkins, *Dialogue* and *Timely Articles;* and J. H. Hopkins. See also Armistead 40–107; Barnes; Elihu Coleman's "Testimony against Making Slaves of Men" in Lay 42; Sewall; Clarkson 178; Cobb; Stringfellow in McKitrick 86–91; McLeod 29–31; Poole's entry on Gen. 9:25; Remy 24–25; and Thomas 33–35.

5. See Dunston; Sewall; Snowden, both books; and Ullendorff for more on the sociological significance of the Ethiopian as a symbol for freedom.

6. For supplementary discussions of the implications of the skin color black in eighteenth-century Western culture, see Baltazar 5–53; Burr, *Narratives* 285–86, 308–12, 393, 420; Heather, 169–70; Jordan, *Negro vs. Equality* 44–49; Jordan, *White Man's* 4–25, 106–110; Kobrin 20–21; C. Mather, *On Witchcraft* 70–71; and Taylor 81, 115.

7. The "respecter of persons" phrase was a familiar one for eighteenth-century abolitionists. For more examples of its use and interpretation, refer to Mather's discussion of the conversions of African-Americans in Greene, *The Negro* 265; and Sewall 7–8.

8. This is covered in Cheever, 94–99; and J. H. Hopkins.

9. See Francis E. W. Harper's poem "Bury Me in a Free Land" (Redding and Davis 103–4); Brent's discussion of white Christians (115); "David Walker's Appeal" (Stuckey 39–117); and of course, Frederick Douglass's eloquent sections on white Christians (93–97, 117–24). Contemporary hypocrisy of some Christians is also discussed in Bragg 71–74; T. M. Cooley 88–95; and Tracy 52.

10. See also Berlin and Hoffman; Kaplan; McLeod; and "The Apparent Bystanders" in Marty 4:3–33.

11. For more on eighteenth-century eschatology, see Beveridge, *Works* 7:100–102; Burkitt 2:242, 108–9; and J. Edwards, *Works* 4:284.

12. Most of these men were eighteenth-century Quaker abolitionists. For more on their lives and work, see Lay.

13.   For more on eighteenth-century theology about the judgment of the rich, see Beveridge, *Works* 6:146–62 and *Private Thoughts* 286, as well as Poole's remarks on Matt. 5:11, 19:21, and James 2:9.

An Evening's Improvement

Behold the Lamb of God which taketh away the sins of the World.
—John 1:29

In the beginning of this chapter John bears testimony that Jesus is the Son of God: "In the beginning was the Word, and the Word was with God, and the Word was God" (John 1:1). This is that Lamb of God which I now invite you to behold. My brethren, we are to behold the Son of God as our Lord and Giver of Life; for he "was made flesh, and dwelt among us, . . . " (verse 14 of the context), and here he is declared to be the Son of God, "full of grace and truth." And here in the first place I mean to show the necessity of beholding the Lamb of God in the sense of the text. Second, I will endeavor to show when we are said to behold the Son of God in the sense of the text. Third, I shall show when we may be said not to behold the Lamb of God as we should do. In the fourth place I shall endeavor to show how far we may be mistaken in beholding the Lamb of God. In the fifth place I shall endeavor to rectify these mistakes.

My brethren, since I wrote my *Winter Piece,* it hath been requested that I would write something more for the advantage of my friends, by my superiors, gentlemen whose judgment I depend on, and by my friends in general. I have had an invitation to give public exhortation but did not think it my duty at that time; but now my brethren, by divine assistance, I shall endeavor to show the necessity of beholding the Lamb of God.

My brethren, we must behold the Lamb of God as taking away the sin of the world, as in our text; and it is necessary that we behold the Lamb of God as Our King: ah! as the King immortal, eternal, invisible,[1] as the only Son of God, for he has declared him, as in the eighteenth verse of the context: "No man hath seen God at any time; the only begotten Son, which is in the bosom of the Father, he hath declared him."

My brethren, let us strive to behold the Lamb of God with faith and repentance; to come weary and heavy-laden with our sins, for they have made us unworthy of the mercy of the Lamb of God.[2] Therefore, we see how necessary it is that we behold the Lamb of God in the sense of the text—that is, in a spiritual manner, not having our own righteousness. But we must be clothed with the unspotted robes of the Lamb of God; we must work out our salvation with fear and trembling, always abounding in the works of the Lord;[3] we must remember the vows of our baptism, which are to follow the Lamb of God. John, speaking of baptism, saith:

> Upon whom thou shalt see the spirit descending, and remaining on him, the same is he which baptizeth with the Holy Ghost. And I saw, and bare record that this is the Son of God. Again the next day after John stood, and two of his disciples; and looking upon Jesus as he walked, he saith, Behold the Lamb of God! And the two disciples heard him speak, and they followed Jesus. (John 1:33–37)

Thus, my dear brethren, we are to follow the Lamb of God at all times, whether in prosperity or adversity, knowing that "all things work together for good for them that love God . . . " (Rom. 8:28). Now let us manifest that we love God, by a holy life; let us strive to glorify and magnify the name of the most high God.

It is necessary that we behold the Lamb of God by taking heed to our ways, that we sin not with our tongues (Ps. 39:1). Here, my brethren, we have the exhortation of David, who beheld the Lamb of God with faith and love, for he cries out a most humble petition: "O Lord, rebuke me not in thine anger, neither chastise me in thy hot displeasure" (Ps. 6:1). And now, my brethren, have we not great reason to cry out to the Lamb of God, that taketh away the sin of the world, that He may have mercy on us and forgive us our sins, and that he would give us his Holy Spirit, that we may have such hungerings and thirsting as may be acceptable in the sight of God. For "As the hart panteth after the water brooks," so should our souls pant for the living God (Ps. 42:1).

And now my brethren, we must behold the Lamb of God, as expressed in John 1:51: "And he saith unto him, Verily, verily I say unto you, Hereafter ye shall see heaven open, and the angels of God ascending and descending upon the Son of man." This is a representation of the great day when the Lamb of God shall appear. "And then shall appear the sign of the Son of man in Heaven: and then shall all the tribes of the earth mourn, and they shall see the Son of man coming in the clouds of heaven with power and great glory" (Matt. 24:30). Here, my brethren, we have life and death set before us, for if we mourn with the tribes for our sins, which have made us unworthy of the least favor in the sight of God, then he will have mercy and he will give us his Holy Spirit. Then we shall have hearts to pray to the Lamb of God, as David did when he was made sensible of his imperfections, when he cried to the Lamb of God: "Have mercy on me, O God, according to thy loving-kindness: according unto the multitude of thy tender mercies blot out my transgressions" (Ps. 51:1).

This, my brethren, is the language of the penitent, for he hath a desire that his heart may be turned from darkness to light, from sin to holiness. This none can do but God, for the carnal mind is enmity against God, for it is not subject to the law of God, neither can be.[4] Here we see that we must behold the Lamb of God as calling to us in a most tender and compassionate manner, saying, "O Jerusalem, Jerusalem, . . . how often would I have gathered thy children together, even as a hen gathereth her chickens under her wings, and ye would not!" (Matt. 23:37). As much as if God had said, "O ye wicked and rebellious people, have I not sent the ministers of the gospel to teach you, and you will not receive the doctrine of the gospel, which is faith and repentance."[5] "I tell you, Nay: but, except ye repent, ye shall all likewise perish" (Luke 13:5).

And now my dear brethren, have we repented of our sins? Have we not neglected to attend divine service? Or if we have attended to the word of God, have we been sincere? For "God is a Spirit: and they that worship him must worship him in spirit and in truth" (John 4:24). When we have heard the word of God sounding in our ears, inviting us to behold the Lamb of God, O my dear brethren, have we, as it were, laid up these words in our hearts, or have we not been like the stony ground hearers?

> But he that received the seed into stony places, the same is he that heareth the word, and anon with joy receiveth it; Yet hath he not root in himself, but dureth for a while: for when tribulation or persecution ariseth because of the word, by and by he is offended. (Matt. 13:20–21)

This is the effect of a hard heart.

There is such a depravity in our natures that we are not willing to suffer any reproach that may be cast on us for the sake of our religion; this, my brethren, is because we have not the love of God shed abroad in our hearts; but our hearts are set too much on the pleasures of this life, forgetting that they are passing away; but the children of God are led by the Spirit of God.[6]

> Therefore, brethren, we are debtors, not to the flesh to live after the flesh. For if ye live after the flesh, ye shall die: but if ye through the Spirit do mortify the deeds of the body, ye shall live. For as many as are led by the Spirit of God, they are the sons of God. (Rom. 8:12–14)

Here, my brethren, we see that it is our indispensable duty to conform to the will of God in all things, not having our hearts set upon the pleasures of this life; but we must prepare for death, our great and last change.[7] For we are sinners by nature, and are adding thereunto by evil practices; for man is prone to evil as the sparks fly upward;[8] and there is nothing short of the divine power of the most high God that can turn our hearts to see the living and true God.

And now we ought to behold the Lamb of God, as it is expressed in Isa. 7:14: " . . . a virgin shall conceive and bear a son, and shall call his name Immanuel." This, my brethren, is the Son of God, who died to save us guilty sinners; and it is only by the mercy of the blessed Jesus we can be saved. Therefore, let us cast off self-dependence and rely on a crucified Saviour, whose blood was shed for all that came unto him by faith and repentance. This we cannot do of ourselves, but we must be found in the use of means.[9] Therefore we ought to come as David did: "Have mercy upon me, O God, according to thy loving-kindness" (Ps. 51:1). This, my brethren, is the duty of all flesh: to come to the divine fountain and to confess our sins before the most high God. For if we say we have no sin, we deceive ourselves and the truth is not in us; but if we confess our sins, he is faithful and just to forgive us our transgressions.[10]

And now my brethren, seeing I have had an invitation to write something more to encourage my dear fellow servants and brethren, Africans, in the knowledge of the Christian religion, I must beg your patience. For I mean to use the most brevity that so important a subject will allow. And now my brethren, we have, as I observed in the foregoing part of this discourse, life and death set before us, for we are invited to come and accept of Christ on the terms of the gospel. "Ho, every one that thirsteth, come ye to the waters, and he that hath no money; come ye, buy and eat . . . wine and milk, without money and without price" (Isa. 55:1).

Here is life, and if we search our hearts, and try our ways, and turn again unto the Lord, he will forgive us our sins and blot out our transgressions (Lam. 3:40). But if we continue in our sins, having our hearts set on the pleasures of this life, we forget that we must give an account for the deeds done in the body. Also unto the Lord belongeth mercy, for he rendereth to every man according to his works (Ps. 62:12). Here we see that we should behold the Lamb of God by a holy life. "God judgeth the righteous, and God is angry with the wicked every day. If he turn not, he will whet his sword; he hath bent his bow, and made it ready" (Ps. 7:11–12). Here we see that the wrath of God abideth on the unbelievers and unconverted sinners. And now my brethren, should not a sense of these things make us cry out in the apostle's language: "Men and brethren, what shall we do to be saved?"[11]

We must be found in the use of means and pray that God would be pleased to rain down a rain of righteousness into our souls; then we shall behold the Lamb of God as taking away the sins of the world. Let us, my brethren, examine ourselves whether we have had a saving change wrought in our hearts and have been brought to bow to the divine sovereignty of a crucified Saviour. Have we been brought to behold the Lamb of God, by obeying the precepts of Isaiah, and turning from evil and learning to do well? "Wash you, make you clean; put away the evil of your doings from before mine eyes; cease to do evil; learn to do well . . . " (Isa. 1:16–17a). Here we have the admonition of the prophet Isaiah who was inspired with the knowledge of divine things so that he calls heaven and earth to witness against the wicked and rebellious sinner. "Hear, O heavens, and give ear, O earth: for the Lord hath spoken, I have nourished and brought up children, and they have rebelled against me" (Isa. 1:2). Is not this the case? Have we not been going astray like lost sheep (Luke 15:6)? Have we not great reason to lay our hands on our mouths and our mouths in the dust, and come upon the bended knees of our souls and beg for mercy as the publican did, saying, "God be merciful to me a sinner" (Luke 18:13)?

This, my dear brethren, should be the language of our conversation: to have a life void of offense towards God and towards man. Have we beheld the Lamb of God, by taking up our cross, denying ourselves, and following the blessed Jesus? "Then said Jesus unto his disciples, If any man will come after me, let him deny himself, and take up his cross, and follow me" (Matt. 16:24). Here we see that we should behold the Lamb of God as our only Saviour and mighty Redeemer, and we are to take up our cross and follow the Lamb of God at all times, not to murmur at the hand of Divine Providence. And we have our example set before us: "And he was withdrawn from them about a stone's cast, and kneeled down, and prayed, Saying, Father, if thou be willing, remove this cup from me: nevertheless not my will, but thine, be done" (Luke 22:41–42).

We should behold the Lamb of God as coming in the clouds of heaven with great power and glory, whom our heavenly

Father hath declared to be his only Son. "While he yet spake, behold, a bright cloud overshadowed them: and behold a voice out of the cloud, which said, This is my beloved Son, in whom I am well pleased, hear ye him" (Matt. 17:5). Should not a sense of these things inflame our hearts with fear and love to God; knowing that there is no other name given by which we can be saved, but by the name of Jesus?[12]

Let us behold the Lamb of God as having power to make the blind to see, the dumb to speak, and the lame to walk, and even to raise the dead. But it may be objected and said by those that have had the advantage of studying, "Are we to expect miracles at this day?" These things were done to confirm that Jesus was the Son of God and to free us from the burden of types and ceremonies of the Jewish law; and this by way of instruction, which I desire to receive with a humble spirit. Others may object and say, what can we expect from an unlearned Ethiopian? And this by way of reflection. To this I answer: "Pray, Sir, give me leave to ask this question. 'Doth not the raising of Lazarus give us a sight of our sinful natures?' "

> And when he thus had spoken, he cried with a loud voice, Lazarus come forth. And he that was dead came forth, bound hand and foot with graveclothes: and his face was bound about with a napkin. Jesus saith unto them, Loose him, and let him go. (John 11:43–44)

Is this not a simile of our deadness by nature? And there is nothing short of the power of the most high God can raise us to life.

Sirs, I know we are not to expect miracles at this day, but hear the words of our Saviour:

> And Simon Peter answered and said, Thou art the Christ, the Son of the living God. And Jesus answered and said unto him, Blessed art thou, Simon Barjona, for flesh and blood hath not revealed it unto thee, but my Father which is in heaven. (Matt. 16:16–17)

Sirs, this may suffice to prove that it is by grace we are saved, and that not of ourselves: it is the gift of God.[13]

But, my brethren, for whom this discourse is designed, I am now in the second place to show when we are said to behold the Lamb of God in the sense of the text. When we are brought humbly to confess our sins before the most high God and are calling on our souls and all that is within us to bless his holy name; this is the duty of all flesh, to praise God for his unmerited mercy in giving his Son to save lost man, who by the fall of Adam became guilty in the sight of God. "But God commendeth his love toward us, in that, while we were yet sinners Christ died for us" (Rom. 5:8). Here we are to behold the Lamb of God as suffering for our sins, and it is only by the precious blood of Christ we can be saved, when we are made sensible of our own imperfections and are desirous to love and fear God; this we cannot do of ourselves, for this is the work of God's Holy Spirit. "And he said, Therefore I said unto you that no man can come unto me, except it were given unto him of my Father" (John 6:65).

Here we see to behold the Lamb of God, in the sense of the text, as the gift of God; we should come as David did, saying "O Lord, rebuke me not in thine anger, neither chasten me in thy hot displeasure" (Ps. 6:1). And we should put our whole trust in the Lord at all times; we should strive to live a religious life, to avoid the very appearance of evil, lest we incur the wrath of God.[14] "Upon the wicked he shall rain snares, fire and brimstone, and an horrible tempest: this shall be the portion of their cup" (Ps. 11:6). Here we see the unhappy state of the sinner; for he is not only led away by that subtle adversary, the devil, but he hath the word of God pronounced against him. "Then shall he say also unto them on the left hand, Depart from me, ye cursed, into everlasting fire, prepared for the devil and his angels" (Matt. 25:41).

Here, my brethren, we are to behold the Lamb of God as being crucified for us. "Pilate therefore, willing to release Jesus, spake again to them. But they cried, saying, Crucify him, crucify him" (Luke 23:20–21). Here we see the effect of sin; the blood of Christ was shed for all that came unto him by faith and repentance. O my brethren, when those things have a proper influence on our minds, by the power of the most high God, to say as David did, "Bless the Lord, O my soul, and forget not all his benefits" (Ps. 103:2)—then we may be said to behold the Lamb of God in the sense of the text.

And we are to behold the Lamb of God as it is expressed in Matt. 17:22–23: "And while they abode in Galilee, Jesus said unto them, The Son of Man shall be betrayed into the hands of men: And they shall kill him, and the third day he shall be raised again." And now should not a sense of these things have a tendency to make us humble in the sight of God, and we should see the place and situation of Christ suffering? "And when they were come to the place, which is called Calvary, there they crucified him, and the malefactors, one on the right hand, and the other on the left" (Luke 23:33). Here we see the boundless riches of free grace; he is numbered with the transgressors, whose blood speaks better things than the blood of Abel; for the blood of Abel calls for justice on the sinner, but the blood of Christ calls for mercy. Then said Jesus, Father, forgive them; for they know not what they do" (Luke 23:34). Here we have the example of our Saviour, that we should forgive our enemies and pray that God would forgive them also. Or how shall we say the Lord's Prayer, "Forgive us our trespasses as we forgive those that trespass against us"? Now when we are enabled to do these things, as we should do them, then may we be said to behold the Lamb of God in the sense of the text.

And now my dear brethren, I am to remind you of a most melancholy scene of providence; it hath pleased the most high God, in his wise providence, to permit a cruel and unnatural war to be commenced. Let us examine ourselves whether we have not been the cause of this heavy judgment: have we been truly thankful for mercies bestowed? And have we been humbled by afflictions? For neither mercies nor afflictions proceed from the dust, but they are the works of our heavenly Father; for it may be that when the tender mercies of God will not allure us, afflictions may drive us to the divine fountain.

Let us now cast an eye back for a few years and consider how many hundreds of our nation and how many thousands of other nations have been sent out of time into a never-ending eternity, by the force of cannon and by the point of the sword. Have we not great cause to think this is the just deserving of our sins? For this is the word of God. "Woe unto the wicked! it shall be ill with him: for the reward of his hands shall be given unto him" (Isa. 3:11). Here we see that we ought to pray that God may hasten the time when the people shall beat their swords into plowshares and their spears into pruning hooks, and nations shall learn war no more.[15]

And now my dear brethren, have we not great reason to be thankful that God in the time of his judgments hath remembered mercy, so that we have the preaching of the gospel and the use of our Bibles, which is the greatest of all mercies; and if after all these advantages we continue in our sins, have we not the greatest reason to fear the judgments of God will be fulfilled on us? "He, that being often reproved hardeneth his neck, shall suddenly be destroyed, and that without remedy" (Prov. 29:1). Have we not great reason to praise God that he is giving us food and raiment, and to say as David did, "O give thanks unto the Lord; for he is good: for his mercy endureth for ever" (Ps. 136:1)? And now my brethren, when these things make us more humble and more holy, then we may be said to behold the Lamb of God in the sense of the text.

And now, in the third place, I am to show when we may be said not to behold the Lamb of God in the sense of the text. When we are negligent to attend the word of God, and unnecessarily, or are living in any known sin, either of omission or commission, or when we have heard the word preached to us and have not improved that talent put into our hands by a holy life, then we may be said not to behold the Lamb of God in the sense of the text.

And now my brethren, I am, in the fourth place, to show how in some things we may be mistaken in beholding the Lamb of God while we are flattering ourselves with the hopes of salvation on the most slight foundation—that we live in a Christian land and attend to divine service. These things are good in themselves; but there must be a saving change wrought in our hearts, and we must become as new in Christ Jesus. We must not live after the flesh but after the Spirit. "For as many as are led by the Spirit of God, they are the sons of God" (Rom. 8:14). And we are to pray that God would keep us from all evil, especially the evil of sin.

Bishop Beveridge, in his second Resolution, speaking of sin, says, "For as God is the center of All good, so sin is the fountain of all evil in the world, all strife and contention, ignominy and disgrace." Read a little further, and he goes on to protest against sin, "I resolve to hate sin [says he] wherever I find it, whether in myself or in others, in the best of my friends as well as in the worst of my enemies."[16] Here we see, my brethren, that if we commit any willful sin, either of omission or commission, we become the servants of sin and are deceiving ourselves, for the Apostle hath told us that "the wages of sin is death":

> But now being made free from sin, and become servants to God, ye have your fruit unto holiness, and the end everlasting life. For the wages of sin is death; but the gift of God is eternal life through Jesus Christ our Lord. (Rom. 6:22–23)

We are to behold the Lamb of God by reading the Scriptures, and we must believe that he hath power to give everlasting life. "Verily, verily, I say unto you, He that believeth on me hath everlasting life" (John 6:47). Do we, my brethren, believe in the blessed Jesus, as we ought? Are we not going the broad way to utter destruction? Are we not leaving the blessed Jesus, who hath the bread of life and is that bread? "I am that bread of life" (John 6:48). Here we see that the blessed Jesus hath power to give eternal life to all that come unto him by faith and repentance; and we see that he is calling to us as he did to his disciples, saying, "Will ye also go away?" For this is the language of the Scriptures. "Then Simon Peter answered him, Lord, to whom shall we go? thou hast the words of eternal life" (John 6:67–68).

And we are, my brethren, to behold the Lamb of God as being the door of eternal life, for this he hath declared in his word to us. "I am the door: by me if any man enter in, he shall be saved, and shall go in and out, and find pasture" (John 10:9). But it is very plain, my brethren, that if we come in our sins, God will not hear us, but if we come and worship him in spirit and in truth, he will have mercy on us. "Now we know that God heareth not sinners: but if any man be a worshipper of God, and doeth his will, him he heareth" (John 9:31).

My dear brethren, as I am drawing to a conclusion, let me press on you to prepare for death—that great and irresistible king of terrors—by a holy life, and make the word of God the rule of your life. But it may be objected that we do not understand the word of God. Mr. Burkitt, a great divine of our church, says that in the Scriptures there are depths that an elephant may swim, and shoals that a lamb may wade.[17] Therefore we must take the plainest text as a key to us.

And now my brethren, I am, in the fifth place, to endeavor to rectify any mistake we may labor under, when we are taking on us the form of godliness, without the power thereof, because then we cannot be said to behold the Lamb of God in the sense of the text. We must pray earnestly to God for his Holy Spirit to guide us in the way to eternal life; this none can do but God. Let us, my brethren, lay up treasure in heaven, where neither moth doth corrupt nor thieves break through and steal. "But seek ye first the kingdom of God, and his righteousness; and all these things shall be added unto you" (Matt. 6:33).

And now my dear brethren, we must pray earnestly to God for the influence of his Holy Spirit to guide us through this howling wilderness and sea of trouble to the mansions of glory, and we should pray that God would give us grace to love and fear him. For if we love God, Black as we be and despised as we are, God will love us. "Then Peter opened his mouth, and said, Of a truth I perceive that God is no respecter of persons: But in every nation he that feareth him, and worketh righteousness, is accepted with him" (Acts 10:34–35).

"O taste and see that the Lord is good: blessed is the man that trusteth in him" (Ps. 34:8). "The eyes of the Lord are upon the righteous, and his ears are open unto their cry" (Ps. 34:15). Let us, my dear brethren, remember that the time is hastening when we shall appear before the Lamb of God to give an account for the deeds done in the body, when we shall be stumbling over the dark mountains of death looking into an endless eternity. O that we may be of that happy number that shall stand with their lamps burning. "Then all those virgins arose, and trimmed their lamps" (Matt. 25:7).[18] Come now, my brethren, let us examine ourselves whether we have had a saving change wrought in our hearts and have been brought to bow to the divine sovereignty of the most high God and to flee to the armies of Jesus, for he is the author of our peace, and the finisher of our faith (Heb. 12:2).

Come now, my brethren, we are one flesh and bone; let us serve the one living and true God.[19] Come, let us behold the Lamb of God by an eye of faith, for "without faith it is impossible to please him" (Heb. 11:6). For faith, my brethren, is of the things not seen.[20] Let us, my brethren, strive by the grace of God to become new creatures. "Therefore if any man be in Christ, he is a new creature" (2 Cor. 5:17). Let us come to the divine fountain, by constant prayer. "Give ear to my words, O Lord, consider my meditation" (Ps. 5:1). Let us improve our talents by our holy life, striving to make our calling and election sure,[21] for "now is the accepted time; behold, now is the day of salvation" (2 Cor. 6:2). Let us pray that God give us of the waters that the woman of Samaria drank. "But whosoever drinketh of the water that I shall give him shall never thirst; but the water that I shall give him shall be in him a well of water springing up into everlasting life" (John 4:14). O my dear brethren, we should be brought humbly to submit to the will of God at all times and to say, "God be merciful to us sinners." "Repent . . . and be converted, that your sins may be blotted out" (Acts 3:19).

My dear brethren, we are many of us seeking for a temporal freedom, and I pray that God would grant your desire. If we are slaves, it is by the permission of God. If we are free, it must be by the power of the most high God. Be not discouraged, but cheerfully perform the duties of the day, sensible that the same power that created the heavens and the earth and causeth the greater light to rule the day and the lesser to rule the night can cause a universal freedom. And I pray God may give you grace to seek that freedom which tendeth to everlasting life. "And ye shall know the truth, and the truth shall make you free" (John 8:32). "If the Son therefore shall make you free, ye shall be free indeed" (John 8:36). But as I am advanced to the age of seventy-nine years, I do not desire temporal freedom for myself.

My brethren, if we desire to be a happy people, we must be a holy people and endeavor to keep the commandments of God, and we should pray that God would come and knock at the door of our hearts, by the power of his Holy Spirit, and give us a steadfastness in the merits of Christ, and we are to believe in Christ for eternal salvation. Mr. Stoddard, a great divine, says in speaking of appearing in the righteousness of Christ, when men believe, it is a part of God's covenant to make them continue to believe.[22] And again he saith, since God hath promised life unto all that believe in this righteousness, it must needs be safe to appear before God in this righteousness (Job 6:12).[23] "Return, ye backsliding children, and I will heal your backslidings. Behold, we come unto thee; for thou art the Lord our God" (Jer. 3:22).

My dear brethren, let not your hearts be set too much on the pleasure of this life. For if it were possible for one man to gain a thousand freedoms and not an interest in the merit of Christ, where must all the advantage be? "For what is a man profited, if he should gain the whole world, and lose his own soul?" (Matt. 16:26). My brethren, we know not how soon God may send the cold hand of death to summon us out of this life to a neverending eternity, there to appear before the judgment seat of Christ. "For we must all appear before the judgment seat of Christ" (2 Cor. 5:10).

And now I conclude with a few words—let me tell you, my dear brethren, that in a few days we must all appear before the judgment seat of Christ, there to give an account for the deeds done in the body. Let us, my brethren, strive to be so prepared for death by the grace of God, that when the time shall come when we are shaking off the shackles of this life and are passing through the valley of the shadow of death, O may we then be enabled to say, "Come, Lord Jesus, come quickly, for thou art the Lamb of God, in whom my soul delighteth."[24] Then, my dear brethren, all those who have repented of their sins shall hear this voice, "Come unto me." "Then shall the King say unto them on his right hand, Come, ye blessed of my father, inherit the kingdom prepared for you from the foundation of the world" (Matt. 25:34). But if we do not repent of our sins, we must hear this voice, "Then shall he say also unto them on the left hand, Depart from me, ye cursed, into everlasting fire, prepared for the devil and his angels" (Matt. 25:41). Then will our souls waft away into endless eternity and our bodies be lodged in the cold and silent grave, there to remain till Christ's Second Coming.

My brethren, we believe in the word of God, we must believe this:

> Behold, I shew you a mystery; We shall not all sleep, but we shall all be changed, In a moment, in the twinkling of an eye, at the last trump: for the trumpet shall sound, and the dead shall be raised incorruptible, and we shall all be changed. For this corruptible must put on incorruption, and this mortal must put on immortality. (1 Cor. 15:51–53)

And now my brethren, let me persuade you to seek the Lord.

> Seek ye the Lord while he may be found, call ye upon him while he is near: Let the wicked forsake his way, and the unrighteous man his thoughts: and let him return unto the Lord, and he will have mercy upon him; and to our God, for he will abundantly pardon. (Isa. 55:6–7)

Therefore do not be contented with the form of godliness without the power thereof. *Amen.*

Emendations

Page	Line		
160	1:	beginning]	begining]R
		testimony.]	testimony]R
	2:	God:]	God. Verse 1st.]R
		beginning]	begining]R
		Word]	word]R

3:	Word]	word]R
	Word]	word]R
	God (John 1:1).]	God]R
5:	brethren]	Brethren]R
6:	Giver]	giver]R
	Life;]	life;]R
	flesh,]	flesh.]R
7:	(verse 14 of the	.verse 14 of the
	context)]	context.]R
10:	Second, I will	2nd. Endeavor]R
	endeavor]	
11:	Third,]	3.]R
16:	*Winter Piece*]	Winter Piece.]R
18:	gentlemen.]	gentlemen,]R
19:	general.]	general,]R
20:	exhortation.]	exhortation;]R
21:	now. my brethren]	now, my brethren]R
22:	God.]	God. My]R
23:	brethren,]	brethren.]R
27:	eighteenth]	eighth]R
	context: No]	context, no]R
161 1:	time;]	time:]R
2:	him.]	him. My]R
3:	God.]	God,]R
4:	heavy-laden]	heavy laden]R
5:	sins]	sin]R
6:	God. Therefore]	God; therefore]R
7:	God.]	God,]R
	text—]	text,]R
8:	righteousness. But]	righteousness; but]R
9:	clothed with]	cloathed upon,]R
12:	are]	is]R
	God. John,]	God. John Chap. 1. 33,]R
13–14:	saith: Upon]	saith, upon]R
14:	descending,]	descending.]R
15:	Ghost. And]	Ghost, and verse 34, and]R
16:	record.]	record,]R
	God. Again]	God, verse 35, again]R
17:	after.]	after,]R
	stood,]	stood.]R
	disciples;]	disciples, verse 36,]R
18:	Jesus.]	Jesus,]R
	he saith]	and saith]R
	God! And]	God, verse 37, and]R
19:	speak,]	speak.]R
19–20:	Jesus (John 1:33–37)]	Jesus. Thus]R

21:	God.]	God,]R
22:	or]	of]R
23:	good.]	good,]R
23–24:	God . . . (Rom. 8:28).Now]	God, or as in Rom. viii. 28. now.]R
26:	God.]	God. It]R
27:	God.]	God,]R
28:	tongues (Ps. 39:1)]	tongues; Psalm xxxix.1 [39:1].]R
29:	my]	by]R
30:	cries]	crys]R
31:	petition:]	petition,]R
	anger,]	anger;]R
32:	displeasure (Ps. 6:1). And]	displeasure. Psalm vi. 1 [6:1]. and]R
35:	Holy Spirit]	holy spirit]R
162 1:	God. For]	God; for]R
	hart]	heart]R
	after]	for]R
2:	brooks]	brook]R
2–3:	God (Ps. 42: 1).]	God. Psalm xlii. 1 [42.1]. and]R
4:	now.]	now,]R
	Lamb of God]	law of God]R
5:	expressed. in John 1:51:]	is exprest, John I. 51 [1:51].]R
	Verily]	verily]R
6:	Hereafter ye]	hereafter you]R
7:	man]	Man]R
8:	day.]	day,]R
9:	appear. And]	appear. Matt. xxiv. 30 [24:30], and]R
	man]	Man]R
10:	Heaven:]	heaven,]R
	all the]	the]R
11:	man	Man]R
	heaven.]	heaven,]R
12:	glory (Matt. 24:30).]	glory.]R
	Here,]	Here.]R
16:	Holy Spirit. Then]	holy spirit; then]R
18:	when he cried]	then he cryed]R
	God: Have]	God, have]R
19:	me,]	me.]R
	God,]	God, Psal. lxi. 1 [51:1],]R
	loving-kindness:]	loving kindness,]R
	according unto]	according to]R
20:	mercies.]	mercies,]R
20–21:	transgressions (Ps. 51:1)]	transgressions. This]R
22:	, my brethren,]	,my brethren.]R

24:	holiness. This]	holiness; this]R
	God,]	God;]R
27:	manner,]	manner, Matt. xxiii.
		37 [23:37],]R
30:	not! (Matt. 23: 37).]	not.]R
34:	repentance.]	repentance,]R
	you, Nay: but,]	you ay; but.]R
	repent,]	repent.]
35:	perish (Luke	perish, Luke xiii. 4
	13:5).]	[13:4].]
163 2:	Spirit:]	spirit,]R
3:	in truth (John	truth, John iv. 24
	4:24).]	[4:24].]R
4:	us]	of us]R
	God,]	God;]R
6:	hearers?]	hearers? Matt. xii.
		20 [12:20].]R
8:	it;]	it. Ver. 21]R
8–9:	hath he not]	hath not]
9:	while:]	while]R
11:	offended. (Matt.	offended. This]R
	13:20–21)]	
12:	heart.]	heart. There]R
15:	, my brethren,]	,my brethren]R
18:	Spirit]	spirit]R
	God.]	God. Rom. viii. 12
		[8:12],]R
19:	, brethren,]	,brethren]R
20:	flesh.]	flesh. Ver. 13.]R
	flesh,]	flesh]R
	die:]	die;]R
	if ye through]	if through]R
21:	Spirit]	spirit]R
	live.]	live, Ver. 14,]R
22:	many as]	many]R
	Spirit]	spirit]R
22–23:	God. (Rom. 8:12–	God. here]R
	14)]	
24:	, my brethren,]	,my brethren]R
	indispensable]	indispensible]R
30:	that can]	can]R
31:	God.]	God; and]R
33:	Isa. 7:14 . . . a]	Isaiah vii. 14
		[7:14],A]R
34:	Immanuel]	Emanuel]R
	, my brethren,]	,my brethren]R
164 1:	saved.]	saved:]R
2:	self-dependence]	self-dependence,]R
3–4:	repentance. This]	repentance; this]R
5:	means. Therefore]	means;
		therefore]R
	did:]	did, Psal. li. 1
		[51:1],]R

6:	me,]	me.]R
6–7:	loving-kindness	lovingkindness
	(Ps. 51:1). This]	(Ps. 51:1). This .]R
7:	flesh:]	flesh.]R
8:	fountain.]	fountain,]R
9:	God. For]	God; for]R
	sin,]	sin.]R
10:	sins,]	sins.]R
11:	transgressions.]	transgressions.
		And]R
15:	patience. For]	patience, for]R
16:	will allow. And]	will admit of;
		and]R
19:	gospel. Ho,]	gospel. Isaiah xliv.
		1 (44:1), O.]R
20:	money;]	money,]R
21:	come ye, buy]	come ye, buy]R
	eat . . . wine]	eat, ye come ye
		buy.]R
22:	price (Isa. 55:1)]	price. Here]R
24:	Lord,]	Lord.]R
25:	transgressions	transgressions,
	(Lam. 3:40)]	Lamen. iii. 40
		[3:40].]R
26:	we forget that]	forgetting that]R
27:	body.]	body. Psal. lxii. 12
		[62:12],]R
29:	works (Ps. 62:12)]	works,]R
30:	life.]	life. Psal. vii. 11
		(7:11),]R
31:	righteous,]	righteous.]R
	God is]	is]R
	day. If]	day, ver. 12, if]R
32:	not, he]	not. He]R
	sword;]	sword,]R
	bow,]	bow.]R
33:	ready (Ps. 7:11–	ready]R
	12).]	
34:	sinners.]	sinner.]R
36:	language:]	language,]R
	brethren,]	brethren.]R
37:	saved?]	saved? We]R
165 1:	means.]	means,]R
4:	, my brethren,]	.my brethren.]R
5:	hearts.]	hearts,]R
7:	Saviour. Have]	Saviour; have]R
9:	well? Wash you]	well. Isaiah i. 16
		[1:16], Wash ye]R
10:	doings]	doing]R
	evil;]	evil.]R
11:	well . . . (Isa. 1:16–	well. Here]R
	17a).]	

14:	sinner. Hear,]	sinner. Isaiah i.2 [1:2], Here.]R
	heavens,]	heavens]R
15:	ear, O earth:]	ear.O earth;]R
15–16:	nourished and brought]	nourished]R
16–17:	me (Isa. 1:2).]	me.]R
18:	sheep (Luke 15:6)?]	sheep? Luke xv. 6 [15:6],]R
21:	sinner (Luke 18:13)?]	sinner, Luke viii 13 [8:13].]R
22:	, my dear brethren,]	.my dear brethren.]R
22–23:	conversation:]	conversation;]R
23:	offense]	offence]R
25:	Jesus?]	Jesus. Matt. xvi 24 [16:24],]R
26:	If]	if]R
	come after me,]	be my disciple]R
27:	and take]	take]R
	cross,]	cross.]R
27–28:	me" (Matt. 16:24).]	me.]R
31:	Providence. And]	Providence; and]R
32:	us:]	us, Luke xxii. 41,42 [22:41,42],]R
33:	kneeled]	he kneeled]R
	down,]	down.]R
	Saying]	saying]R
	Father]	my Father]R
34:	me:]	me,]R
	will,]	will.]R
35:	thine,]	thine.]R
	done (Luke 22:41–42).]	done. We]R
166 1:	Son. While]	Son. Matt. xvii. 5 [17:5], And]R
	spake]	spoke]R
2:	behold,]	behold.]R
	them:]	them;]R
3:	cloud,]	cloud.]R
	This]	this]R
	Son,]	Son.]R
4:	pleased,]	pleased;]R
	ye him (Matt. 17:5).]	him.]R
7:	Jesus?]	Jesus; let]R
10:	dead.]	dead:]R
11–12:	"Are . . . day?"]	.are . . . day?.]R
13:	God.]	God,]R
	burden]	burthen]R
15:	a]	an]R
17:	answer]	answer,]R
	"Pray]	.Pray]R

18–19:	question. 'Doth . . . natures?' '']	question,,Doth . . . natures?· John xi. 12, 13 (11:12–13),]R
20:	thus had]	had thus]R
	cried]	said]R
21:	forth.]	forth. Ver. 4,]R
22:	graveclothes:]	grave clothes,]R
	face]	head]R
23:	napkin.]	napkin;]R
	Loose him,]	loose him,]R
23–24:	go. (John 11:43–44)]	go.]R
27:	life.]	life. Sirs]R
28:	day,]	day;]R
29:	Saviour:]	Saviour Matt. xvi. 16 [16:16]]R
30:	Thou]	thou]R
	the Christ,]	Christ.]R
31:	God.]	God. Ver. 17,]R
32:	thou,]	thou,]R
	Barjona,]	Barjona:]R
33:	heaven.]	heaven. (Matt. 16:16–17)]R
35:	ourselves:]	ourselves,]R
	God.]	God. But]R
167 1:	But,]	But.]R
3:	God,]	God,]R
8:	God.]	God. Rom. v. 8 [5:8],]R
	commendeth]	commandeth]R
9:	toward]	towards]R
	that,]	that.]R
	yet sinners]	sinners]R
10:	us (Rom. 5:8).]	us.]R
14:	Holy Spirit.]	holy spirit. John vi. 64 [6:64],]R
15:	Therefore]	therefore]R
	me,]	me.]R
16–17:	Father (John 6:65).]	Father. Here]R
20:	Lord,]	Lord,]R
	chasten]	chastise]R
21:	displeasure (Ps. 6:1).]	displeasure, Psal. vi. 1 [6:1].]R
23:	lest]	least]R
24:	God.]	God. Psal. xi. 6 [11:6],]R
	snares,]	showers of]R
25:	tempest:]	tempest;]R
26:	cup'' (Ps. 11:6).	cup.]R
27:	adversary,]	adversary,]R

28:	him.]	him. Matt. xxv. 40 [25:40],]R
29:	also unto]	unto]R
	hand, Depart from me,]	hand. depart from me.]R
30:	cursed,]	cursed.]R
	fire,]	fire.]R
31:	angels (Matt. 25:41).]	angels. Here]R
32:	, my brethren,]	,my brethren.]R
33:	us.]	us. Matt. xxiii. 20 [23:20],]R
	therefore,]	therefore.]R
	Jesus,]	Jesus.]R
34:	them.]	them. ver 22,]R
	cried]	cryed]R
	saying, Crucify]	saying. crucify]R
168 2:	did,]	did, Psal. cii. 1 [103:1],]R
	Lord,]	Lord.]R
3:	benefits (Ps. 103:2)—then]	benefits. Then]R
4:	text.]	text: And]R
6:	Matt. 17:22–23:]	Matt. xvii. 22 [17:22],]R
	Galilee,]	Galilee.]R
7:	The]	the]R
8:	men:]	men; and ver. 23,]R
	be raised]	rise]R
11:	suffering?]	suffering. Luke xxii. 33 [22:33],]R
12:	place,]	place.]R
	which is called]	called]R
13:	malefactors,]	malefactors.]R
	hand,]	hand.]R
15:	with the]	with]R
18:	mercy.]	mercy. Luke xxiii. 34 [23:34],]R
	Father,]	Father.]R
	them;]	them,]R
19:	do (Luke 23:34).]	do.]R
20:	enemies,]	enemies,]R
21:	also. Or]	also, or]R
22:	those]	them]R
23:	us"?]	us.']R
25:	text.]	text. And]R
27:	providence]	Providence]R
29:	commenced. Let]	commenced; let]R
30:	judgment:]	judgment;]R
35:	fountain.]	fountain. Let]R
169 3:	sins? For]	sins; for]R

4:	God.]	God. Isaiah iii. 11 [3:11],]R
	wicked! it]	wicked, It]R
5:	him:]	him,]R
5–6:	him (Isa. 3:11).]	him.]R
6:	pray.]	pray,]R
7–8:	plowshares]	plough-shares]R
8:	pruning hooks]	pruning-hooks]R
10:	brethren,]	brethren.]R
12:	gospel]	Gospel]R
13:	Bibles]	bibles]R
16:	us?]	us.]R
	He,]	He.]R
	neck,]	neck.]R
17:	remedy (Prov. 29:1).]	remedy.]R
19:	did,]	did, Psal. cxxxvii. 1 [137:1],]R
20:	Lord;]	Lord,]R
	for he is good: for his mercy]	for his mercy]R
20–21:	ever (Ps. 136:1)?]	ever.]R
23:	text.]	text. And]R
25:	text.]	text:]R
31:	text.]	text. And]R
32:	am,]	am]R
34:	God.]	God,]R
35:	foundation—that]	foundation, because]R
36:	service. These]	service; these]R
170 1:	Jesus. We]	Jesus; we]R
2:	flesh.]	flesh,]R
	Spirit. For]	spirit, for]R
3:	Spirit]	spirit]R
	God, they are]	God, are]R
3–4:	God (Rom. 8:14). And]	God, Rom. vii. 14 [8:14]. and]R
5:	sin.]	sin. Bishop]R
6:	Beveridge]	Bevrage]R
7:	says]	he says]R
	center]	centre]R
10:	[says he]]	(says he)]R
12:	, my brethren,]	,my brethren.]R
13:	sin.]	sin,]R
15:	Apostle]	apostle]R
	us.]	us,]R
15–16:	death: But]	death, Rom. vi. 22,23 [6:22,23]; but]R
16:	become]	are become]R
	servants to God,]	the servants of God.]R
17:	fruit unto]	fruits into]R

	and the]	and in the]R
	everlasting life. For]	eternal life; for]R
18:	death;]	death,]R
19:	Lord. (Rom. 6:22–23)]	Lord. We]R
20:	Scriptures]	scriptures]R
21:	life.]	life. John vi. 47 [6:47],]R
22:	verily,]	verily.]
	He]	he]R
23:	life (John 6:47).]	life.]R
	, my brethren,]	,my brethren]R
26:	bread?]	bread? John vi. 48 [6:48],]R
	that]	the]R
30:	Will ye also go away? For]	Wilt thou go away also; for]R
31:	Scriptures.]	scriptures, John vi. 67, 68 [6:67,68],]R
	Simon Peter]	Simon]R
	Lord,]	Lord.]R
32:	thou]	Thou]R
	life (John 6:67–68)]	life. And]R
33:	, my brethren,	,my brethren.]R
35:	us.]	us. John x.9 [10:9],]R
	door:]	door,]R
	enter.]	enter in,]R
171 1:	out,]	out.]R
	pasture (John 10:9).]	pasture.]R
2:	, my brethren,]	,my brethren.]R
	sins,]	sins.]R
3:	truth,]	truth.]R
4:	us.]	us. John ix. 31, 32 [9:31, 32],]R
5:	sinners:]	sinners,]R
	God,]	God.]R
	doeth]	doth]R
6:	heareth (John 9:31).]	heareth.]R
7:	brethren,]	brethren.]R
8:	death—]	death,]R
	irresistible]	irresistable]R
9:	terrors—]	terrors,]R
10:	life. But]	life; but]R
	that we]	we]R
11:	Burkitt]	Burkit]R
11–12:	church, says.]	in]R
12:	Scriptures]	scriptures]R
	are]	is]R

14:	us.]	us. And]R
15:	brethren,]	brethren.]R
	am,]	am.]R
	place,]	place.]R
17:	godliness]	Godliness]R
17–18:	because then]	then]R
19:	Holy]	holy]R
21:	, my brethren,]	,my brethren.]R
22:	steal.]	steal. Matt. vi. 20–
		23 [6:20–23],]R
22–23:	But seek ye]	Seek]R
23:	God,]	God.]R
	righteousness;]	righteousness.]R
24:	you (Matt. 6:33).]	you.]R
26:	Holy Spirit]	holy spirit]R
29:	him. For]	him, for]R
	Black]	black]R
	be.]	be,]R
30:	us.]	us. Acts x. 34
		[10:34],]R
	mouth,]	mouth.]R
31:	Of]	of]R
31–32:	is no respecter of	has no respect to
	persons: But in]	persons. Ver. 35,
		In]R
32:	him, and worketh	him.]R
	righteousness]	
33:	with him" (Acts	of him. Psalm
	10:34–35).]	xxxiv. 8 [34:8], O]R
34:	good: blessed]	good, and]R
35:	him (Ps. 34:8).]	him. Ver. 15,]R
36:	open unto]	open to]R
	cry (Ps. 34:15).]	cry.]R
37:	, my dear	,my dear
	brethren,]	brethren.]R
5:	burning.]	burning. Matt. xxv.
		7 [25:7],]R
	arose,]	rose.]R
5–6:	lamps (Matt.	lamps.]R
	25:7).]	
6:	now,]	now.]R
8:	hearts.]	hearts,]R
9:	God.]	God,]R
10–11:	faith (Heb. 12:2).]	faith. Heb. xii.
		[12:2], Looking to
		Jesus the author
		and finisher of our
		faith.]
12:	now,]	now.]R
	bone;]	bone,]R
13:	Come,]	Come.]R
14:	faith,]	faith.]R

172

15:	him (Heb. 11:6).]	God. Heb. xi. 5
		[11:5],]R
	, my brethren,]	,my brethren.]R
16:	, my brethren,]	,my brethren.]R
17:	creatures.	creatures; for]R
	Therefore]	
	Christ,]	Christ.]R
18:	creature (2 Cor.	creature, 2 Cor. iv.
	5:17).]	17 [4:17].]R
19:	prayer.]	prayer. Psal. iv. 1
		[4:1],]R
	words,]	words.]R
20:	meditation (Ps.	meditations, ver.
	5:1).]	2,3.]R
22:	behold,]	behold.]R
22–23:	salvation (2 Cor.	salvation. 2 Cor.
	6:2).]	vi. 2 [6:2].]R
24:	drank]	drank. John xiv. 19
		[14:19],]R
	drinketh]	shall drink]R
25:	that I]	I]R
	thirst;]	thirst,]R
	that I]	I]R
27:	life (John 4:14).]	life.]R
27:	brethren,]	brethren.]R
29:	say,]	say.]R
	sinners.]	sinners, Acts iii. 19
		[3:19:,]R
29–30:	converted,]	converted.]R
30:	out (Acts 3:19).]	out. My]R
31:	brethren,]	brethren.]R
32:	desire. If]	desire; if]R
33:	slaves,]	slaves.]R
	God. If]	God; if]R
	free,]	free.]R
34:	God. Be]	God; be]R
37:	night.]	night,]R
173 1:	freedom. And]	freedom; and]R
2:	life.]	life. John viii. 32
		[8:32].]R
3–4:	free (John 8:32).]	free. Ver. 36,]R
4:	therefore shall]	shall]R
	ye]	then you]R
5:	indeed (John	indeed" (John
	8:36).]	8:36).]R
6:	myself.]	myself. My]R
7:	people.]	people,]R
10:	hearts,]	hearts.]R
	Holy Spirit]	holy spirit]R
11:	steadfastness]	steadfastness]R
14:	covenant.]	covenant,]R
15:	believe.]	believe. Job. vi.
		12.]R

18:	righteousness (Job 6:12).]	righteousness. Jer. iii. 22 [3:22],]R
	Return,]	Return,]R
	backsliding	back-sliding
	children,]	children,]R
19:	backslidings.]	back-slidings;]R
	Behold,]	behold,]R
	thee;]	thee,]R
20:	art]	are]R
	God (Jer. 3:22).]	God.]R
21:	brethren,]	brethren,]R
22:	pleasure]	pleasures]R
	life. For]	life; for]R
23:	freedoms.]	freedoms,]R
24:	be? For]	be; for]R
	is a man profited,]	would it profit a man]R
25:	world,]	world,]R
	lose]	loose]R
25–26:	soul? (Matt. 16:26).]	soul, Matt. xvi. 26 [16:26].]R
26:	brethren,]	brethren,]R
28:	Christ.]	Christ. 2 Cor. v. 10 [5:10], For]R
29:	we must all]	all must]R
29–30:	Christ (2 Cor. 5:10).]	Christ. And]R
31:	you,]	you,]R
34:	us,]	us,]R
35:	death.]	death,]R
36:	life.]	life,]R
37:	death,]	death.]R
174　1:	Come,]	come,]R
	Jesus,]	Jesus,]R
2:	delighteth.]	delighteth;]R
2–3:	, my dear brethren,]	, my dear brethren,]R
3:	who]	which]R
4:	Come]	come]R
	me.]	me. Matt. xxv. 34 [25:34],]R
5:	hand, Come,]	hand; come,]R
6–7:	world (Matt. 25:34).]	world.]R
7:	sins,]	sins,]R
8:	voice,]	voice, Matt. xxv. 41 [25:41],]R
	the]	his]R
9:	Depart]	depart]R
	, ye cursed,]	, ye cursed,]R
	fire,]	fire,]R
10:	angels (Matt. 25:41).]	angels.]R

11:	eternity.]	eternity,]R
	be lodged]	lodged]R
12:	Coming.]	coming. My]R
13:	in the]	the]R
14:	this:]	this. 1 Cor. xiii. 41
		(13:41).]R
15:	Behold,]	Behold,]R
	mystery;]	mistery,]R
15–16:	shall all]	shall]R
16:	changed, In]	changed, in]R
	moment,]	moment.]R
17:	trump:]	trumpet;]R
	sound,]	sound,]R
18:	raised	raised, Ver. 35,]R
	incorruptible, and	
	we shall all be	
	changed]	
18–19:	corruptible]	corruptable]R
20:	immortality. (1	immortality.
	Cor. 15:51–53)]	And]R
21:	Lord.]	Lord. Isaiah lv. 6
		[55:6],]R
22:	ye the]	the]R
	call ye upon]	and call on]R
23:	near:]	near; ver.7]R
24:	thoughts:]	thoughts,]R
25:	upon him;]	on him,]R
	God,]	God,]R
	for he]	and he]R
26:	pardon. (Isa. 55:6–	pardon.]R
	7)]	
27:	Therefore do not]	Therefore, not]R

Notes

1. Here Hammon is paraphrasing the Apostle Paul's benediction in 1 Tim. 1:17: "Now unto the King eternal, immortal, invisible, the only wise God, be honour and glory for ever and ever. Amen." The reference reinforces Hammon's premise about the divinity of Christ.

2. A partial quote from Matt. 11:28, the "weary and heavy-laden" phrase is used often in Negro spirituals, and is one of Hammon's favorite texts. Frazier 19–23 and Southern give more on well-known catchphrases in Black spirituals.

3. This clause is taken from Phil. 2:12: "work out your own salvation with fear and trembling." The next phrase in the sentence is part of 1 Cor. 15:58: "Therefore, my beloved brethren, be ye steadfast, unmoveable, always abounding in the work of the lord, for as much as ye know that your labour is not in vain in the Lord."

4.   Hammon is paraphrasing a familiar text of Scripture from Rom. 8:7: "Because the carnal mind is enmity against God: for it is not subject to the law of God, neither indeed can be."

5.   Although not a direct quote from Scripture, the language and the rhythm are similar to other passages in Matthew 23, for example, vv. 33–36. See also Matt. 12:39.

6.   Here Hammon alludes to Rom. 5:5: "And hope maketh not ashamed; because the love of God is shed abroad in our hearts by the Holy Ghost which is given unto us," and to the Romans 8 text that he quotes next.

7.   Hammon is referring to the Apostle Paul's description of the Resurrection of the Just, from 1 Cor. 15:51–52: "We shall not all sleep, but we shall all be changed, in a moment, in the twinkling of an eye, at the last trump: for the trumpet shall sound, and the dead shall be raised incorruptible, and we shall be changed." This is just one of the many instances wherein Hammon alludes to a physical change at death, a change that would obviate slavery but would not extinguish the African identity of black skin. See Dick 267.

8.   This is a paraphrase of Job 5:7: "Yet man is born unto trouble; as the sparks fly upward."

9.   With "use of means," Hammon is referring to what he and other eighteenth-century theologians considered to be the necessary steps to individual salvation. These included faith, repentance, and Christian behavior. P. M. Jones explores these steps from a colonial religious perspective in her "Puritan's Progress: The Story of the Soul's Salvation in the Early New England Sermons" 14–28. But for Hammon these steps had social and political implications that reached beyond the church doors to affect conditions for American slaves.

10.   This is an almost word-for-word quotation of John 1:8–9, "He was not that Light, but was sent to bear witness of that Light. That was the true Light, which lighteth every man that cometh into the world." Often when he mentions Christ as the Light, Hammon has in mind the Quakers' identification of the Inner Light that was given to guide all men. See Brinton; G. Fox, *Doctrines and Ministry* and *Journal;* and Van Etten.

11.   The quoted words are a combination of Acts 2:37 and 16:30. These are not Peter's words but the query of those who had heard his message for the first time on the day of Pentecost. The second exclamation was when the Macedonian jailer asked the apostles Paul and Silas about salvation.

12.   This language is an allusion to Peter's sermon on the Name of Jesus that was delivered before the Sanhedrin as described in Acts

4:12: "Neither is there salvation in any other: for there is none other name under heaven given among men, whereby we must be saved."

13. Here Hammon remembers a verse of Scripture that was famous in eighteenth-century evangelical circles, Eph. 2:8–9: "For by grace are ye saved through faith; and that not of yourselves: it is a gift of God: not of works, lest any man should boast."

14. Hammon is summarizing 1 Thess. 5:22: "Abstain from all appearance of evil."

15. This familiar verse, commonly used by peace advocates during wartime, is taken from Isa. 2:4: "And he shall judge among the nations, and shall rebuke many people: and they shall beat their swords into plowshares, and their spears into pruninghooks: nation shall not lift up sword against nation, neither shall they learn war any more."

16. Beveridge, *Works* 1:235. Bishop Beveridge was the leading Anglican bishop of the seventeenth century; his volumes, included in the Lloyds' library, were a primary source for Hammon's theological training.

17. William Burkitt (1650–1703) was a popular British theologian—a rector, a divine, and a commentator in the Anglican church. Hammon often quotes from a Burkitt volume found in the Lloyds' library, *Expository Notes with Practical Observations on the New Testament*. The eleven editions of this book were a doctrinal wellspring in England and the colonies.

18. In this paragraph, Hammon gives a synopsis of his nonextant broadside, *An Essay on the Ten Virgins*. The text here, and in the lost work, was taken from Christ's parable on the ten bridesmaids (in Matthew 25) who were unprepared for the return of the bridegroom. The text was a popular tool in England and the colonies. Both Shepard and Seiss had texts with the same title as Hammon's. Poole's and Burkitt's entries for Matthew 25 give interesting background on some of the themes that Hammon's essay might have included.

19. Here Hammon is alluding to Gen. 2:23: "And Adam said, This is now bone of my bones, and flesh of my flesh: she shall be called Woman, because she was taken out of Man." Another possible source is Eph. 5:30.

20. Here Hammon is summarizing Heb. 11:1: "Now faith is the substance of things hoped for, the evidence of things not seen."

21. Here Hammon alludes to 2 Pet. 1:10: "Wherefore the rather, brethren, give diligence to make your calling and lection sure."

22. Hammon is referring to *The Safety of Appearing at the Day of Judgement, in the Righteousness of Christ: Open and Applied,* by Solomon Stoddard, pastor of the church in Northampton, Massachu-

setts. A well-known eighteenth-century preacher and evangelist, Stoddard was a maverick among the Puritans because he offered "open Communion" to the unconverted as well as to church members. This practice sparked a revival that swept through the middle colonies, including Long Island. By the time of Hammon's maturity, Stoddardism would have been an accepted factor in the Oyster Bay congregation, a milieu giving Hammon—and other slaves, Native Americans, white redemptioneers, and other social outcasts—a somewhat greater access to church life. For more on Stoddard see Carr, Coffman, Keller, and Pope.

23.   Although Hammon's quotation of Job 6:12 is incorrect, he may be referring to Job's willingness to withstand grave adversity in order to keep his covenant with God. Thus the poet could be telling the slaves in his audience that if they are persistent in their faith in Christ, God will eventually vindicate them just as he did Job.

24.   In "Come, Lord Jesus," Hammon echoes the plea of the Apostle John who wrote in the book of Revelation, "He which testifieth these things said, Surely I come quickly. Amen. Even so, come, Lord Jesus" (Rev. 22:20).

6. A Dialogue, Entitled, The Kind Master and Dutiful Servant

Introduction: Veneer and Reality

This poem is Jupiter Hammon's artistic zenith. It is a dramatic exchange between a dictatorial slaveholder and a clever Servant whom the Master thinks he owns. Hammon created personae who were stereotypical of the eighteenth-century slaveholder and slave. On the surface, the slave feigns placid obedience to the Master. Yet beneath the poetic line, the slave (or "Servant," as Hammon prefers to call him) articulates subtle rebellion against the Master's position. The Master, on the other hand, overtly represents the typical interests and beliefs of his aristocratic class. Both profess Christianity, but their views of God and theology differ vastly.

Hammon bases the poem's tensions on an adaptation of such biblical adages as "Can two walk together, except they be one?" (Amos 3:3). The Master continually questions the Servant's salvation. He believes that the Servant's spiritual state hinges upon the latter's willingness to stay in the place that a hierarchical society has carved out for him. Thus, the Master tells the slave to "follow after grace," but in his understanding of the New Testament covenant, this admonition means to follow after him. The Servant retorts that God offers grace to every man on an unconditional basis and that therefore he will not follow the Master; instead, he will follow God.

According to William Beveridge, an Anglican bishop, only deferential service to an earthly master evinces a servant's obedience and reverence to God. In Resolution 4, "Concerning My

Relations," taken from his *Private Thoughts on Religion,* Beveridge concludes:

> And to these ends, I think it my duty to allow my servants some time every day wherein to serve God, as well as to see they spend their other hours in serving me; and to make them sensible that they do not serve me only for myself, but ultimately and principally in reference unto God; their serving me making way for my better serving God. . . . There is a strict injunction upon all servants, that they should be "obedient to their masters according to the flesh, with fear and trembling, in singleness of heart, as unto Christ," Ephes. vi. 5. But how with fear and trembling? Why, fearing lest they should offend God in offending them, and trembling at the thoughts of being disobedient to the divine command, which enjoins them to "be obedient to their master in all things, not answering again," Tit. ii. 9. (*Works* 1:270–72)

Hammon would disagree with Beveridge's claim that constraint and force should be used to evoke "God's will." The dichotomies provide an underlying theme of the poem. Within Hammon's dramatic arena, the Servant holds the Master at bay with rhetoric, while the Master uses the persuasive coercion of guilt (a mental rather than a physical violence) to contrive the Servant's submission.[1]

Such manipulative behavior convinced colonial slaves of their masters' perverse Christianity. In the Servant's prayer for his Master's salvation, Hammon subtly makes this charge: "I will . . . pray that God may be with me, and save thee in the Lord." In tone ranging from terse graciousness to bitter invective, Blacks writing from the eighteenth century until the eve of the Civil War frequently pointed out the un-Christian behavior of purportedly Christian masters.[2] Only Hammon had the finesse, through subtle but subversive art, to make the same charge against white Christians while enslaved.

Thus, each speaker's perspective becomes the tantamount critical tool analyzing the poem. The Master thinks in terms of an imperial ruling class preordained by God. The Servant believes that the Bible neither sanctions the hierarchy nor those who support it. Each character suspects the other's sincerity and feels that his own position best concurs with the teachings of Christ and the Bible. In fact, both views do seem scriptural; the Bible refers to Christ as Servant and Bondservant as well as Master and King.

As the "Dialogue" continues, the Master tells the Servant to view Christ as King, the ultimate image in the British aristocratic philosophy of the Great Chain. He further sees himself as the British monarchy's patriarchal representative. Samuel Davies' sermon, "The Necessity and Excellence of Family Religion," articulates the Master's "fatherly" theology and is representative of the hierarchical tenor of the age:

> In all societies there must be subordination, and particularly in families, and it is the place of the head of such societies to rule and direct. Particularly it belongs to the head of a family, when there is no fitter person present, to perform worship in it, to use proper means to cause all his domestics to attend upon it. . . . That you are authorized and obligated to all this, is evident from God's commending Abraham for commanding his children, &c., from Joshua's resolving that not only he, but also his house, to compel them, at least externally, to serve the Lord, (Josh. xxiv. 15) and which enables you to command them in this case, as well as in your own affairs. (2:59)

Edward Long, a British aristocrat who made his fortune by working slaves on a Jamaican plantation, recalls the typical eighteenth-century slaveholder's response to accusations that his treatment of slaves was anything but fatherly:

> A planter smiles with disdain to hear himself calumniated for tyranical behaviour to his Negroes. He would wish the defamer might be present, to observe with what freedom and confidence they address him; not with the abject prostration of real slaves, but as their common friend and father. His authority over them is like that of an ancient patriarch: conciliating affection by the mildness of its exertion, and claiming respect by the justice and propriety of its decisions and discipline, it attracts the love of the honest and good; while it awes the worthlessness into reformation. (2:270–72)

Thus, within the colonial hierarchy, social practice places slaves on the same level or beneath that of white children. Therefore, when the Servant insists on an agreement between him and the Master called a convenant—an important eighteenth-century idea based upon the Bible—he attempts to remove himself from a subservient position under the patriarchal umbrella, commanding the right to rule as an adult Christian male even if circumstances will allow him to rule no one but himself. As the poem progresses, other doctrinal differences emerge. Reflecting the kinetic religious polemics of the Great Awakening, the Servant speaks of free will, universal salvation, and unlimited atonement—all in sharp contrast to the Master's aristocratic assurances.

No contact between Black and white colonists dissolved the rules of established socialization, because of the whites' view of the universe as a "Great Chain of Being." According to Arthur Lovejoy, principles which underlay the Great Chain concept included "plentitude, continuity, gradation." And, he continues, these concepts "attained their widest diffusion and acceptance" in the eighteenth century (183). Scientifically, the theory explored the plurality and interrelatedness of all existence and, as evidenced in conclusions by Thomas Jefferson, Edward Long, and the Reverend Samuel Stanhope Smith, it led to assumptions that Blacks were the link between animals and humans.[3]

Socially and politically, Chain logic fostered beliefs that within such a divinely sanctioned social order, the Anglo-aristocracy was second only to a ruling king. Black slaves came least in social considerations after all economic classes of whites, including indentured servants. Additionally, most of the eighteenth-century colonial middle class and aristocracy belonged to Christian denominations of Calvinist persuasion which required adherence to theology—such as the doctrines of election, predestination, and total depravity—that reinforced the Chain's social controls. Again applying gradation to Christian cosmology, white colonists assured themselves that Blacks were God's least chosen people. Thus, the Master enters the "Dialogue" with a range of preconceptions, all concluding that the Servant's proper "scientific" and religious role, in a well-ordered Christian society, is to follow, and to follow only him.[4]

When seeking to educate Blacks, the Society for the Propagation of the Gospel in Foreign Parts, the missionary arm of the Anglican church, assured worried masters that Christianity would produce more obedient slaves. In his letter to slave owners in the Americas (May 19, 1727), urging masters to give missionaries egress for Christian instruction, the bishop of London expresses the mind-set of a pseudo-Christian oligarchy:

> But it is further pleaded, That the Instruction of Heathens in the Christian Faith, is in order to their Baptism; and that not only the *Time* to be allowed for *Instructing them,* would be an Abatement from the Profits of their Labour, but also that the *Baptizing* them when instructed, would destroy both the Property which the Masters have in them as Slaves ought with their Money, and the Right of selling them again at Pleasure; and that the making them Christians, only makes them less diligent, and more ungovernable. . . . And so far is Christianity from discharging Men from the Duties of the Station and Condition in which it found them, that it lays them under stronger Obligations to perform those duties with the greatest Diligence and Fidelity, not only from the Fear of men, but from a Sense of Duty to God. . . . As to their being more ungovernable after Baptism, than before; it is certain that the Gospel every where enjoins, not only Diligence and Fidelity, but also *Obedience,* for Conscience sake. (Humphreys 264–66)

Having the same motive, Cotton Mather insisted, in his *Rules for the Society of Negroes,* that Christian conversion, instead of inciting resistance, would mold more subservient slaves. Thus, Mather tried to manipulate Christian religion to produce a "chosen" class even among slaves. Rather than proposing mercy because of the conditions of slavery, Mather wrote a complex system of retribution that banished any Blacks who fell "into the sin of drunkenness, or swearing or cursing, or lying or stealing or notorious disobedience or unfaithfulness," including "fornication" (Greene, *The Negro* 266). Like the Master in the poem, Mather posited that obedience to the slave system was the slave's only guarantee of salvation in the life hereafter:

> But then, there is a voice of Heaven to the slaves, in what this poor creature is left with—
> • To beware of the sins which may provoke the Glorious One to leave them unto the last degrees of wickedness and misery.
> • To study a dutiful behavior unto their superiors, and that they may be blessings to the family they belong unto.
> • To be patient in their low and bad condition.
> • To become the servants of Christ.
> • Then, what they shall very shortly see at the end of their short servitude—else, a worse thing. (Silverman 368–69)[5]

The Master in Hammon's play is a pragmatic religionist. Like his seventeenth-century counterpart John Saffin, an ardent slave apologist, the Master perceives slavery as an earthly, economic venture, one needed for society's survival.[6] In accordance with the doctrine of all contemporary colonial denominations (except the Quakers), missionary teachers were to instruct Africans on the love of God so that they could be better servants. The Master travels a one-way street of personal insecurity beneath a facade of aristocratic confidence. He wants the slave to love him with wholehearted devotion, but it never occurs to him to love the slave with the same zeal.[7]

Thus, while some more religious colonial masters endeavored to promote the spiritual growth of their charges with this benign, fatherly approach, they were nonetheless just as nonchalant about the slave institution as the most virulent proslaver. For instance, in November 1716, while grieving over a dying daughter, Mather wrote in his diary: "A new Negro servant, (a little Boy) is come into my Family. What, what shall I do? what Cares must be used, that GOD may have Service from him?" (*Diary* 8:384). Even an approaching familial death could not penetrate or redirect his conscience from its master/slave psyche.

When he has the Master remind the Servant of "thy place," Hammon makes his character utter the standard religious jargon that establishment ministers like Mather preached to their congregations continually. One could say that in his own writing Jupiter Hammon advocated the same moral "righteousness" for slaves, but several differences exist. Men like Mather believed that they were morally perfect. But, because of slavery, Hammon had already judged their morality to be a facade to true Christianity. He could therefore tell his readers to establish a relationship with God that transcended the example or advice of Cotton Mather or any other slave master. Secondly, Hammon had no vested interest in having good slaves. He had no power to ingratiate and no rewards to give. As a Black leader, he desired to channel his people through the quagmire of slavery by directing their view to Christ, whom he believed would eventually lead them out of it.

Hammon's choice of the word "grace" to end stanza 1 is fitting. The Master's view of grace inculcates an ironic twist of Christian dogma. A contemporary theologian defined grace as that love of God which comes with salvation and is free for all. The Master assumes that definition for himself. He never mentions any condition that he must meet for his own salvation, but he demands obedience and subservience as conditions for the slave's salvation. One view is based on grace as a free gift; the other is based on grace as attained by works.[8]

Tradition, church dogma, and political and economic expediency inform the Master's vision. He is not influenced by urgent personal need or spiritual experience. But the Servant charts a new course. In his walk of revelation, he must not trust man's guidance but have "grace and truth's insight." Thus, throughout the poem, the Servant tells the Master that, while he may appear to be a "normal," dutiful, and obedient slave, in actuality, he seeks solely to please God, to whom he looks for vindication and judgment. The Servant says that his "whole delight" in serving the Master is sustained by his ultimate faith, not in the Master's righteousness but in God's goodness and reward.

The Master represents a classic Anglican-Puritan speaker. Very much like him, Hammon's "owners" were loyal Anglicans, but as this British denomination did not have a parish in their nearby hamlet, they worshiped with a Puritan congregation. Both denominations staunchly adhered to Calvinism. The Master uses these doctrines variously in the poem to explain the cosmology of slavery. His theological phraseology, "we are sinners all," represents the first principle of Calvinism: total depravity, or man's inability to save himself or reorient his fate without divine intervention. However, illustrating typical eighteenth-century slave psychology, the Master assumes that the slave's depravity carries more weight than his own. This assumption is then merged into Great Chain's scientific and religious thought. These and other interdependent theories of race and color allowed the Master, and other members of his class, to excuse the practice of slavery while ostensibly building a Christian society.

When the Servant, who earnestly prays for the Master's salvation, persists in bringing the "Dialogue" back to issues of death and judgment, the Master acknowledges that he must one day stand before God and answer for his sins (as in Rev. 20:11–15).[9] The issue, though, is whether he will be judged with repentant saints or hardened sinners. In his essays, Hammon implies that unrepentant slaveholders, regardless of their professions of Christianity, inevitably will be condemned at the Great White Throne Judgment, the final reckoning for sinners, and that they will be sentenced to a degree of punishment in hell appropriate for injustices against African slaves.

The Master is myopic. He insists that the Servant's salvation, indeed the whole social order ("that Christ may love us all"), precariously depends upon the Servant's obedience. Yet without compunction, he himself willingly belongs to a social stratum presently rebelling against its British king. In his essays, Hammon lambastes this moral blindness—the irony of slavery during the zeal for Revolution—and he tells his African readers that they must seek a freedom of more lasting integrity: "when the Son shall set you free you are free indeed."[10]

Toward the end of the poem, the Master slightly repents of his caustic stand. He had previously acknowledged (stanza 13) that both he and the Servant had to face the heavenly King together in judgment. But in stanza 19 he admits that if God does have sovereign power, then the Almighty may have permitted the war's fervor to humble proud America. But his general advice that all nations pray for peace, rather than any specific sorrow over his own failures and those of his nation, makes the Master's call for repentance a hollow one. His perspective, however, is taken from another Calvinist doctrine prevalent in mid-eighteenth-century theology—that God holds sovereign responsibility for all events in the world of men. Thus when he says, "This is the work of God's own hand, / We see by precepts given; / To relieve distress and save the land, / Must be the pow'r of heav'n," the speaker assumes no accountability for what he or those members of his class may have done to precipitate the war.[11]

When the Servant answers the Master the first time, he attempts to move the relationship from one of manipulation and guilt to one wherein he, although a slave, can somewhat control his own motives and actions. That does not mean that he acquiesces to slavery; he merely bides his time until emancipation, and attempts to create an atmosphere that allows him to deal with the Master on a man-to-man, not a man-to-slave, basis. Because of both his slave state and his Christian commitment, Hammon could not advocate violent insurrection to end slavery. However, as the first published Black preacher in America, he was the progenitor of such Black churchmen as Dr. Martin Luther King, Jr., who advocated nonviolent change through faith and a sense of self that transcended immediate circumstances. Throughout national history this political psychology has forced the dominant class to negotiate agreement whether its leaders wanted to or not. In both religious and civil terms, such a negotiated settlement was called a "covenant" in colonial society.

The covenant, or the right of unforced participation, formed the foundation of colonial American church life. This system of social commitment, however, remained a biblical directive for a Christian society that white men reserved for themselves. Byington says of New England citizens:

> The essential thing in a church, in their opinion, was a company of believers associated together by a mutual covenant, living in Christian love and fellowship with each other, and with all other Christians, and observing the ordinances which are set forth in the New Testament. (*Puritan in England* 98)

Perry Miller says "the conception of a covenant was . . . the master idea of the age" (*Mind: From Colony* 21). In his companion work, *Mind: Seventeenth Century,* he again explains the nature and spirit of the covenant ideal:

> Through the maze of dialectic with which the covenant theologians rephrased conventional tenets runs one consistent purpose: they were endeavoring to mark off an area of human behavior from the general realm of nature, and within it substitute for the rule of necessity the rule of freedom. They were striving to push as far into the background as possible the order of things that exists by inevitable equilibrium, that is fulfilled by unconscious and aimless motions, that is determined by inertia and inexorable law, and in its place to set up an order founded upon voluntary choice, upon the deliberate assumption of obligation, upon unconstrained parts, upon the sovereign determination of free wills. . . . Obedience was no longer to be wrung from subjects by might, but accepted as a spontaneous token; a man was to be good or bad, not because he could never have been otherwise, but because he wholeheartedly preferred his course. Certainty in human affairs was to rest not upon inexplicable decrees but upon the seal that attested the sworn covenant and insured the fulfillment of covenant terms. (398–99)[12]

This inherent meaning of "covenant"—peace and reward as a result of fulfilled agreement—does not suggest that the Servant in the poem must approve of his own enslavement. Rather, Hammon's speaker tries to renegotiate the circumstances of an otherwise choiceless existence and to convince the Master that his submission to service fulfills motives far different than those the Master has in mind.

When the Servant says, "I will follow thee, / According to thy word," he uses covenant language which the society, and the Master, deem acceptable in work agreements with indentured servants. Such contracts were arranged for lower-class English and German immigrants, some for the completion of criminal sentences, others for the payment of debt. A few simply indentured themselves to pay for their passage to America. In all cases of indentured servitude, colonist and servant worked under labor agreements wherein both parties made certain commitments for performance: the worker to serve, the master to provide basic necessities. Sometimes the agreement even included an apprenticeship for the indentured party. Generally, an indentured servant volunteered to serve a temporary term while slavery forced the African to work for life. Treated much better than Blacks, "retired" white indentured servants entered the mainstream of American life, many becoming successful businessmen, professionals, and politicians. Even one signer of the Declaration of Independence was a former indentured servant. Thus, the Slave in Hammon's poem subsumes for himself the principles of covenant agreement, as translated from church doctrine to social spheres.[13]

But, as the Servant does not share the Master's cosmological vision of heaven or of God, the proposed agreement would be strictly a temporary accommodation because of the undeniable presence of slavery. Of paramount importance to the Servant, the Master, and more importantly the poet's larger audience, one must correctly identify the person and function of God even in the midst of these temporal situations. To the Servant, Christ is primarily the Lamb of God: the Great Sacrificer, God, King of all, who himself gave up his life for all mankind. For the Servant that is true kingship: the gracious act of a heavenly aristocrat coming down to the level of common men, becoming one with them, and shedding his life's blood to create a new brotherhood in his image. The Master in Hammon's poem never accepted that kind of royal condescension as an example that he should follow.[14]

The Servant's image of a heavenly abode is one where Christ welcomes penitents in an attitude that New World missionaries, visitors to the continent themselves, should have offered to Native Americans and Africans. Hammon's reference to Christ as the welcoming "King / . . . standing on some distant land, / Inviting sinners in" (stanza 12) imbues his vision with deep implications for Africans abducted to the colonies, their own "distant land" from where they yet hoped to be rescued. Colonists frequently invoked the titles "Master" or "King" to emphasize that saving power, not to interpret God as the ultimate ruler of slaves. The zealous Quaker founder and missionary, George Fox, for example, expounded that "among Us Christ is King, who bringeth the Blessing, and destroyeth that which brought the Curse" ("God Save the King" [August 8, 1665], Epistle 242, *Day Book* 171).

The Servant does agree with the Master on their souls' imminent appearance before God at the Second Coming. Hammon's use of "summons" pointedly reminds his audience of a moral accounting at the end-time judgment. The poet invokes the connotation of summons elsewhere in his writings, always with a multileveled warning. Slaves must look to God, every man's final judge, for ultimate reclamation. And slave owners must realize that they are already condemned for enslaving their fellowmen. Also Hammon warns his readers often in the poem that God's judgment can come on earth as in war or natural disaster. Thus the Servant tells the Master that although the war has ended, many colonists are "still in some distress" (stanza 18). Who else could those distressful ones be in the midst of this "happy end" but slaves? Likewise while "the distant foes" are in one sense England and the colonies, they could also be the characters in Hammon's "Dialogue," the antiphonal Master and Slave.

Much has been written on the consequences of the American Revolution in the lives of those white men and women who supported it in council halls and battlefields. However, the war changed opportunities and conditions for numerous Black slaves and freedmen as well. A free woman and a new mother after the war, Phillis Wheatley found herself in possession of no marketable skill, struggling against an unstable economy for whatever menial or domestic labor she could find (Richmond 42). Her unfamiliarity with the financial insecurity that free Blacks in the colonies often suffered eventually contributed to her death. The war also affected Jupiter Hammon's life. He fled to Connecticut with the Lloyds when British troops invaded Long Island. Yet even amid the havoc that the war heaped on all Americans, Hammon perceived the irony in the patriots' deafness to the slaves' cries for freedom.

In stanza 24, the Servant becomes the main speaker and remains so until the poem's end. He asserts that all professing Christians, not just servants, must obey God's word. Ironically, the Servant now is the one in the controlling position: as the narrator he has the last word. In this reversal of the Chain of Being structure, where supposedly only whites are intellectually competent enough to create art, Hammon posits that the Master's hierarchical position—and the psyche that lends credence to his "Great Chain" scale—is suspect.

There is a definite pattern in each of the first fifteen stanzas of the poem. In the first two lines each speaker relates to the other, while in the next two lines he speaks of his, or sometimes their, relationship with God. In stanza 2 the Servant tells the Master that as slaveholder, he is not saved: "And pray that God may be with me, / And save thee in the Lord." In stanza 6 the Servant tells the Master that he is praying that the latter will even see inside heaven: "And pray that God would bless thy soul, / His heav'nly place to see." After telling the Master politely that he may follow him on earth, "According to thy word" (stanza 2), the Servant cries that really, "The only safety that I see, / Is Jesus' holy word" (stanza 8). The implication here of course is that while the Servant does have a trustworthy covenant with God, he does not have such an assurance or covenant with the Master.

Finally, in stanza 12, the Servant simply tells the Master that in reality he, the slave, is not listening to the voice of the Master at all; he is in reality listening only to God: "Dear Master, I shall follow then, / The voice of my great King." This faith in his unseen Master is the thrust of Jupiter Hammon's work. He dismisses slavery as evil, temporal, and under the harsh sentence of God's judgment. The crucial purpose of his art is that his readers would join him in this assessment and go about reordering the priorities of their lives. If those readers were white, they would work to end the institution. If those readers were Black, they would follow him in this biblical knowledge that led at once to the freedom of the soul and that would lead ultimately to freedom from earthly bondage.

Notes

1. For additional information on the patriarchal zeal with which masters attempted to prepare their servants, Black and white, for salvation, refer to E. S. Morgan, *Puritan Family* 115–18.
2. Consider Wheatley's letter to Samson Occom in Lay, *Am I Not* 306–8; Article 1 of David Walker's *Appeal . . . to the Coloured Citizens of the World* (1829) in Stuckey 56; Nat Turner's *Confession* (1831), an abridged version of which is in Kinnamon and Barksdale, particularly 167; Frederick Douglass's speech in Rochester, New York, on July 5, 1852, also in Kinnamon and Barksdale 97; Francis Watkins Harper's poem, "Bury Me in a Free Land," Kinnamon and Barksdale 225; and Brent 76–77.
3. Their statements can be found in Jordan, *White Man's,* 194–204 and his *White over Black,* 482–511.
4. For more on the politicization of the Great Chain of Being theory in eighteenth-century society, see Craig 1–32.
5. Mather's system is based on Old Testament law, not New Testament grace. Additionally, for the Calvinist grace was the call of God which man supposedly could not refuse. The Westminster Confession defines grace as "effectually drawing [sinners] to Jesus Christ; yet so as they come most freely, being made willing by his grace" (Steele and Thomas 49). Under either definition, clearly Hammon has created a dramatic character who, like Cotton Mather, contorts theology so that it will accommodate slavery.
6. See Saffin, "Brief and Candid," in Moore 251–56.

7. Both Greene, *The Negro* 285–86 and Klingberg 224 canvass slaveholders' use of Christianity to justify their manipulation of human souls for economic gain.

8. To understand the difference between these injunctions and Hammon's moral direction, see C. Mather, *Negro Christianized,* in Ruchames, 59–70.

9. Also see the entry "Judgement" in Brown's *Dictionary,* 343–44.

10. This was indeed Phillis Wheatley's message to Samson Occom and Samuel Hopkins' message to his Rhode Island congregation: a Christianity that freed some, while enslaving others, was not genuine, nor was a democratic country truly functioning unless all of its citizens were free. See Wheatley's letter in Lay, *Am I Not* 306–8; S. Hopkins' antislavery sermons and tracts in *Timely Articles,* especially 565–68; also read McPherson and Katz's introduction of S. Hopkins' *Dialogue.* For other sociopolitical and religious statements on the Revolutionary War by and about slaves and Black abolitionists, see Quarles 283–301; D. B. Davis 273–84; and Kaplan's entire work, *Black Presence.*

11. Davies writes, "God is the supreme disposer of the fates of kingdoms, and of the events of war" (3:236).

12. See also Beveridge, *Works* 1:270; Brown 161–63; Cherry 328–40; Emerson 136–42; P. Miller's article, "From the Covenant to the Revival," in Jamison and Smith 322–68; Niebuhr 132–33; Schafer 51–66; and Thomas 90–91, for more delineations of the religious, political and social ramifications of "covenant."

13. For an example of a contemporary covenant between an employer and his indentured servant in colonial New York, see McKee 103. Also, further background on these work agreements throughout the colonies is provided by Herrick; A. E. Smith; and W. B. Smith.

14. See Phil. 2:1–11. For views of Christ as Servant, see Brown's entry on "Servant," 525–26.

"A Dialogue, Entitled, The Kind Master and Dutiful Servant"

1
Master.
Come my Servant, follow me,
According to thy place;
And surely God will be with thee,
And send thee heav'nly grace.

2
Servant.

Dear Master, I will follow thee,
    According to thy word,
And pray that God may be with me,
    And save thee in the Lord.

3
Master.

My Servant, lovely is the Lord,
    And blest those servants be,
That truly love his holy word,
    And thus will follow me.

4
Servant.

Dear Master, that's my whole delight,
    Thy pleasure for to do;
As for grace and truth's insight,
    Thus far I'll surely go.

5
Master.

My Servant, grace proceeds from God,
    And truth should be with thee;
Whence e'er you find it in his word,
    Thus far come follow me.

6
Servant.

Dear Master, now without control,
    I quickly follow thee;
And pray that God would bless thy soul,
    His heav'nly place to see.

7
Master.

My Servant, Heaven is high above,
    Yea, higher than the sky:
I pray that God would grant his love,
    Come follow me thereby.

8
Servant.

Dear Master, now I'll follow thee,
    And trust upon the Lord;
The only safety that I see,
    Is Jesus' holy word.

9
Master.

My Servant, follow Jesus now,
    Our great victorious King;
Who governs all both high and low,
    And searches things within.[1]

10
Servant.

Dear Master, I will follow thee,
    When praying to our King;
It is the Lamb I plainly see,
    Invites the sinner in.

11
Master.

My Servant, we are sinners all,
    But follow after grace;
I pray that God would bless thy soul,
    And fill thy heart with grace.

12
Servant.

Dear Master, I shall follow then,
    The voice of my great King;
As standing on some distant land,
    Inviting sinners in.

13
Master.

My Servant, we must all appear,
    And follow then our King;
For sure he'll stand where sinners are,
    To take true converts in.

14
Servant.

Dear Master, now if Jesus calls,
 And sends his summons in;
We'll follow saints and angels all,
 And come unto our King.

15
Master.

My Servant, now come pray to God,
 Consider well his call;
Strive to obey his holy word,
 That Christ may love us all.

A Line on the present war.[2]

16
Servant.

Dear Master, now it is a time,
 A time of great distress;[3]
We'll follow after things divine,
 And pray for happiness.

17
Master.

Then will the happy day appear,
 That virtue shall increase;
Lay up the sword and drop the spear,[4]
 And Nations seek for peace.

18
Servant.

Then shall we see the happy end,
 Tho' still in some distress;
That distant foes shall act like friends,
 And leave their wickedness.

19
Master.

We pray that God would give us grace,
 And make us humble too;
Let ev'ry Nation seek for peace,
 And virtue make a show.

20
Servant.
Then we shall see the happy day,
    That virtue is in power;
Each holy act shall have its sway,
    Extend from shore to shore.

21
Master.
This is the work of God's own hand,
    We see by precepts given;
To relieve distress and save the land,
    Must be the pow'r of heav'n.

22
Servant.
Now glory be unto our God,
    Let ev'ry Nation sing;
Strive to obey his holy word,
    That Christ may take them in.

23
Master.
Where endless joys shall never cease,
    Blest Angels constant sing;
The glory of their God increase,
    Hallelujahs to their King.

24
Servant.
Thus the Dialogue shall end,
    Strive to obey the word;
When ev'ry Nation acts like friends,
    Shall be the sons of God.

25
Believe me now my Christian friends,
    Believe your friend call'd Hammon:
You cannot to your God attend,
    And serve the God of Mammon.

26

If God is pleased by his own hand
      To relieve distresses here;
And grant a peace throughout the land,
      'Twill be a happy year.

27

'Tis God alone can give us peace;
      It's not the pow'r of man:
When virtuous pow'r shall increase,
      'Twill beautify the land.

28

Then shall we rejoice and sing
      By pow'r of virtue's word
Come sweet Jesus, heav'nly King,
      Thou art the Son of God.

29

When virtue comes in bright array,
      Discovers ev'ry sin;
We see the dangers of the day,
      And fly unto our King.

30

Now Glory be unto our God,
      All praise be justly given;
Let ev'ry soul obey his word,
      And seek the joy of heav'n.

FINIS

Emendations

Stanza	Line			
1	1:	Servant]	servant] R	
4	3:	insight]	in sight] R	
8	4:	Jesus']	Jesus's] R	
12	1:	Master,]	Master,] R	
13	1:	Servant,]	servant,] R	
15	1:	Servant,]	servant,] R	
16	1:	Master,]	Master,] R	
17	1:	appear,]	appear.] R	
22	2:	Nation]	nation] R	
26	3:	the]	the the [sic]] R	the the] H
28	2:	virtue's]	virtues] R	

Notes

1.   The Master's aphorism that God knows the heart is taken from Rev. 2:23: "and all the churches shall know that I am he which searcheth the reins and hearts: and I will give unto every one of you according to your works." Notice that this knowledge of God's omniscience in no way influences his assessment of the rightness of the social scale. He is to be "high" and the Servant "low," and this, he knows, is God's order of domestic government.

2.   America's Revolutionary War was fought between 1775 and 1782. This poem was published in 1783.

3.   As M. A. Richmond suggests in her account of Phillis Wheatley's struggle as an ex-slave in the Revolution, the War of Independence was not just a series of battles conducted while civilians nestled in their homes until the cannons ceased to fire and the smoke cleared. It was an extended pattern of "flight, death, and pillage" marked by increased joblessness in an unstable economy and by unreliable communications networks (38, 40–42). The country's population was ever shifting: Tories fled defeat on London-bound ships and patriots abandoned farms that both sides had transformed into battlefields. This backdrop of upheaval was proof to Hammon that God was exerting judgment against colonists who vehemently fought for liberty from England while shipping Blacks around the hemisphere in chains.

4.   Used often in America during the Revolutionary and Civil wars, these very familiar biblical words are allusions to Isa. 2:4: "and they shall beat their swords into plowshares, and their spears into pruning hooks: nation shall not lift up sword against nation, neither shall they learn war any more."

7. An Address to the Negroes in the State of New York

Introduction: The Elder Advises; The Younger Misjudges

In this his final publication, Hammon speaks most directly to his concern for fellow slaves. While he was aware of Christ's commandment that the message of Christian love be disseminated to all nationalities without partiality, he also knew that the American evangelical movement did little to evangelize his people and even less to make them equal members of the Body of Christ. Hammon takes his first text from Rom. 9:2–3 wherein the Apostle Paul laments in loving sorrow over those Jews who had not accepted Christ: "That I have great heaviness and continual sorrow in my heart. For I could wish that myself were accursed from Christ for my brethren, my kinsmen according to the flesh."

Hammon wrote that he could relate to the Apostle Paul's sorrow on two levels. While most of his evangelical work was among non-Jewish peoples, Paul, as a Jew, desired that more of those of his own religion would hear and accept the Gospel. Similarly, Hammon wanted other Africans to experience the psychological and spiritual escape from slavery's oppression that he had found. While he did not have the arsenal or troops to influence their physical freedom, he could at least offer them freedom for the soul. He also wanted them to know more about slavery than what their masters had taught them. The masters held that the Bible sanctioned the institution, but he believed that precisely the opposite was true, that true Christians would

212

not have slaves nor would they have supported the slave system.

Second, Hammon related to Paul's concern about intrachurch relationships. Many of the Jews who had embraced Christianity tried to synthesize the new religion with Judaic laws and rituals. They would impose these restrictions on Gentile converts but would not allow full participation in church activities until those converts conformed to their standards of behavior. Paul vehemently disagreed with this practice and the prejudice against Gentiles that it perpetuated (see Gal. 2:11–21). Like those Gentiles, Hammon and his fellow slaves suffered segregation within the colonial church, both in the pulpit and in the pew. Along with his contemporaries, Richard Allen and Absalom Jones, Hammon knew that he had no possible chance for leadership within the eighteenth-century evangelical movement. Allen and Jones, who were years younger than Hammon, eventually had to establish separate Black churches where they could teach their people freely without the interference of those who had extrareligious motives. But—because of his age, the ruralness of his village, and the unwillingness of established churches to accept his potential when he was a younger man— Hammon could gain autonomy only through his pen, with which he nonetheless created a wider pulpit than that offered by occasional opportunities to preach among slaves.

Raboteau and Blassingame rightly speak of the antebellum Black church as an invisible institution. Before the success of Jones and Allen, the Black church was a "cosmic" structure of emotional understanding between the slave in the pulpit and the slave in the pew. Whether in Southern groves or Northern hollows, when they could get together for secret meetings to moan Black hymns and spirituals, African-Americans praised God with their own unique style. Even when it could not be done surreptitiously (such as those times when attendance by unsympathetic whites tended to thwart Black expression), they still used covert codes to tell one another, and to petition God publicly, about their longings for freedom. Thus, Hammon knew the techniques of the secret code well; he simply transferred them from pulpit and choir loft—positions of code expression which twentieth-century critics seem to have an easier time comprehending—to the printed page.[1]

This *Address* clearly indicates that Hammon's major audience was the New England slave community. He evidently felt secure that networks of whites would distribute this text among their own slaves and among other Africans in their vicinities. That the Quakers published this *Address* several times after the first printing identifies them as that network or at least as its principal agency. Because Northern slaves were just as accustomed as Southern slaves to white clergymen's manipulating the Bible in order to justify slavery, Hammon establishes early in this essay that, while the Bible is his major textual reference, he, as a slave himself, has no interest in deceiving his fellow slaves. Rather he tells them that the Scriptures have given him hope and consolation about slavery and that he would have them enjoy this knowledge also.

Education and labor in a house of immense wealth, along with access to that influential class of white Christian abolitionists through his preaching avocation, sometimes separated Hammon and other Black preachers in New England from their potential slave constituency. The intended effect was to inhibit the vital service they wished to render to their own people. Of those Black preachers known to history, only Hammon, Allen, and Jones managed to steer their ministries predominantly toward Black Americans. "Black" Harry Hosier and Tom Coker were well known to white evangelicals through their association with the Methodist bishop, Francis Asbury. John Murrant and Lemuel Haynes also mainly ministered among whites.[2] And even Hammon, Allen, and Jones often depended upon whites for an underground network of political, financial, and publishing support, as in the preservation of several editions of this *Address*.

Also like Hammon, many eighteenth-century Black spokesmen commented upon the state of hopelessness that slavery imposed upon their fellow slaves. They admitted that it was a test of their faith to watch their African brothers suffer such a fate in a "Christian" land. For consolation, Hammon could only conclude that the practice at best was in God's permitted will and that God would overturn it in his own time. While Hammon's language in this essay may seem harsh, consider the wording of an anonymous slave writer who referred to himself as "Othello." In an "Essay on Negro Slavery" he wrote:

> Whoever examines into the condition of the slaves in America will find them in a state of the most uncultivated rudeness. Not instructed in any kind of learning, they are grossly ignorant of all refinement, and have little else about them belonging to the nature of civilized man than the mere form. They are strangers to almost every idea that doth not relate to their labor or their food, and though naturally possessed of strong sagacity and lively parts are, in all respects, in a state of the most deplorable brutality. This owing to the iron hand of oppression, which ever crushes the bud of genius and binds up in chains every expansion of the human mind. Such is their extreme ignorance that they are utterly unacquainted with the laws of the world—the injunctions of religion—their own natural rights, and the forms, ceremonies and privileges of marriage originally established by the Divinity. Accordingly they live in open violations of the precepts of Christianity and with as little formality or restriction as the brutes of the field unite for the purpose of procreation. (Ducas 36)[3]

In an effort to counter such perceptions and for their own edification, Hammon encouraged his slave audience to master reading and then to apply this skill to Scripture for two reasons: first, they could hardly understand his coded messages without some knowledge of biblical symbolism, of narrative, and of ethics (about outcasts like the Samaritans, publicans, the poor, etc.) and of God's special concern for all pariahs; and second, they could not comprehend the pretentiousness of colonists who professed Christianity while continuing the slave system. Further, only through the Bible could they know just how much God condemns rich men who oppress the poor.

In the middle section of this essay Hammon paraphrases and alludes to several biblical references, the contents of which, as a slave, he could not publicly explore. For instance, when he writes "God hath not chosen the rich of this world," Hammon directly confronts the Anglican-Calvinist theological oligarchy with a position converse to their doctrine, and simultaneously gives one of his most stinging pronouncements against slavery and its enforcers. When he quotes from the Apostle James, Hammon argues that God did not just elect the Puritan sect, but that, conversely, God had *chosen* the *poor* for salvation: "Hath not God chosen the poor of this world rich in faith, and heirs of the kingdom which he hath promised to them that love him? But ye have despised the poor" (James 2:5–6). If he could get his audience to acquire the skill of reading and then turn them to the Bible, he knew they could also read the first chapter, wherein James says that the rich man will fade away like grass and flowers, and his scouring indictment of rich oppressors (slaveholders) in 5:1–5: "The hire of the labourers who have reaped down your fields, which is of you kept back by fraud, crieth: and the cries of them which have reaped are entered into the ears of the Lord of Sabaoth. Ye have lived in pleasure on the earth, and been wanton; ye have nourished your hearts, as in a day of slaughter."

Herein lies Hammon's encouragement. He could not be so direct as he would have liked. But he knew that those who read would eventually understand the biblically cosmic determinations of slaveholders. In addition to the text from James, Hammon used wording from 1 Cor. 1:19–29, which again provides him with surreptitious ammunition: "Not many wise men after the flesh, not many mighty, not many noble, are called: But God hath chosen the foolish things of the world to confound the wise; and God hath chosen the weak things of the world to confound the things which are mighty; And base things of the world, and things which are despised, hath God chosen, yea, and things which are not, to bring to nought things that are." Hammon thus fashioned his own eschatology, one that would give African slaves a vision of reality and a system of law and justice both foreign to and opposed by white Christian practice in the colonies.[4]

Throughout his work, Hammon struggled to reconcile the reality of slavery with the controversial doctrine of the absolute will of God. Tangential to the doctrine of the sovereign will of God is the concept of God as the supreme cause of all natural phenomena and the final arbiter of all human affairs. As with a familiar phrase often shouted in the Black church, Hammon believed "we shall understand it better by and by." He believed that God is just, that slavery is unjust, and that therefore as a separate corporate nation within a nation, Africans in America will not be held responsible for their own enslavement at God's judgment. Elsewhere he writes that slavery is a satanic phenomenon. In spite of his belief that God is the final causality of all things, Hammon always comes short of saying that God approves of slavery. He especially does so by ending his essays with the promise of a final accounting for earthly actions at the end of the age. With this assurance and with his concept of evil personified as a power working within the hearts of ungodly persons, Hammon further distanced himself from the Calvinistic doctrine of the absolutely sovereign will of God.

Whether due to his enslavement, his race, or his theological methodology, Hammon viewed life and death in perpetual duality. Like contemporary conditions for slavery—submission or death, slavery or freedom, knowledge or ignorance—his dichotomous answers were as absolute and opposite as "black" and "white." To have a naive or weak approach toward the negative opposite was, to Hammon, as dangerous as positioning oneself in the center of that opposite. In this essay, Hammon quietly urges Blacks to be cognizant of their white counterparts. Using the ambiguity necessary for a publishing slave, he nonetheless draws clear but subtle images of the "master" class. He does not want slaves to imitate masters because, he writes, whites are deceived by their riches and power; they have merely covered themselves with a thin veil of Christianity which they believe will be sufficient for final salvation. But for Hammon this position is the mercurial opposite: to hypothesize the religion is worse than not having belief in it at all.

Therefore the preacher believes that he and not his captors will "awaken to the resurrection of life" and "reign with Christ for all eternity"; and he would have all believing Africans reign with him. Although quite simplistic, his answers were after all his, not ones that he mimicked from his captors. Further they reflected the representative position for antebellum slaves who endured bondage, not only because it was not feasible to do otherwise, but because they had faith that God had a better life in store in eternity.

Therefore, Hammon advises his readers that the true path to freedom is superior moral behavior and, further, that slaveholders attempted to establish their own moral standard, disregarding God's standard. In admonishing slaves to live above examples set by their masters, Hammon next suggests that many slave masters actually commit murder; he then asks slaves if they would carry imitation to that extent:

> Some of you, to excuse yourselves, may plead the example of others, saying that you hear a great many white people, who know more than such poor ignorant Negroes as you are, and some who are rich and great gentlemen, swear and talk profanely. And some of you may say this of your masters and say no more than is true. But all this is not a sufficient excuse for you. You know that murder is wicked. If you saw your master kill a man, do you suppose this would be any excuse for you if you should commit the same crime. You must know it would not; nor will your hearing him curse and swear and take the name of God in vain, or any other man, be he ever so great or rich, excuse you. God is greater than all other beings, and him we are bound to obey. To him we must give an account for every idle word that we speak. He will bring us all, rich and poor, white and black, to his judgement seat. If we are found among those who feared his name and trembled at this word, we shall be called good and faithful servants. Our slavery will be at an end, and though ever so mean, low, and despised in this world, we shall sit with God in his kingdom, as kings and priests, and rejoice forever and ever.

Hammon's accusations were not new to the era, but they were particularly dangerous when spoken by a Black slave. A white abolitionist, John Cooper of New Jersey, made a similar statement in 1780:

> Slavery is worse than death. He, therefore, who enslaves his fellow-creatures, must in our esteem be worse than he who takes his life and yet, surprizing [sic] as it may seem, we hold thousands of our fellow-men in slavery, and slumber on under the dreadful load of guilt—worse than murderers and yet at ease! (Lay, *Am I Not* 456–59)

Despite his bravery, modern readers assume that Jupiter Hammon was an Uncle Tom. Yet history shows that Hammon did not merely call for Christian submissiveness; he tried to keep slaves alive and out of jail. All the seemingly petty societal infringements that Hammon warns of in this essay were serious crimes for which slaves were flogged, jailed, and hung. Greene says that "of the specifically named crimes committed by Negroes, stealing and breach of peace were perhaps the most common" (*The Negro* 150). In the late seventeenth century, a slave named Silvanus Wano was found guilty of stealing from his master. He was whipped with twenty stripes, fined twenty pounds, and put in jail. Hannah, a female slave, was accused of stealing surgical instruments from a Boston store. She was "whipped with ten stripes" and fined ten pounds (151).

In 1786, just one year before the appearance of Hammon's essay, a notorious mulatto, Johnson Green, gained fame throughout New England by a series of rather minor thefts: "thirty weight of salt pork," "a pair of trousers, three pair of stockings and a shirt," "three cheeses, one small firkin of butter, and some chocolate," but never more than "food, money, clothing and liquor." Records indicate that his thefts were always petty, returning him little profit. Jailed several times, once Green was given one hundred stripes. Finally in Worcester, Massachusetts, when he was twenty-nine years old, on August 17, 1786, Green was hanged "for the atrocious crime of burglary" (Greene, *The Negro* 150–53).

Even profanity could have resulted in criminal punishment. Most colonies had very harsh laws against profanity and blasphemous conversation. Trumbull reports one:

> That no man blaspheme God's holy name, upon pain of death; or
> use unlawfull oaths, taking the name of God in vain, curse, or
> ban, upon pain of severe punishment for the first offence commit-
> ted, and for the second, *to have a bodkin thrust through his
> tongue;* and if he continue the blaspheming of God's holy name,
> for the third time so offending he shall be brought to a martial
> court, and there receive censure of death for his offence. (321)

Hammon especially extended his moral instructions to free
Blacks because whites used any behavior by them as an excuse
not to free those still enslaved. As early as 1713 one New England slave code concluded: "It is found by experience that free
negroes are an idle, slothful people, and prone very often to a
charge to the place where they are" (Hurd 284). MacLeod explains that as the antislavery movement increased in influence,
persuading more masters to free their slaves, the burgeoning free
Black population caused a torrential white backlash. "One conse-
quence was that there were many who were led to question the
wisdom of freeing them in the first place" (152). MacLeod concludes that any "abnormal" action by free Blacks precipitated
fears of riot and insurrection. Other laws forbade free Blacks
from employment in lucrative trades, or owning "any houses,
lands, tenements or hereditaments" (Higginbotham 122–23).
Clearly, along with other Black leaders like Booker T. Washington and Dr. Martin Luther King, Jr., whom some likewise brand
as "Toms," Jupiter Hammon was enjoining his Black American
audience to exhibit superior moral behavior, not just so they
would be the ideal Christians but so they could stay alive as well.[5]

As this and other auras of discrimination pervaded the society, free Blacks swelled the poverty rolls and increased the tax
burden. In the North, MacLeod says, "political and legal arguments in favor of slavery followed the same kind of pattern as
they had in the South. Even the opinion that free blacks were
improvident and criminal found a central place in the proslavery position" (99). Although there was no evidence to support
their suspicions, "colonial New Yorkers were convinced that
free Negroes not only joined their unfree brethren in acts of

violence, but that they also provided leadership for insurrection and the focal point for unrest" (Kobrin 25). Actually most free Negroes avoided slaves and kept to themselves, but the societal prejudice which fostered this behavior was only another form of slave control. Woodson (*The History*) says:

> There were efforts also to restrict contact of slaves with the free Negroes. One means employed was the embittering of one against the other. The free Negro was encouraged to think himself better than the slave. On the other hand, the slave was taught to hate the free Negro because of his haughtiness in his superior position. (115)[6]

Many modern readers have been critical of Hammon for saying that he did not wish to be free and for suggesting emancipation only for slaves who were much younger than he. However, he was voicing a plan of gradual emancipation, which New York abolitionists had often suggested to the state legislature as a compromise plan to end slavery. Not that Hammon or the Quakers (those abolitionists with whom he had the closest relationship) or any other abolitionists in the state merely wanted gradual emancipation. But political leaders in New York, the largest slaveholding state north of Maryland, had such a vested interest in continuing slavery that they recalcitrantly refused to follow the trend of emancipation sweeping the Northern colonies in the last decade of the century. Finally in 1799, the State of New York adopted the precise plan that Hammon suggests in this essay. A significant first step, gradual emancipation was all that Hammon had as a ray of hope. New York slaves were not fully manumitted until 1821, several years after his death. It became the last state in the North to end slavery.[7]

When Hammon argues that slaves of his age did not need to be freed—because "many of us who are grown-up slaves and have always had masters to take care of us should hardly know how to care of ourselves and it may be more for our own comfort to remain as we are"—he is again responding to realities in his era. This statement perhaps more than any other has been the cause of the negative reception of all of Hammon's work, and it has led to the denial of his place as the father of Black American protest literature. However, once more a sense of history is needed to inform literary criticism. It was a common practice by the end of the eighteenth century for masters to "free" older slaves who had served families faithfully for sixty or seventy years. Of no more utility to masters, these elderly slaves were set out in the street with no home or visible means of support (Kobrin 15). Thus, Hammon is being ironic when he says "and it may be more for our own comfort to remain as we are." Realistically, a seventy-six-year-old slave in the colonial era had little other choice.

Most colonial historians discuss the legislation enacted to stop this malicious practice as clearly intended to perpetuate slavery. Higginbotham says, "Slaveholders were expressly forbidden to abandon slaves who had become too old or too sick to be of further service" (123). To stem the tide of additional slaves' being put on public rolls, legislation was finally passed requiring owners to put up a bond of at least "200 pounds, guaranteeing the freeman's ability to be self-supporting" (Higginbotham 129). Masters were further ordered to pay freed slaves twenty pounds for tax.[8]

Thus, those looking backward at history should not judge Hammon too harshly for his statement about his own freedom. The Oyster Bay Manor had been his home for over seventy years. The Lloyds had an obligation to care for him in his old age, as he had worked for them, without gratuity, for all those years. While he says that he could "do most any kind of work," there is no evidence that salaried work was available in the small community. We know of no wife, children, or other younger family members, either slave or free, who could have cared for him or provided a home; nor is there evidence that housing was available. The law required that the former master pay a bond and an annual stipend for the manumitted older slave. Yet the Lloyd records do not show that they ever paid such a bond or fee; thus, there is no reason to believe that they were willing to give Hammon this security.

Hammon is also countering a tendency prevalent among whites to excuse the behavior of slaves on the grounds that Africans were too ignorant or innocent to know better. In the white male moral order, slaves were placed on the same level of accountability as white children. As long as slaves were not free to function as adults but condemned to lives of perpetual dependency, colonists could reinforce their own perceptions of a God-ordained social order. Thus, in all of his writing, Hammon challenges Blacks to redefine concepts of responsibility and adulthood even while in the vice of slavery. He urges slaves to throw off the yoke of dependency and to exercise at least those freedoms of choice that no man could take away from them—that is, choices about the soul and its eternal resting place.

Within the Black-as-child motif is an additional assumption of white society: namely, that it functioned on a system of superior morality that the slave had not adopted. When they debated emancipation in the nineteenth century, some Kentucky Presbyterians argued that slavery (1) depraves and degrades its subjects; (2) "dooms thousands of human beings to hopeless ignorance"; and (3) "produces general licentiousness among the slaves." Even in arguing for emancipation, the Kentucky Synod tended to view Africans like mice in a maze. With all good intentions, they did not likewise label as licentious the moral code of the enslavers. Although writing as a "perpetual servant" himself, Hammon constantly tried to make his fellow slaves view not their own culpability, but that of the slave masters. He believed that such an awakening was the beginning of inward growth and maturity, despite slavery's bonds. A companion strategy was to encourage the slave to live above the "Christianity" that the master practiced.

Because of their treatment of Black colonists, Hammon wrote, whites proved themselves not to be Christians at all. This premise was in part based on correlated biblical instructions to masters in Ephesians and Colossians, which provided that they were to treat their servants as brothers. Thus Hammon chides masters for nurturing their own children in Christian tutelage while ignoring the children of slaves. These verses demanded that masters "do the same unto them . . . that which is just and equal." But in disobedience to that commandment, whites sought their freedom from England while refusing to free the Africans in America. And in this essay, Hammon takes them to task for it. Other Blacks as well as white abolitionists made the same charge.[9]

While a superficial reading of this essay indicates to some that Hammon acquiesced to slavery, he rather followed a plan for emancipation set forth by the Apostle Paul in three of his epistles (Ephesians, Colossians, and Philemon) and by leading eighteenth-century abolitionists. As peacemakers (Matt. 5:9), both Hammon and Paul wanted to end slavery in a way that would preclude violence. Paul first exhorted slaves to serve masters with a cooperative attitude; then he told masters to treat slaves like brothers. Philemon's slave, Onesimus, had escaped and run away to Rome. After leading him in Christian conversion, Paul writes Philemon, whom he had led to Christ, a letter stressing equality and brotherhood. Realizing Philemon's status of wealth and his "investment" in Onesimus, the apostle reminded Philemon that the Christian message was worth more than earthly wealth. When putting this consideration into the economic balance, Paul could command freedom for Onesimus: "Therefore receive him . . . Not now as a servant, but above a servant, a brother beloved, specially to me, but how much more unto thee, both in the flesh, and in the Lord?" (Phil., vv.12, 16). Typically, proslavery writers ignored the book of Philemon and the commandments to masters in Ephesians and Colossians.[10] Even abolitionists avoided discussion of Philemon as a source to explore master/slave relationships because it seems to admit the presence of slavery in New Testament church life.[11]

Like other Black colonial writers, Hammon noted how eagerly white colonists fought for their own freedom while enslaving others:

> That liberty is a great thing we may know from our own feelings, and we may likewise judge so from the conduct of the white people in the late war. How much money has been spent and how

many lives have been lost to defend their liberty! I must say that I have hoped that God would open their eyes, when they were so much engaged for liberty, to think of the state of the poor blacks and to pity us.

With the same forthrightness, in his well-publicized letter to Thomas Jefferson, Black mathematician and architect Benjamin Banneker wrote:

> Here, Sir, was a time in which your tender feelings for your selves engaged you thus to declare, you were then impressed with proper ideas of the great valuation of liberty, and the free possession of those blessings to which you were entitled by nature; but Sir how pitiable is it to reflect, that altho you were so fully convinced of the benevolence of the Father of mankind, and of his equal and impartial distribution of those rights and privileges which he had conferred upon them, that you should at the Same time counteract his mercies, in detaining by fraud and violence so numerous a part of my brethren under groaning captivity and cruel oppression, that you should at the Same time be found guilty of that most criminal act, which you professedly detested in others, with respect to yourselves. (Kaplan 120)

After her emancipation, Wheatley wrote a searing letter with a similar opinion to Native American preacher Samson Occom. In his compatible declaration, Hammon reflects the thoughts of the two most prominent Black abolitionists of his day. Yet today these two Black leaders are lauded, while Hammon, the only one among them who was a slave all of his life, is denigrated.[12]

Continuing in his message of subterfuge against the colonial economic system, Hammon cites the Kingdom Feast parable from Luke 14. Prosperous citizens were too occupied with business ventures to attend the dinner, so the master of the house told his servant to "Go out quickly into the streets and lanes of the city, and bring in hither the poor" (14:21). Therefore, Hammon tells Africans that they—not whites who profess Christianity while ignoring God's commandments concerning the poor (that is, the slaves)—will inherit the kingdom of heaven.

For Hammon, evangelism was not just empty, ethereal dogma; it descended even unto the least of all mankind with the offer of hope and freedom. As he does throughout his writing, in this essay Hammon equates slavery to the anguish of hell and lays the responsibility for the practice on Satan. Thus he tells unchurched Africans that if they do not accept Christ they will "be slaves here, and slaves forever." Hammon also chides slaveholders that money is the underpinning of the slave institution. He tells the slaves that, as they have no earthly freedom or wealth, they will not be so concerned with worldly goods as to ignore God's invitation to the heavenly celebration. His note about the "drowning" of the rich comes from 1 Tim. 6:9–10: "But they that will be rich fall into temptation and a snare, and into many foolish and hurtful lusts, which drown men in destruction and perdition. For the love of money is the root of all evil." That some could claim Christian conversion while surrendering to this temptation is shown in other texts from which Hammon drew his theme of punishment: "For the wrath of God is revealed from heaven against all ungodliness and unrighteousness of men, who hold the truth in unrighteousness" (Rom. 1:18).

He also selects a familiar passage from 1 Corinthians, but he rewords it and rearranges its images of "the rulers of this world" to include "the rich," recrafting the text to enumerate "what God had not chosen." The KJV reads:

> For ye see your calling, brethren, how that not many wise men after the flesh, not many mighty, not many noble, are called: But God hath chosen the foolish things of the world to confound the wise; and God hath chosen the weak things of the world to confound the things which are mighty; And base things of the world, and things which are despised, hath God chosen, yea, and things which are not, to bring to nought things that are: That no flesh should glory in his presence. (1 Cor. 1:26–29)

As echoed by gospel singers for the next several decades, Black preachers said that because they were not so concerned with "the affairs of this world," slaves had a great assurance of heaven.[13]

Hammon relied on Judgment to absolve his people from individual and corporate responsibility for slavery and to vindicate their lot against their enemies. He believed that saints and sinners would receive two different judgments: that of Christians, referred to as the Judgment Seat of Christ, and that of unbelievers, called the Great White Throne Judgment.[14] That this was accepted theology in colonial times is reflected in the works of a contemporary poet, Michael Wigglesworth, who says of the great judgment bar:

> Thus one and all, thus great and small,
>   the Rich as well as Poor,
> And those of place as the most base,
>   do stand the Judge before.
> They are arrign'd and there detain'd,
>   before Christ's Judgement-seat
> With trembling fear, their Doom to hear,
>   and fell his anger heat.
>
>   (*Day of Doom* 22)[15]

As he attended a Puritan church with the Lloyds, Hammon would have heard repeated strains of the judgment scene. The last chapter of the joint doctrinal statement of all Puritan and/or Congregational churches was a concise tenet entitled "Of the Last Judgement":

> God both appointed a day wherein he will judge the World in righteousness by Jesus Christ, to whom all Power and Judgement is given of the Father; in which day not onely [sic] the Apostate Angels shall be judged, but likewise all persons that have lived upon the earth shall appear before the Tribunal of Christ, to give an account of their thoughts, words and deeds, and to receive according to what they have done in the body, whether good or evil. (Walker 402)[16]

It is unfortunate that a dearth of information about slavery in the North hindered critics of Black American literature from knowing the true living conditions of early Black writers like Jupiter Hammon. This dearth has led to a critical misinterpretation of *An Address to the Negroes in the State of New York*. And the prevalence of this misinterpretation has done much to damage Hammon's integrity and to prevent his veneration as the first Black writer of America.

Notes

1.   For more on Jones and Allen, see George; Porter 335–42; and Allen's autobiography. See also Blassingame; Frazier; Mitchell; Raboteau; and Woodson *The History,* for more on the Black church and the early Black American preacher.

2.   See T. M. Cooley; George; Morse 22–32; and Woodson, *The History* 56–58, 75–78.

3.   Other evangelical writers who recognized Blacks as the poor of America include Beveridge, *Works* 2:487–506; S. Hopkins, *Timely Articles* 591–92; J. C. Lovejoy 61–67; and C. Mather, *Bonifacius* 107–19.

4.   For more instances of identification with Blacks as the poor, see Weimer 74–76. Brown's entries on both the poor and the rich (464, 496), established the theological backdrop from which Hammon's questions arose.

5.   See also Greene, "Slave-Holding" 510–19; and Kobrin 14–15. For additional background on the punishments from which Hammon sough to protect slaves, see Hurd 1:270–72, 293; and Trumbull 67–69, 89–91, 276–78, 293–95.

6.   See also Dumond 119–25; Greene, *The Negro* 290–333; Hirsch; and Schenell.

7.   As proof of how stubborn post-Revolutionary colonists in New York held on to the slave institution, Arthur Zilversmit explains that gradual emancipation actually became a way to support and prolong slavery:

> The act would take effect on July 4, 1799. All Negro children born after that date would be free, but would have to serve the masters of their mothers until they were twenty-eight (males) or twenty-five (females). Slaveowners could abandon these Negro children a year after their birth, and they would be considered paupers, bound out to service by the overseers of the poor. The state would reimburse the towns for the support of abandoned children at a monthly rate of up to $3.50 per month for every Negro child, over one year old, born to one of their slaves. Because the overseers of the poor would be inclined to bind out the child to the owner of the child's mother, masters could expect

to derive a lucrative income from abandonments. This abandonment clause was, therefore, a disguised scheme for compensated abolition, and it undoubtedly served to make gradual abolition more acceptable to slaveowners conscious of their property rights. (182)

8. Edwin Olson in "Social Aspects of Slave Life in New York" offers a cogent example:

> Slaves who by reason of old age or infirmity were no longer capable of performing labor were sometimes disposed of either by setting them adrift to shift for themselves or by executing a pretended sale of them. The case of Sarah is pertinent. Peter Van Rensselaer, of Claverack, in 1814 "sold" his woman slave, Sarah, to Asel Woodworth, also of Claverack, who was poor and unable to support the woman. Van Rensselaer paid Woodworth the sum of forty dollars to take her off his hands, Sarah being infirm, subject to fits, and unable to work. These infirmities were clearly set forth in the bill of sale. Woodworth profited by selling Sarah to David McKinstry for ten dollars. Since Sarah was an economic liability it is apparent that Woodworth did not reveal to the purchaser her true condition. A few days following the acquisition of the woman, McKinstry sold her and she thereafter passed from one master to another until ultimately she was left on the streets of Claverack to make her own way. A clash betwen the authorities of two towns over her maintenance brought the case of Sarah to the New York Supreme Court, in 1818, which held that her sale by Van Rensselaer to Woodworth was collusive by law and hence was void. (77)

See also Epps; Hirsch; and Ovington for further study of neglected elderly slaves.

9. For additional discussion on the education of Blacks, both children and adults, read reports of the SPG's missionary activities by Mabee 3–10; Pasco 57–78; Pierre; and Vibert. The specific education of the children of Puritans is discussed in Byington (both works); and E. S. Morgan, *Puritan Family.* For more on master/slave relationships, see Beveridge, *Works* 6:162–77; Beveridge, *Private Thoughts* 127–29; J. H. Hopkins 99–115, 129–35; S. Hopkins, *Timely Articles* 565–68; E. J. McManus, *History* 12–17; MacLeod; C. Mather, *Negro Christianized,* in Ruchames 61–70; and Woodson, *Negro in History* 110–16.

10. For various interpretations, see Barnes 318–38; J. H. Hopkins 137–38, 170; and Thomas 40–42.

11. See, for instance, Burkitt 2:539–44. For information about gradual emancipation plans in the colonies, read Dumond 46–52; Locke; and Zorn.

12. For thorough studies of free Black leaders during the Revolutionary era, see Quarles' book and his essay in Berlin and Hoffman 283–301; D. B. Davis 273–84; and Kaplan's entire work. For Wheatley's letter, see Lay, *Am I Not* 306.

13. Poole's commentary gives contemporary discussion of the warnings to the rich in James 1:10–11, 618; 1 Cor. 1:17–22; 2 Tim. 9–10.

14. See Tucker 126, 132–41. See also Seiss 155–82.

15. The approaches of both Hammon and Wigglesworth contrast with that of the last great Calvinist, Jonathan Edwards. Rather than show unconverted sinners writhing before God in a divine court, Edwards has them shipped directly into hell. Hammon may have perceived the idea of angels present at this type of trial from Edward's treatment of a scene from the Book of Revelation:

> you shall be tormented in the presence of the holy angels, and in the presence of the Lamb; and where you shall be in this state of suffering, the glorious inhabitants of heaven shall go forth and look on the awful spectacle. (*Apocalyptic Writings*)

Hammon's speculation that this judgment period may take a thousand years is based on 2 Pet. 3:8: "One day is with the Lord as a thousand years, and a thousand years as one day."

16. For more on colonial views of judgment, see Foster 189–223; J. Edwards, *Works* 4:219–20; and P. Miller, *Mind: From Colony.*

An Address to the Negroes in the State of New York

When I am writing to you with a design to say something to you for your good and with a view to promoting your happiness, I can with truth and sincerity join with the Apostle Paul, speaking in his own nation, the Jews, and say: "That I have great heaviness and continual sorrow in my heart . . . for my brethren, my kinsmen according to the flesh" (Rom. 9:2–3). Yes, my dear brethren, when I think of you, which is very often, and of the poor, despised, and miserable state you are in as to the things of this world, and when I think of your ignorance and stupidity and the great wickedness of the most of you, I am pained to the heart. It is at times almost too much for human nature to bear, and I am obliged to turn my thoughts from the subject or endeavor to still my mind by considering that it is permitted thus to be by that God who governs all things, who setteth up one and pulleth down another. While I have been thinking on this subject, I have frequently had great struggles in my own mind and have been at a loss to know what to do. I have wanted exceedingly to say something to you, to call upon you with the tenderness of a father and friend, and to give you the last and, I may say dying, advice of an old man who wishes your best good in this world and in the world to come. But while I have had such desires, a sense of my own ignorance and unfitness to teach others has frequently discouraged me from attempting to say anything to you. Yet when I thought of your situation, I could not rest easy.

When I was at Hartford in Connecticut, where I lived during the war,[1] I published several pieces, which were well received not only by those of my own color but by a number of the white people, who thought they might do good among their servants. This is one consideration, among others, that emboldens me now to publish what I have written to you. Another is that I think you will be more likely to listen to what is said when you know it comes from a Negro, one of your own nation and color, and who therefore can have no interest in deceiving you or in saying anything to you but what he really thinks is in your interest and is your duty to comply with.

My age gives me some right to speak to you and reason to expect that you will harken to my advice. I am now upwards of seventy years old and cannot expect, though I am well and able to do almost any kind of business, to live much longer.[2] I have passed the common bounds set for man and must soon go the way of all the earth. I have had more experience in the world than most of you, and I have seen a great deal of the vanity and wickedness of it. I have great reason to be thankful that my lot has been so much better than that of most slaves. I suppose I have had more advantages and privileges than most of you who are slaves have ever known and more, I believe, than many white people have enjoyed—for which I desire to bless God, and pray that he may bless those who have given them to me. I do not, my dear friends, say these things about myself to make you think that I am wiser or better than others but that you might harken prejudice to what I have to say to you on the following particulars.

First. Respecting obedience to masters. Now whether it is right and lawful in the sight of God for them to make slaves of us or not, I am certain that while we are slaves, it is our duty to obey our masters in all their lawful commands and mind them unless we are bid to do that which we know to be sin, or forbidden in God's word.[3] The Apostle Paul says:

> Servants, be obedient to them that are your masters according to the flesh, with fear and trembling, in singleness of your heart, as unto Christ; Not with eyeservice, as menpleasers; but as the servants of Christ, doing the will of God from the heart; With good will doing service, as to the Lord, and not to men: Knowing that whatsoever good thing any man doeth, the same shall he receive of the Lord, whether he be bond or free. (Eph. 6:5–8)

Here is God's plain command for us to obey our masters. It may seem hard for us, if we think our masters wrong in holding us slaves, to obey in all things, but who of us dares dispute with God! He has commanded us to obey, and we ought to do it cheerfully and freely.[4]

This should be done by us, not only because God commands but because our own peace and comfort depend upon it. As we depend upon our masters for what we eat and drink and wear and for all our comfortable things in this world, we cannot be happy unless we please them. This we cannot do without obeying them freely, without muttering or finding fault. If a servant strives to please his master and studies and takes pains to do it, I believe there are but few masters who would use such a servant cruelly. Good servants frequently make good masters. If your master is really hard, unreasonable, and cruel, there is no way so likely for you to convince him of it, as always to obey his commands and try to serve him, and take care of his interest and try to promote it insofar as it is in your power. If you are proud and stubborn and always finding fault, your master will think the fault lies wholly on your side; but if you are humble and meek and bear all things patiently, your master may think he is wrong: if he does not, his neighbours will be apt to see it and will befriend you and try to alter his conduct.[5] If this does not do, you must cry to Him who has the hearts of all men in his hands and turneth them as the rivers of water are turned.

Second. The particulars I would mention are honesty and faithfulness. You must suffer me now to deal plainly with you, my dear brethren, for I do not mean to flatter or omit speaking the truth, whether it is for you or against you. How many of you are there who steal from your masters? It is wicked for you not to take care of your masters' goods, but how much worse is it to pilfer and steal from them whenever you think you shall not be found out? This, you must know, is very wicked and provoking to God. There are none of you so ignorant but that you must know that this is wrong. Though you may try to excuse yourselves by saying that your masters are unjust to you and though you may try to quiet your consciences in this way, yet if you are honest in owning the truth, you must think it as wicked, and on some accounts more wicked, to steal from your masters as from others.[6]

We cannot certainly have any excuse, either for taking anything that belongs to our masters, without their leave, or for being unfaithful in their business. It is our duty to be faithful, "not with eyeservice, as menpleasers." We have no right to stay, when we are sent on errands, any longer than to do the business we were sent upon. All the time spent idly is spent wickedly and is unfaithfulness to our masters. In these things I must say that I think many of you are guilty. I know that many of you endeavor to excuse yourselves and say that you have nothing to call your own and that you are under great temptations to be unfaithful and take from your masters. But this will not do; God will certainly punish you for stealing and for being unfaithful. All that we have to mind is our own duty. If God has put us in bad circumstances, that is not our fault, and he will not punish us for it. If any are wicked in keeping us so, we cannot help it; they must answer to God for it. Nothing will serve as an excuse for not doing our duty. The same God will judge both them and us. Pray then, my dear friends, fear to offend in this way, but be faithful to God, to your masters, and to your own souls.[7]

Third. The next thing I would mention and warn you against is profaneness. This you know is forbidden by God. Christ tells us, "Swear not at all" (Matt. 5:34). And again it is said: "Thou shalt not take the name of the Lord thy God in vain; for the Lord will not hold him guiltless that taketh his name in vain" (Exod. 20:7). Now, though the great God has forbidden it, yet how dreadfully profane are many, and I don't know but I may say the most of you! How common is it to hear you take the terrible and awful name of the great God in vain—to swear by it and by Jesus Christ, his Son. How common is it to hear you wish damnation to your companions and to your own souls—and to sport with, in the name of heaven and hell, as if there were no such places for you to hope for or to fear. Oh my friends, be warned to forsake this dreadful sin of profaneness. Pray, my dear friends; believe and realize that there is a God, that he is great and terrible beyond what you can think, that he keeps you in life every moment, and that he can send you to that awful hell that you laugh at, in an instant, and confine you there forever, and that he will certainly do it if you do not repent. You certainly do not believe that there is a God or that there is a heaven or hell, or you would never trifle with them. It would make you shudder, when you hear others do it, if you believe in them as much as you believe anything you see with your bodily eyes.

I have heard some learned and good men say that the heathen and all that worshipped false gods never spoke lightly or irreverently of their gods; they never took their names in vain or jested with those things which they held sacred. Now, why should the true God, who made all things, be treated worse in this respect than those false gods that were made of wood and stone? I believe it is because Satan tempts men to do it. He tried to make them love their false gods and to speak well of them; but he wishes to have men think lightly of the true God, to take his holy name in vain, and to scoff at and make a jest of all things that are really good. You may think that Satan has not the power to do so much and have so great an influence on the minds of men. But the Scripture says that he, "as a roaring lion walketh about, seeking whom he may devour"; that he is "the prince of the power of the air, the spirit that now worketh in the children of disobedience"; and that wicked men are "taken captive by him, at his will" (1 Pet. 5:8; Eph. 2:2; 2 Tim. 2:26).[8]

All of those of you who are profane are serving the devil. You are doing what he tempts and desires you to do. If you could see him with your bodily eyes, would you like to make an agreement with him to serve him and do as he bid you? I believe most of you would be shocked at this, but you may be certain that all of you who indulge yourselves in this sin are as really serving him and to just as good purpose as if you met him and promised to dishonor God and serve the devil with all your might. Do you believe this? It is true, whether you believe it or not. Some of you, to excuse yourselves, may plead the example of others, saying that you hear a great many white people, who know more than such poor ignorant Negroes as you are, and some who are rich and great gentlemen, swear and talk profanely.

And some of you may say this of your masters and say no more than is true. But all this is not a sufficient excuse for you. You know that murder is wicked. If you saw your master kill a man, do you suppose this would be any excuse for you if you should commit the same crime? You must know it would not; nor will your hearing him curse and swear and take the name of God in vain, or any other man, be he ever so great or rich, excuse you. God is greater than all other beings, and him we are bound to obey. To him we must give an account for every idle word that we speak.[9] He will bring us all, rich and poor, white and black, to his judgement seat. If we are found among those who feared his name and trembled at his word, we shall be called good and faithful servants. Our slavery will be at an end, and though ever so mean, low, and despised in this world, we shall sit with God in his kingdom, as kings and priests, and rejoice forever and ever. Do not then, my dear friends, take God's holy name in vain or speak profanely in any way. Let not the example of others lead you into the sin, but reverence and fear that great and fearful name, the Lord our God.[10]

I might now caution you against others sins to which you are exposed. But as I meant only to mention those you were exposed to more than others, by your being slaves, I will conclude what I have to say to you by advising you to become religious and to make religion the great business of your lives.

Now I acknowledge that liberty is a great thing and worth seeking for if we can get it honestly and by our good conduct prevail on our masters to set us free. For my own part, I do not wish to be free, yet I should be glad if others, especially the young Negroes, were to be free. Many of us who are grown-up slaves and have always had masters to take care of us should hardly know how to take care of ourselves, and it may be more for our own comfort to remain as we are. That liberty is a great thing we may know from our own feelings, and we may likewise judge so from the conduct of the white people in the late war. How much money has been spent and how many lives have been lost to defend their liberty! I must say that I have hoped that God would open their eyes, when they were so much engaged for liberty, to think of the state of the poor blacks and to pity us. He has done it in some measure and has raised us up many friends, for which we have reason to be thankful and to hope in his mercy. What may be done further, he only knows, for known unto God are all his ways from the beginning.

But this, my dear brethren, is by no means the greatest thing we have to be concerned about. Getting our liberty in this world is nothing to our having the liberty of the children of God. Now the Bible tells us that we are all, by nature, sinners, that we are slaves to sin and Satan, and that unless we are converted, or born again, we must be miserable forever. Christ says that except a man be born again, he cannot see the kingdom of God and all that do not see the kingdom of God must be in the kingdom of darkness.[11] There are but two places where all go after death, white and black, rich and poor: those places are heaven and hell. Heaven is a place made for those who are born again and who love God, and it is a place where they will be happy forever. Hell is a place made for those who hate God and are his enemies and where they will be miserable for all eternity.

Now you may think you are not enemies to God and do not hate him, but if your heart has not been changed and you have not become true Christians, you certainly are enemies to God and have been opposed to him ever since you were born. Many of you I suppose, never think of this and are almost as ignorant as the beasts that perish.[12] Those of you who can read, I must beg you to read the Bible. Whenever you can get time, study the Bible. And if you can get no other time, spare some of your time from sleep and learn the mind and will of God. But what shall I say to them who cannot read? This lay with great weight on my mind when I thought of writing to my poor brethren, but I hope that those who can read will take pity on them and read what I have to say to them. In hopes of this, I will beg of you to spare no pains in trying to learn to read. If you are once engaged, you may learn. Let all the time you can get be spent in trying to learn to read. Get those who can read to teach you; but remember that what you learn for is to read the Bible.

If there were no Bible, it would be no matter whether you could read or not. Reading other books would do you no good. But the Bible is the word of God and tells you what you must do to please God; it tells you how you may escape misery and be happy forever. If you see most people neglect the Bible, and many that can read never look into it, let it not harden you and make you think lightly of it and that it is a book of no worth. All those who are really good love the Bible and meditate on it day and night. In the Bible, God had told us everything it is necessary we should know in order to be happy here and hereafter. The Bible is a revelation of the mind and will of God to men. Therein we may learn what God is, that he made all things by the power of his word, and that he made things for his own glory, and not for our glory. That he is over all and above all his creatures and more above them than we can think or conceive—that they can do nothing without him—that he upholds them all and will overrule all things for his own glory.

In the Bible likewise, we are told what man is. That he was at first made holy, in the image of God, that he fell from that state of holiness and became an enemy to God, and that since the fall, all the imaginations of the thoughts of his heart are evil, and only evil and that continually. That the carnal mind is not subject to the law of God, neither indeed can be.[13] And that all mankind was under the wrath and curse of God and must have been forever miserable if they had been left to suffer what their sins deserved. It tells us that God, to save some of mankind, sent his Son into this world to die in the place and stead of sinners, and that now God can save from eternal misery all that believe in his Son and take him for their Savior, and that all are called upon to repent and believe in Jesus Christ.[14]

It tells us that those who do repent and believe and who are friends to Christ shall have many trials and sufferings in this world but that they shall be happy forever, after death, and reign with Christ for all eternity. The Bible tells us that this world is a place of trial and that there is no other time or place for us to alter, but in this life. If we are Christians when we die, we shall awake to the resurrection of life; if not, we shall awaken to the resurrection of damnation. It tells us we must all live in heaven or hell, be happy or miserable, and that without end. The Bible does not tell us of but two places for all to go to.

There is no place for innocent folks that are not Christians. There is no place for ignorant folks that did not know how to be Christians. What I mean is that there is no place besides heaven and hell. These two places will receive all mankind; for Christ says, there are but two sorts: "He that is not with me is against me; and he that gathereth not with me, scattereth abroad" (Matt. 12:30).

The Bible likewise tells us that this world and all things in it shall be burnt up and that God has appointed a day in which he will judge the world; he will bring every secret thing, whether it be good or bad, into judgement; that which is done in secret shall be declared from the housetops.[15] I do not know, nor do I think any can tell, but that the day of judgement may last a thousand years. God could tell the state of all his creatures in a moment, but then, everything that everyone had done, through his whole life, is to be told before the whole world of angels and men. Oh how solemn is the thought! You and I must stand and hear every thing we have thought or done, however secret, however wicked and vile, told before all the men and women that ever have been or ever will be, and before all the angels, good and bad.

Now, my dear friends, seeing that the Bible is the word of God and everything in it is true and that it reveals such awful and glorious things, what can be more important than that you should learn to read it? And when you have learned to read, that you should study it day and night? There are some things very encouraging in God's word for such ignorant creatures as we are. For God hath not chosen the rich of this world. Not many rich, not many noble are called, but God hath chosen the weak things of this world, and things which are not, to confound the things that are.[16] And when the great and the rich refused to come to the gospel feast, the servant was told to go into the highways and hedges, and compel those poor creatures that he found there to come in. Now, my brethren, it seems to me that there are no people that ought to attend to the hope of happiness in another world so much as we. Most of us are cut off from comfort and happiness here in this world and can expect nothing from it. Now seeing this is the case why should we not take care to be happy after death? Why should we spend our whole lives in sinning against God and thus be miserable in this world and in the world to come? If we do thus, we shall certainly be the greatest fools. We shall be slaves here and slaves forever. We cannot plead so great a temptation to neglect religion as others. Riches and honours, which drown the greater part of mankind, who have the gospel, in perdition, can be little or no temptation to us.

We have so little time in this world that it is no matter how wretched and miserable we are if it prepares us for heaven. What is forty, fifty, or sixty years when compared with eternity? When thousands and millions of years have rolled away, this eternity will be no nigher coming to an end. Oh how glorious is an eternal life of happiness! And how dreadful an eternity of misery! Those of us who have had religious masters, and have been taught to read the Bible and have been brought by their example and teaching to a sense of divine things, how happy shall we be to meet them in heaven, where we shall join them in praising God forever. But if any of us have had such masters and yet have lived and died wicked, how will it add to our misery to think of our folly? If any of us who have wicked and profane masters should become religious, how will our estates be changed in another world?

Oh, my friends, let me entreat you to think on these things and to live as if you believed them to be true. If you become Christians, you will have reason to bless God forever that you have been brought into a land where you have heard the gospel, though you have been slaves. If we should ever get to heaven, we shall find nobody to reproach us for being black or for being slaves. Let me beg of you, my dear African brethren, to think very little of your bondage in this life, for your thinking of it will do you no good. If God designs to set us free, he will do it in his own time and way; but think of your bondage to sin and Satan, and do not rest until you are delivered from it. We cannot be happy, whether we are ever so free or ever so rich, while we are servants of sin and slaves to Satan.[17] We must be miserable here and to all eternity.

I will conclude what I have to say with a few words to those Negroes who have their liberty.[18] The most of what I have said to those who are slaves may be of use to you; but you have more advantages than they, on some accounts, if you will improve your freedom, as you may do. You have more time to read God's Holy Word and to take care of the salvation of your souls. Let me beg of you to spend your time in this way, or it will be better for you if you had always been slaves. If you think seriously of the matter, you must conclude that if you do not use your freedom to promote the salvation of your souls, it will not be of any lasting good to you. Besides all this, if you are idle and take to bad courses, you will hurt those of your brethren who are slaves and do all in your power to prevent their being free. One great reason that is given by some for not freeing us, I understand, is that we should not know how to take care of ourselves and should take to bad courses, that we should be lazy and idle, and get drunk and steal. Now all those of you who follow any bad courses and who do not try are doing more to prevent our being free than anybody else. Let me beg of you then, for the sake of your own good and happiness in time and for eternity, and for the sake of your poor brethren who are still in bondage, to "lead a quiet and peaceable life in all godliness and honesty" (1 Tim. 2:2). And may God bless you and bring you to his kingdom, for Christ's sake. Amen.

Emendations

Page	Line		
230	2:	good.]	good,] R
		promoting]	promote] R
	3:	Apostle]	apostle] R
		speaking]	when speaking] R
	4:	nation,]	nation.] R
	5:	heart. . .]	heart,] R
	6:	flesh (Rom. 9:2–3).]	flesh.] R
		Yes,]	yes.] R
	8:	despised,]	despised.] R
		in.]	in,] R
231	1:	stupidity.]	stupidity,] R
	3:	times.]	times,] R
	5:	mind.]	mind,] R
		to be.]	to be,] R
	8:	mind.]	mind,] R
	11:	last.]	last,] R
		and,]	and.] R
		dying,]	dying.] R
	12:	advice.]	advice,] R
		man.]	man,] R
		world.]	world,] R
	14:	ignorance.]	ignorance,] R
	14:	others.]	others,] R
	15:	anything]	any thing] R
	16:	you. Yet]	you; yet] R
	18:	pieces,]	pieces.] R
		received.]	received,] R
	19:	color.]	colour,] R
	22:	is. that]	is,] R

	23:	said.]	said,] R
	24:	Negro]	negro] R
	25:	who therefore]	therefore] R
		you.]	you,] R
	26:	anything]	any thing] R
		you.]	you,] R
		is in]	is] R
		interest.]	interest,] R
	27:	is your duty]	duty] R
		with.]	with. My] R
	28:	age.]	age, I think,] R
		you.]	you,] R
	29:	that]	expect you] R
		harken]	hearken] R
	30:	old.]	old,] R
		well,]	well,] R
	32:	man.]	man,] R
	35:	it.]	it,] R
	36:	that of most	most slaves have
		slaves]	had] R
232	37:	you.]	you,] R
	1:	slaves.]	slaves,] R
		known.]	known,] R
		and more, I	and. I believe.
		believe,]	more] R
	2:	—for]	, for] R
	4:	myself.]	myself,] R
	5:	others.]	others;] R
	6:	harken.]	hearken,] R
		prejudice.]	prejudice,] R
	8:	First.]	1st.] R
	8–9:	right. and	right, and
		lawful.]	lawful,] R
	9:	God.]	God,] R
	10:	not,]	not.] R
	11:	masters.]	masters,] R
		commands.]	commands,] R
	13:	Apostle]	apostel] R
	14:	Servants,]	Servants.] R
	15:	trembling,]	trembling.] R
		of your]	in your] R
		heart,]	heart.] R
	16:	Christ;]	Christ:] R
		eyeservice]	eye service] R
		menpleasers;]	men pleasers,] R
	17:	Christ,]	Christ.] R
	18:	service,]	service to] R
	19:	whatsoever good]	whatever] R
		any]	a] R
		doeth,]	doeth.] R
	20:	free. (Eph. 6:5–	free."—] R
		8)]	

	21:	God's plain command]
	23:	dares]
	25:	cheerfully.]
		freely.]
	26:	commands.]
	28:	masters]
		wear.]
	30:	happy.]
	35:	unreasonable,]
233	1:	commands.]
		interest.]
	2:	insofar as it is in your power.]
	4:	humble. and meek.]
	5:	wrong:]
	6:	it.]
	7:	you.]
	8:	Him]
		hands.]
	10:	Second.]
		mention.]
		are]
	11:	faithfulness. You]
	13:	you.]
	14:	there.]
		steal]
		masters?]
	15:	goods,]
	16:	them]
	17:	out? This, you must know,]
	20:	you. and]
	22:	wicked,]
	23:	masters. as]
	25–26:	anything]
	28:	eyeservice, as menpleasers]
	30:	wickedly.]
	31:	say.]
	33:	yourselves.]
		to call]
	34:	own.]
	36:	stealing.]
	37:	mind.]
234	3:	excuse]
	7:	Third. The]
	9:	all (Matt. 5:34). And]
		said:]

a plain command of God] R
dare] R
cheerfully,] R
freely. This] R
commands,] R
masters.] R
wear,] R
happy,] R
unreasonable,.] R
commands,] R
interest,] R
all in your power.] R
humble, and meek,] R
wrong;] R
it,] R
you,] R
him,] R
hands,] R
2nd] R
mention, is] R
is] R
faithfulness.] R
you, or] R
there,] R
allow yourselves in stealing] R
masters.] R
goods;] R
them,] R
out. This. your must know.] R
you, and] R
wicked.] R
masters, than] R
any thing] R
eye service. as men pleasers] R
wickedly,] R
say,] R
yourselves,] R
that you can call] R
own,] R
stealing,] R
mind,] R
excuse to us] R
The] R
all," and] R
said,] R

	10:	vain;]
	11:	vain" (Exod.
		20:7).]
	15:	vain—to]
		it,]
	16:	Son.]
	17:	companions]
	18:	heaven and hell]
	20:	friends;]
	21:	God,]
	22:	think,]
	23:	moment,]
		hell]
	24:	forever,]
	25:	it,]
	26:	God.]
		heaven or hell]
	27–28:	shudder, when]
	28:	believe in]
	29:	anything]
	30:	heathen.]
	31:	gods.]
	32:	vain.]
	35:	gods.]
235	4:	much.]
		great an]
	5:	men.]
		says that he]
	5–6:	as a roaring lion
		walketh about]
	6:	devour; that]
	7:	air, the spirit
		that now
		worketh in]
	8:	disobedience;]
		taken]
	9:	at]
		will (1 Pet. 5:8;
		Eph. 2:2; 2 Tim.
		2:26).]
	10:	profane.]
		devil]
	12:	him]
	14:	this,]
	15:	indulge]
		sin.]
		him.]
	16:	purpose]
	17:	God.]
		the devil]
	18:	true,]
	19:	you,]
	20:	saying]

Right column readings:

vain,] R
vain."] R
vain!—To] R
it,] R
Son.—] R
companions,] R
heaven and Hell] R
friends,] R
God] R
think—] R
moment—] R
Hell] R
for ever;] R
it,] R
God] R
Heaven or Hell] R
shudder, if] R
believe them] R
any thing] R
heathen,] R
gods,] R
vain;] R
gods,] R
much,] R
great influence] R
men:] R
says] R
goeth about like a
roaring Lion] R
devour—That] R
air—and that
he rules in
the hearts of] R
disobedience,—] R
led] R
to do] R
will. All] R
profane,] R
Devil] R
him,] R
this;] R
allow] R
sin,] R
him,] R
purpose,] R
God,] R
him] R
true.] R
you.] R
and say] R

	22:	swear, and talk	swear, and talk
		profanely.]	profanely; and] R
	23:	masters,]	masters,] R
	26:	you,]	you,] R
	28:	swear,]	swear,] R
		name,]	name,] R
	36:	low,]	low] R
	37:	kings and priests]	Kings and Priests] R
		forever]	for ever] R
236	1:	vain,]	vain,] R
	6:	exposed. But]	exposed; but] R
		to,]	to,] R
	8:	you,]	you, by] R
		religious,]	religious,] R
	10:	thing,]	thing,] R
	11:	for,]	for,] R
		honestly,]	honestly;] R
	12:	free. For]	free: though for] R
		part,]	part,] R
	14:	free. Many]	free; for many] R
		grown-up]	grown up] R
	15:	slaves,]	slaves,] R
		us,]	us,] R
	16:	ourselves,]	ourselves;] R
	20:	spent,]	spent,] R
	23:	blacks]	blacks,] R
	24:	measure,]	measure,] R
	25:	friends,]	friends;] R
		thankful,]	thankful,] R
	27:	beginning.]	beginning. But] R
	31:	sinners,]	sinners;] R
	33:	forever]	for ever] R
	33:	says , that]	says,] R
	34:	God,]	God,] R
	35:	God]	God,] R
	37:	poor:]	poor;] R
		heaven and hell]	Heaven and Hell] R
237	1:	again,]	again,] R
	2:	God,]	God;] R
		forever]	for ever] R
	3:	God,]	God,] R
		enemies,]	enemies,] R
	4:	for]	to] R
		eternity.]	eternity. Now] R
	5:	God]	God,] R
	6:	him,]	him:] R
		changed,]	changed,] R
	7:	God,]	God,] R
	9:	this,]	this,] R
	11:	Bible. Whenever]	Bible; and whenever] R
	12:	Bible. And]	Bible; and] R
	13:	sleep,]	sleep,] R
		learn]	learn what] R

	God.]	God is] R
15:	mind.]	mind,] R
	brethren,]	brethren;] R
16:	them]	them,] R
20:	read.]	read,] R
	teach]	learn] R
	remember.]	remember,] R
21:	for.]	for,] R
	Bible.]	Bible. If] R
22:	were]	was] R
24:	God.]	God,] R
25:	misery.]	misery,] R
26:	forever]	for ever] R
27:	you.]	you,] R
28:	it.]	it,] R
29:	Bible.]	Bible,] R
30:	Bible,]	Bible.] R
	everything]	every thing] R
31:	know.]	know,] R
33:	is, that]	is. That] R
34:	word,]	word;] R
35:	all.]	all,] R
	creatures.]	creatures,] R

238

	all]	all,] R
1:	all]	all,] R
2:	glory.]	glory. In] R
3:	likewise,]	likewise.] R
4:	God,]	God;] R
5:	holiness.]	holiness,] R
	God,]	God;] R
6:	evil.]	evil,] R
9:	was]	were] R
	God.]	God,] R
10:	forever]	for ever] R
	miserable.]	miserable,] R
12:	die]	die,] R
	place and stead]	room and stead] R
	sinners,]	sinners;] R
14:	Son.]	Son,] R
	Savior,]	Saviour;] R
15:	repent.]	repent,] R
	Christ.]	Christ. It] R
16:	believe.]	believe,] R
	who are]	are] R
17:	Christ.]	Christ,] R
18:	world.]	world,] R
	forever]	for ever] R
19:	for]	to] R
20:	trial.]	trial,] R
23–24:	heaven or hell]	Heaven or Hell] R
25:	places.]	places,] R
	to.]	to. There] R
26:	folks.]	folks,] R
27:	folks.]	folks,] R

28:	is.]	is.] R
29:	heaven and hell]	Heaven and Hell] R
30:	sorts: He]	sorts, he] R
32:	abroad (Matt.	abroad.—The] R
	12:30).]	
33:	world.]	world,] R
	it.]	it,] R
34:	up]	up—] R
35:	he will bring]	and that he will bring] R
36:	judgement;]	judgment—] R
37:	from the	on the housetop] R
	housetops]	
239 3:	then,]	then.] R
	everything]	every thing] R
	everyone]	every one] R
5:	stand.]	stand,] R
7:	been.]	been,] R
9:	that the]	the] R
	God.]	God,] R
10:	everything]	every thing] R
	true.]	true,] R
	that it]	it] R
12:	it? And]	it; and] R
13:	night? There]	night. There] R
15:	are. For]	are; for] R
18–19:	to come]	coming] R
21:	there]	there,] R
23:	world.]	world,] R
25:	case.]	case,] R
27:	God.]	God;] R
	thus be]	be] R
	world. and]	world, and] R
29:	here.]	here,] R
	forever]	for ever] R
30:	a temptation]	great temptation] R
31:	honours,]	honours.] R
32:	temptation]	temptations] R
35:	are.]	are,] R
	heaven.]	Heaven.] R
36:	with]	to] R
37:	years	years,] R
240 3:	masters]	matters] R
4:	Bible.]	Bible,] R
6:	heaven]	Heaven] R
7:	forever]	for ever] R
	masters.]	masters,]R
9:	folly?]	folly.] R
	us.]	us,] R
10:	masters.]	masters,] R
11:	world?]	world.] R
12:	entreat]	intreat of] R
	things.]	things,] R
14:	forever.]	for ever,] R

16:	heaven]	Heaven] R
17:	black,]	black,] R
19:	life,]	life;] R
22:	it. We]	it.] R
23:	whether]	if] R
24:	sin,]	sin,] R
	here,]	here,] R
28:	slaves,]	slaves,] R
29:	advantages than they]	advantages] R
30:	do.]	do, than they.] R
31:	Holy Word,]	holy word,] R

Notes

1.   An anti-Loyalist, one descendant of the Lloyd family, Joseph Lloyd, fled to Hartford when the British overran Long Island and used the Manor as an outpost during the Revolutionary War. Lloyd took Hammon with him. The more cosmopolitan urban area was quite agreeable to the poet's productiveness. While there, he published many of his works: "An Address to Miss Phillis Wheatley," 1778; *An Essay on the Ten Virgins,* 1779 (nonextant); and *A Winter Piece,* 1782.

2.   Before Lillian Koppel discovered Hammon's date of birth in the back of a Lloyd ledger (Ransom 10), scholars dated Hammon's birth from this passage, which would mean either that Hammon did not know his own age or that the Koppel date is incorrect. In this text, published in 1787, the poet says that he is about seventy years old, which would indicate that he was born around 1717 instead of 1711. But several explanations can reconcile the statement to the date in the ledger. First, although the essay was published in 1787, he may have written it sometime before then. Second, in the next line he writes, "I have passed the common bounds set for man." In biblical consciousness those "common bounds" were identified by the Psalmist David as "three-score years and ten" (Ps. 90:10), or seventy years. So when Hammon says "I am now upwards of seventy years old" and then again "I have passed the common bounds," he is indicating that he was not *nearing* seventy years of age but *past* it—or in fact around seventy-six (as the ledger records)—when this essay was printed.

3.   Those whites in Hammon's audience knew that in the verse following the one which he quotes God enjoins masters to return the same treatment to servants. It reads: "And ye masters, do the same things unto them, forbearing threatening; knowing that your Master also is in heaven: neither is there respect of persons with him" (Eph. 6:9). The correlated Scripture in Col. 4:1 gives a similar commandment: "Masters, give unto your servants that which is just and equal; knowing that ye also have a Master in heaven." This is the only place

in his work where Hammon yields to a proslavery interpretation that the biblical "servant" may mean "slave."

4. For various contemporary interpretations of this text and the other two, see Barnes 313–38; J. H. Hopkins 137–38, 170; and Thomas 40–42.

5. Hammon was both literary and pastoral progenitor of Black leaders like Dr. Martin Luther King, Jr., who advocated superior moral character within the persuasive view of public opinion to effect racial advancement. Just as Hammon felt that sympathetic neighbors would influence a slaveholder's conduct, King focused the spotlight of world opinion on the segregated South. King told his staff, "Our method will be that of persuasion, not coercion" (*Stride* 62). Later he wrote, "The nonviolent approach does not immediately change the heart of the oppressor. . . . Finally it reaches the opponent and so stirs his conscience that reconciliation becomes a reality" (219). But Hammon made this discovery almost two hundred years before King.

6. Hammon readers today assume that he was delivering Tommish advice in support of the slave system (see Higginbotham 140–41; Kobrin; Mays; Redding, *To Make*). Yet history shows that he was not merely calling for Christian submissiveness; he was trying to keep slaves alive and out of jail. All of the seemingly petty societal infringements that Hammon warns of in this essay were serious crimes for which slaves were flogged, jailed, put in stocks, otherwise abused, and sometimes executed. See Greene's "Slave-Holding" 510–19; and Kobrin 14–15 for examples.

7. Throughout his work Hammon struggles to reconcile the reality of slavery with the controversial doctrine of the absolute will of God. The catalyst of slave psychology in colonial times was guilt, and the Ham-Cain curses were devised as biblical reasons to excuse slavery because the Africans were supposed to have inherited guilt from their ancient forebears. For the impingement of the Ham-Cain myth on American slavery, see Clarkson 178–200; Cobb 25–30; Coleman 24; Epps; S. Mather 20–29; and Sewall.

8. As in *A Winter Piece,* Hammon identifies the power of the spoken word to curse man to effectuate their enslavement. He says that the source of both phenomena is Satan. As Hammon illustrates in "A Dialogue, Entitled, The Kind Master and Dutiful Servant," when a master places himself and his wishes between a slave and God, he attempts to become a false god to the slave. For more on slave naming and other aspects of the power of language to make slaves of men, the following texts are helpful: Branston 110–12; Scherer 65–68, 91–96; Spalding 36–38, 42–43.

9.   The preacher begins this homiletic section on the pending judgments with a warning that Christ gives in the New Testament: "But I say unto you, That every idle word that men shall speak, they shall give account thereof in the day of judgement" (Matt. 12:36).

10.   Again Hammon's standard is creditable moral behavior. Like Harriet Beecher Stowe, Hammon seems to envision the Black man as a Christ figure—perfect, yet rejected by an immoral society. In this scenario, the Black slave, like the African Simon of Cyrene (Luke 23:26), becomes the sacrificial object for the white community. Beecher developed the theory to such an extent that she could argue that Black people will save the world. (Other discussions of the Black man as a Christlike sacrificial symbol are engaged in Washington 146–56.)

11.   Hammon quotes from Christ's meeting with the Jewish ruler, Nicodemus, reported in John 3:3. But his idea of a kingdom of darkness is implied in Eph. 6:12, Col. 1:12, and Rev. 16:10.

12.   As harsh as Hammon's words may sound, most Black spokesmen in the eighteenth century described the plight of the Black masses in similar terms. One year after the first printing of this *Address,* an essay written by a Black man who identified himself only as "Othello" described slaves as rude, ignorant, and uncivilized. In his autobiography, Richard Allen uses the same type of language to make whites aware of the living conditions that slavery forced upon Blacks.

13.   Here Hammon is paraphrasing several scriptural verses that describe the state of man's inward consciousness after the Fall, the most closely notable of which is Gen. 6:5: "And God saw that the wickedness of man was great in the earth, and that every imagination of the thoughts of his heart was only evil continually." See also Jer. 7:24 and Rom. 1:21. This essay clearly reveals that Hammon categorized slavery as an abhorrent act of fallen man and an imitation of Satan's vilest attributes. The injunction on the carnal mind is a portion of Rom. 8:7: "Because the carnal mind is enmity against God: for it is not subject to the law of God, neither indeed can be."

14.   Here Hammon seems to mix both Calvinist and Arminian theology. When he says that Christ died "to save some of mankind" he is echoing Calvin's theory of limited atonement. But when he writes that God can save "all that believe" and that "all are called to repent and believe," he is relating the new wave of Arminianism that spread through the colonies at the end of the century. A close reading of Hammon's work indicates that, to offset the preferential racial selection that he believed Calvinism engendered, he developed his own brand of Arminianism as early as 1760, at least two decades before the advent of Methodist Arminianism in the colonies. For

in-depth discussion of the Calvinist-Arminian debate of those times see Bacon; Burr, *New England's Place* 14–27; Christie 153–72; Goodwin; and Pauck.

15.   Hammon is drawing on several scriptural references for this imagery, including Acts 17:31: "Because he hath appointed a day, in the which he will judge the world in righteousness by that man whom he hath ordained; whereof he hath given assurance unto all men, in that he hath raised him from the dead"; Luke 8:17: "For nothing is secret, that shall not be made manifest; neither any thing hid, that shall not be known and come abroad"; and Matt. 10:26–27: "Fear them not therefore for there is nothing covered, that shall not be revealed; and hid, that shall not be known. What I tell you in darkness, that speak ye in light: and what ye hear in the ear, that preach ye upon the housetops."

16.   Again he uses biblical authority to condemn the slaveholder:

> But they that will be rich fall into temptation and a snare, and into many foolish and hurtful lusts, which drown men in destruction and perdition. For the love of money is the root of all evil: which while some coveted after, they have erred from the faith, and pierced themselves through with many sorrows. (1 Tim. 6:9–10)

He was reminding slaveholders that the Bible promises that rich men who oppress the poor will go to perdition. However, those in the Anglican-Puritan hierarchy assumed that the texts did not apply to them because they were "Christians." Here Hammon makes it explicit that the text applies to oppressive "Christians, or mankind who have the gospel." His irony is that they have heard the Gospel and have simply taken it on as a veneer; because of their commitment to slavery, they do not have true Christianity at all. In addition to the verses from 1 Timothy, Hammon also uses James 5:1–6, which is even more applicable to American slavery:

> Go to now, ye rich men, weep and howl for your miseries that shall come upon you. Your riches are corrupted, and your garments are motheaten. Your gold and silver is cankered; and the rest of them shall be a witness against you, and shall eat your flesh as it were fire. Ye have heaped treasure together for the last days. Behold, the hire of the labourers who have reaped down your fields, which is of you kept back by fraud, crieth: and the cries of them which have reaped are entered into the ears of the Lord of Sabaoth. You have lived in pleasure on the earth, and

been wanton; ye have nourished your hearts, as in a day of slaughter. Ye have condemned and killed the just; and he doth not resist you.

17.　　Hammon is clearly charging that it is white colonists, not Africans, who are slaves because they are so enslaved by their money that they cannot obey the commandments of Christ. He is not really talking to Africans here: they are neither "ever so free" nor "ever so rich." And he is observing that those who do have this freedom and wealth are not made happy thereby. So there must be a source other than money to obtain the true essence of life. Hammon posits that that source is Christ.

18.　　After the Revolutionary War, whites were quite concerned about the growing population of free Blacks in the North. Hundreds were freed because they joined the colonists in fighting the British; others were freed as sentiment for manumission increased. By the beginning of the nineteenth century, in some states one out of every four Blacks was free. To reverse the trend, legislation was passed to discourage manumission. Simultaneously several societies were formed to recolonize the slave in Africa. What the increase of the free Black population did prove was that, although wanting an end to slavery, most Northern whites, even outspoken abolitionists, did not want racial mixing. See "An Address to the Inhabitants of Philadelphia against the Colonization Society," by James Forten (in Ducas 52–57). See also Bragg 53–55; Hurd 1:263–65; Stuckley 18–20; and Zorn.

List of Works Cited

Alighieri, Dante. *The Divine Comedy*. New York: Vintage Books, 1959.

Allen, Richard. *The Life Experiences and Gospel Labors of Rt. Rev. Richard Allen*. 1960. Reprint. New York: Abingdon Press, 1983.

Andrews, Charles C. *The History of the New York African Free-Schools*. 1830. Reprint. New York: Negro Universities Press, 1969.

Anstey, Roger. *The Atlantic Slave Trade and British Abolition, 1760–1810*. Atlantic Highlands, N.J.: Humanities Press, 1975.

Aptheker, Herbert. *American Negro Slave Revolts*. New York: Columbia University Press, 1944.

———. "The Quakers and Negro Slavery." *Journal of Negro Slavery* 25.3 (July 1940): 331–62.

———. "They Began the Fight on Slavery." *Opportunity: A Journal of Negro Life* 17.8 (August 1939): 243–44.

Armistead, W. S. *The Negro Is a Man*. 1903. Reprint. Nashville: Fisk University Library Negro Collection, 1969.

Aykroyd, W. R. *Sweet Malefactor*. London: Heinemann, 1967.

Bacon, Leonard Woolsey. *A History of American Christianity*. New York: Christian Literature Co., 1897.

Bailey, Rosalie Fellows, ed. "The Accounts Book of Henry Lloyd of the Manor of Queens Village." *Journal of Long Island History* 2 (Spring 1962): 26–49.

Baldwin, James. *Notes of a Native Son*. Boston: Beacon Press, 1964.

Baltazar, Eualio. *The Dark Center.* New York: Paulist Press, 1973.

Barck, Dorothy. Introduction to *Lloyd Papers. See* Lloyd Family.

Barnes, Albert. *An Inquiry into the Scriptural Views of Slavery.* Philadelphia: Perkins and Purves, 1846.

Bate, John. *Six Thousand Illustrations of Moral and Religious Truth.* London: Jarrold and Sons, [18xx].

Bayne, Paul. *An Entire Commentary upon the Whole Epistle of the Apostle Paul to the Ephesians.* London: M. Flelber, for I.B., 1647.

Bell, Bernard W. "African-American Writers." In *American Literature, 1764–1789: The Revolutionary Years,* ed. Everett Emerson. Madison: University of Wisconsin Press, 1977.

Bellamy, Joseph. *The Works of the Rev. Joseph Bellamy.* 3 vols. New York: Stephen Dodge, 1812.

Berlin, Ira, and Ronald Hoffman, eds. *Slavery and Freedom in the Age of the American Revolution.* Charlottesville: University Press of Virginia, 1983.

Berwanger, Eugene H. "Negrophobia in Northern Proslavery and Antislavery Thought." *Phylon: The Atlanta University Review of Race and Culture* 33.3 (Fall 1972): 266–75.

Beveridge, William. *The Church Catechism Explained.* London: W. Baxter, 1839.

———. *Private Thoughts upon Religion and upon a Christian Life.* Liverpool: H. Forshaw, 1802.

———. *Thesaurus Theologicus.* London: Rich. Smith, 1710.

———. *The Works of the Right Rev. William Beveridge.* 9 vols. London: James Duncan, 1824.

Blassingame, John H. *The Slave Community.* New York: Oxford University Press, 1972.

Bolt, Christine, and Seymour Drescher, eds. *Anti-Slavery, Religion, and Reform: Essays in Memory of Roger Anstey.* Hamden, Conn.: Archon Books; Folkestone, Kent: William Dawson and Sons, 1980.

Bontemps, Arna Wendell. *Great Slave Narratives*. Boston: Beacon Press, 1969.

Boyer, Paul, and Stephen Missenbaum. *Satan Possessed: The Social Origins of Witchcraft*. Cambridge: Harvard University Press, 1974.

Bragg, George F. *History of the Afro-American Group of the Episcopal Church*. 1922. Reprint. Baltimore: Church Advocate Press, 1968.

Brainerd, David. *An Account of the Life of the Late Rev. Mr. David Brainerd*. 1749.

Branston, Brian. *The Lost Gods of England*. New York: Oxford University Press, 1974.

Brawley, Benjamin. *Early Negro American Writers*. New York: Books for Libraries Press, 1968.

———. *The Negro in Literature and Art in the United States*. New York: Duffield and Co., 1930.

———. *A Short History of the American Negro*. New York: Macmillan, 1913.

Brent, Linda. *Incidents in the Life of a Slave*. Boston: Published for the author, 1861.

Brinton, Howard H. *The Religious Philosophy of Quakerism*. Philadelphia: Pendle Hill Publications, 1973.

Brown, John. *A Dictionary of the Holy Bible*. Berwick, Eng.: W. Lockhead, 1800.

Bruns, Roger. "Anthony Benezet's Assertion of Negro Equality." *Journal of Negro History* 56.3 (July 1971): 230–38.

Bull, George. *Harmonia Apostalica*. London: Sumptibus, Guliel, Wells and Robert Scott, 1670.

Bunyan, John. *The Pilgrim's Progress*. New York: New American Library, 1981.

Burkitt, William. *Expository Notes with Practical Observations on the New Testament*. 2 vols. Philadelphia: John Ball, 1851.

Burleigh, Charles C. "Slavery and the North." *Anti-Slavery Tracts* 10 (1858): 1–12. Westport, Conn.: Negro Universities Press, 1970.

Burr, George Lincoln. *Narratives of the Witchcraft Cases: 1648–1706*. New York: Charles Scribner's Sons, 1914.

———. *New England's Place in the History of Witchcraft*. Freeport, N.Y.: Books for Libraries Press, 1911.

Bushnell, Horace. *Twelve Selections*. Vol. 2, ed. H. Shelton Smith. New York: Oxford University Press, 1965.

Byington, Ezra Hoyt. *The Puritan as a Colonist and Reformer*. Boston: Little, Brown, 1899.

———. *The Puritan in England and New England*. 1900. Reprint. New York: Burt Franklin Press, 1972.

Byles, Mather. *Poems on Several Occasions*. New York: Columbia University Press, 1940.

Cadbury, Henry J. "Negro Membership in the Society of Friends." *Journal of Negro History* 21.2 (April 1936): 151–213.

Caldwell, Patricia. *The Puritan Conversion Narrative*. London: Cambridge University Press, 1983.

Calef, Robert. *More Wonders of the Invisible World*. Salem, Mass.: William Carlton, 1796.

Cantor, Milton. "Image of the Negro in Colonial Literature." *New England Quarterly* 36.4 (December 1963): 452–77.

Carr, James V. "Solomon Stoddard: An American Way of Religion." Ph.D. diss., Hartford Seminary, 1977.

Cheever, George B. *The Guilt of Slavery and the Crime of Slaveholding, Demonstrated from the Hebrew and Greek Scripture*. 1860. Reprint. New York: Negro Universities Press, 1976.

Cherry, Conrad. *The Theology of Jonathan Edwards*. New York: Anchor Books, 1966.

Christie, Francis Albert. "The Beginnings of Arminianism in New England." *The American Society of Church History*. Papers, 2d ser., 3.2 (1912): 151–172.

Christy, David. *Pulpit Politics; or, Ecclesiastical Legislation on Slavery*. New York: Negro Universities Press, 1969.

Clarkson, Thomas. *An Essay on the Slavery and Commerce of the Human Species, Particularly the African*. Dublin: W. Porter, 1785.

Cobb, Howell. *A Scriptural Examination of Slavery in the United States with Its Objects and Purposes.* Georgia: Printed for the author, 1856.

Coffman, Ralph J. *Solomon Stoddard.* Boston: Twayne Publishers, 1978.

Coleman, Elihu. "A Testimony against That Anti-Christian Practice of Making Slaves of Men." *Friends Review* 5.6 (October 25, 1851): 84–85.

Cooley, Henry Scofield. *A Study of Slavery in New Jersey.* Baltimore: Johns Hopkins Press, 1896.

Cooley, Timothy Mather. *Sketches of the Life and Character of the Rev. Lemuel Haynes.* New York: Harper and Sons, 1837.

Costanzo, Angelo. "Three Black Poets in Eighteenth-Century America." *Shippensburg State College Review* 1973, 89–101.

Covel, James. *A Concise Dictionary of the Holy Bible.* New York: Lane and Scott, 1852.

Craig, Hardin. *The Enchanted Glass.* New York: Oxford University Press, 1936.

Cross, F. L., ed. *The Oxford Dictionary of the Christian Church.* London: Oxford University Press, 1974.

Cruden, Alexander. *Cruden's Complete Concordance to the Old and New Testament.* Philadelphia: John C. Winston, 1930.

Crummell, Alexander. *Africa and America.* 1891. Reprint. Miami: Mnemosyne Publishing, 1969.

Curtin, Philip D. *Atlantic Slave Trade: A Census.* Madison: University of Wisconsin Press, 1969.

Dathorne, Oscar Ronald. "Africa Their Africa." In *Neo-African Literature and Culture,* ed. Bernth Lindfors and Ulla Schild. Wiesbaden: B. Heymann, 1976.

Davies, Samuel. *Sermons on Important Subjects.* 3 vols. New York: Dayton and Saxton Publishing, 1841.

Davis, David Brion. *The Problem of Slavery in the Age of Revolution, 1770–1823.* Ithaca: Cornell University Press, 1975.

Davis, Thomas J. "The New York Slave Conspiracy of 1741 as Black Protest." *Journal of Negro History* 56.1 (January 1971): 17–30.

Degler, Carl N. "Slavery and the Genesis of American Race Prejudice." *Comparative Studies in Society and History* 2.1 (October 1959): 49–66.

Devisse, Jean, and Michael Mollat. *The Image of the Black in Western Art.* Vol. 2. New York: William Morrow, 1979.

Dick, David. *All Modern Slavery Indefensible.* 1836. Reprint. Freeport, N.Y.: Books for Libraries Press, 1972.

Dodd, Robert. *History of Long Island.* New York: Sentry Press, 1962.

Douglass, Frederick. *Narrative of the Life of Frederick Douglass, an American Slave.* 1845. Reprint. New York: Anchor Books, 1973.

Drake, Thomas E. *Quakers and Slavery in America.* New Haven: Yale University Press, 1950.

DuBois, W. E. B. *The Souls of Black Folk.* 1953. Reprint. New York: Fawcett Publications, 1969.

Ducas, George. *Great Documents in Black American History.* New York: Praeger Publishers, 1970.

Dumond, Lowell Dwight. *Anti-Slavery: The Crusade for Freedom in America.* Ann Arbor: University of Michigan Press, 1961.

Dunston, Alfred G. *The Black Man in the Old Testament.* Philadelphia: Dorrance, 1974.

Dwight, Timothy. *Travels in New England and New York.* 4 vols. Cambridge: Harvard University Press, 1969.

Edwards, Jonathan. *Apocalyptic Writings.* Vol. 5 of *Works.* New Haven: Yale University Press, 1977.

———. *Collected Writings of Jonathan Edwards,* ed. Virgilius Ferm. New York: Library Publishers, 1953.

———. *Freedom of Will.* Vol. 1 of *Works.* New Haven: Yale University Press, 1957.

———. *The Great Awakening.* Vol. 4 of *Works.* New Haven: Yale University Press, 1972.

————. *A History of the Work of Redemption: Comprising an Outline of Church History.* New York: American Tract Society, 1774.

————. *Representative Selections with Bibliography and Notes,* ed. Clarence H. Faust and Thomas H. Johnson. 1935. Reprint. New York: Hill and Wang, 1962.

————. *The Salvation of All Men.* Boston: Ewer and Bedlington, 1824.

————. *The Works of Jonathan Edwards.* 9 vols. New Haven: Yale University Press, 1957.

Edwards, Paul. *Equiano's Travels.* New York: Frederick A. Praeger, 1966.

"Eighteenth Century Slaves as Advertised by Their Masters." *Journal of Negro History* 1 (1916): 175–216.

Elliott, Emory. *Power and the Pulpit in Puritan New England.* Princeton: Princeton University Press, 1975.

Emerson, Everett H. "Calvin and Covenant Theology." *Church History* 25.2 (June 1956): 136–44.

Epps, Archie. "The Christian Doctrine of Slavery: A Theological Analysis." *Journal of Negro History* 66.4 (1961): 243–49.

Equiano, Olaudah. *The Life of Olaudah Equiano; or, Gustavas Vassa the African.* London: Dawsons of Pall Mall, 1969.

Ernst, Robert. "The Economic Status of New York City Negroes, 1850–1863." *Negro History Bulletin* 12 (March 1949): 131–32, 139–43.

Fisher, Miles Mark. *Negro Slave Songs in the United States.* New York: Cornell University Press, 1953.

Fladeland, Betty. *Men and Brothers.* Urbana: University of Illinois Press, 1972.

————. "Who Were the Abolitionists?" *Journal of Negro History* 66.1 (January 1964): 99–115.

Flint, Martha B. *Long Island before the Revolution: A Colonial Study.* 1896. Reprint. New York: Ira J. Friedman, 1967.

Floyd, Preston L. "An Examination of Theological Concepts in the Negro Spirituals." *Duke Divinity School Review* 4 (Spring 1978): 11–18.

Foster, Frank Hugh. *A Genetic History of the New England Theology*. Chicago: University of Chicago Press, 1907.

Fox, Dixon Ryan. "The Negro Vote in New York." *Political Science Quarterly* 32 (June 1917): 252–75.

Fox, George. *The Day Book of Counsel and Comfort from the Epistle of George Fox*. London: Macmillan, 1937.

———. *The Doctrines and Ministry of George Fox*. Philadelphia: The Friends Bookstore, 1875.

———. *The Journal of George Fox,* ed. John Nickalls. Cambridge: Cambridge University Press, 1952.

———. *A Memoir of George Fox of the Life, Travels, and Gospel Labours*. London: Edward Marsh, Friends, Book and Tract Depository, 1850.

———. *The Works of George Fox*. 3 vols. Philadelphia: Marcus Gould, 1831.

Franklin, John Hope. *From Slavery to Freedom: A History of Negro Americans*. 5th edition. New York: Alfred A. Knopf, 1980.

Frazier, E. Franklin. *The Negro Church in America*. New York: Schocken Books, 1974.

Frost, J. William, ed. *The Quaker Origins of Antislavery*. Norwood, Pa.: Norwood Editions, 1980.

Gabriel, Ralph Henry. *The Evolution of Long Island: A Story of Sea and Land*. New Haven: Yale University Press, 1921.

Garrison, William Lloyd. *Anti-Slavery Pamphlets*. Boston: Garrison and Knapp, 1832.

Genovese, Eugene D. *Roll, Jordan, Roll: The World the Slaves Made*. New York: Pantheon Books, 1974.

George, Carol. *Segregated Sabbaths*. New York: Oxford University Press, 1973.

Gillette, Francis. *Discourse on the Slavery Question in Anti-Slavery Pamphlets*. Hartford: S. S. Cowles, 1839.

———. *A Review of the Rev. Horace Bushnell's Discourse on the Slavery Question, Delivered in the North Church, Hartford, January 10, 1839*. Hartford: S. S. Cowles, 1839.

Goodwin, Gerald, J. "The Myth of 'Arminian-Calvinism' in Eighteenth-Century New England." *New England Quarterly* 41 (June 1968): 213–37.

Greene, Lorenzo J. *The Negro in Colonial New England: 1620–1776.* New York: Columbia University Press, 1942.

———. "Slave-Holding New England and Its Awakening." *Journal of Negro History* 13.4 (October 1928): 492–533.

Griffin, Edward Dorr. *Humble Attempt to Reconcile the Differences of Christians Respecting the Extent of the Atonement.* New York: Stephen Dodge, 1819.

Grimke, Francis J. *The Negro: His Rights and Wrongs, the Forces for Him and against Him.* Washington: n.p., 1898?.

Hammon, Briton. *A Narrative of the Sufferings and Deliverance of Briton Hammon.* New York: Garland Publishing, 1978.

Hastings, James, ed. *Encyclopedia of Religion and Ethics.* Vol. 11. New York: Charles Scribner's Sons, 1921.

Haynes, George Edmund. *The Negro at Work in New York City.* Vol. 49. New York: Columbia University Press, 1912.

Haynes, Henry W. "Cotton Mather and His Slaves." *American Antiquarian Society* 6.2 (October 23, 1890): 191–195.

Haynes, Leonard L., Jr. *The Negro Community within American Protestantism, 1619–1844.* Boston: Christopher Publishing House, 1953.

Heather, P. J. "Color Symbolism." *Folklore* 50 (1949): 165–215.

Hepburn, John. *The American Defense of the Golden Rule.* 1715. In *Racial Thought in America,* ed. Louis Ruchames. Amherst: University of Massachusetts Press, 1969.

Herrick, Chessman A. *White Servitude in Pennsylvania.* Philadelphia: Joseph McVey, 1926.

Hervey, James. *Meditations and Contemplations in Two Volumes.* Philadelphia: Mithra Jones, 1808.

Higginbotham, Leon A. *In the Matter of Color: Race and the American Legal Process.* New York: Oxford University Press, 1978.

Hindson, Louis. *Introduction to Puritan Theology.* Grand Rapids: Baker House, 1976.

Hirsch, Leo H. "The Negro and New York, 1783 to 1865." *Journal of Negro History* 4.16 (October 1931): 382–414.

Hopkins, John Henry. *View of Slavery.* 1864. Reprint. New York: Negro Universities Press, 1969.

Hopkins, Samuel. *A Dialogue Concerning the Slavery of the Africans and Samuel Sewall's "The Selling of Joseph,"* ed. James M. McPherson and William Loren Katz. New York: Arno Press/New York Times, 1968.

———. *Slavery of Africans.* New York: Arno Press/New York Times, 1969.

———. *Timely Articles on Slavery.* 1854. Reprint. Miami: Mnemosyne Publishing, 1969.

———. *The Works of Samuel Hopkins D.D.* Vols. 1–3. Boston: Doctrinal Tract and Book Society, 1854.

Horton, George Moses. *The Poetical Works of George Moses Horton: The Colored Bard of North Carolina.* Hillsborough, N.C.: D. Hearth, 1845.

Humphreys, David. *A Historical Account of the Incorporated Society for the Propagation of the Gospel in Foreign Parts.* New York: Arno Press/New York Times, 1969.

Hurd, John Codman. *The Law of Freedom and Bondage in the United States.* Vol. 1. 1858. Reprint. New York: Negro Universities Press, 1968.

Hutchinson, Thomas. *Witchcraft Delusion of 1692.* Boston: Privately printed, 1870.

Jackson, Samuel Macauley, ed. *The New Schaff-Herzog Encyclopedia of Religious Knowledge.* 2 vols. New York: Funk and Wagnalls, 1908.

Jahn, Janheinz. *A History of Neo-African Literature: Writing in Two Continents,* trans. Oliver Coburn and Ursula Lehrburger. London: Faber and Faber, 1968.

Jamison, A. Leland, and James Ward Smith, eds. *The Shaping of American Religion.* Princeton, N.J.: Princeton University Press, 1961.

Jernegan, Marcus W. *Laboring and Dependent Classes in Colo-*

nial America, 1607–1783. Chicago: University of Chicago Press, 1931.

————. "Slavery and Conversion in the American Colonies," *American Historical Review* 21.3 (April 1916): 504–27.

Johnson, James Weldon. *The Book of American Negro Spirituals*. New York: Viking Press, 1933.

Jones, Phyllis M. "Puritan's Progress: The Story of the Soul's Salvation in the Early New England Sermons." *Early American Literature* 15.1 (Spring 1980): 14–28.

Jones, Rufus M. *George Fox: Seeker and Friend*. London: George Allen and Unwin, 1930.

————. *The Quakers in the American Colonies*. London: Macmillan, 1911.

Jordan, Winthrop D. *The Negro vs. Equality*. Chicago: Rand McNally, 1969.

————. *The White Man's Burden: Historical Origins of Racism in the United States*. New York: Oxford University Press, 1974.

————. *White over Black: American Attitudes toward the Negro, 1550–1812*. Baltimore: Penguin Books, 1968.

Kaplan, Sidney. *The Black Presence in the Era of the American Revolution, 1770–1800*. Washington: New York Graphic Society, 1973.

Katz, Bernard, ed. *The Social Implication of Early Negro Music in the United States*. New York: Arno Press, 1969.

Keller, Karl. "The Loose, Large Principles of Solomon Stoddard." *Early American Literature* 16.1 (Spring 1981): 27–40.

Kerlin, Robert T. *Negro Poets and Their Poems*. Washington: Associated Publishers, 1923.

King, Martin Luther, Jr. *Stride toward Freedom: The Montgomery Story*. New York: Harper and Sons, 1958.

Kinnamon, Keneth, and Richard Barksdale, eds. *Black Writers of America: A Comprehensive Anthology*. New York: Macmillan, 1972.

Kittredge, George Lyman. *Witchcraft in Old and New England.* New York: Russell and Russell, 1956.

Klein, Herbert S. *The Middle Passage.* Princeton: Princeton University Press, 1978.

Klingberg, Frank J. *Anglican Humanitarianism in Colonial New York.* Philadelphia: Church Historical Society, 1940.

Kobrin, David. *The Black Minority in Early New York.* Albany: State University of New York Press, 1971.

Lay, Benjamin. *Am I Not a Man and a Brother?: The Anti-Slavery Crusade of Revolutionary America, 1688–1788,* ed. Roger Bruns. New York: Chelsea House Publishers, 1977.

Levin, David. *What Happened in Salem?* New York: Harcourt Brace and World, 1960.

Littlejohn, David. *Black on White: A Critical Survey of Writing by American Negroes.* New York: Grossman Publishers, 1966.

Litwack, Leon F. "The Abolitionist Dilemma: The Antislavery Movement and the Northern Negro." *New England Quarterly* 34.1 (March 1961): 50–73.

Lloyd Family. *Papers of the Lloyd Family of the Manor of Queens Village, Lloyd's Neck, Long Island, New York, 1654–1826.* Vols. 1, 2. New York: Printed for The New York Historical Society, 1927.

Locke, Mary Stoughton. *Anti-Slavery in America from the Introduction of African Slaves to the Prohibition of the Slave Trade.* Boston: Ginn and Co., 1901.

Loggins, Vernon. *The Negro Author: His Development in America to 1900.* Port Washington, N.Y.: Kennikat Press, 1964.

Long, Edward. *The History of Jamaica.* 3 vols. 1774. Reprint. London: Frank Cass, 1970.

Lovejoy, A. O. *The Great Chain of Being: A Study of the History of an Idea.* Cambridge: Harvard University Press, 1936.

Lovejoy, J. C. *Memoir of the Martyr Torrey.* Boston: John P. Jewett, 1847.

Mabee, Carleton. *Black Education in New York from Colonial to Modern Times*. New York: Syracuse University Press, 1979.

MacEacheren, Elaine. "Emancipation in Massachusetts: A Reexamination." *Journal of Negro History* 55.4 (October 1970): 289–306.

MacFarland, Alan. *Witchcraft in Tudor and Stuart England*. New York: Harper and Row, 1970.

McKee, Samuel. *Labor in Colonial New York, 1664–1776*. New York: Columbia University Press, 1935.

McKitrick, Eric L. *Slavery Defended: The Views of the Old South*. Englewood Cliffs, N.J.: Prentice-Hall, 1963.

McLeod, Alexander. *Negro Slavery*. New York: n.p., 1860.

MacLeod, Duncan J. *Slavery, Race and the American Revolution*. Cambridge: Cambridge University Press, 1974.

McManus, Douglas R. *Colonial New England*. New York: Oxford University Press, 1975.

McManus, Edgar J. *Black Bondage in the North*. New York: Syracuse University Press, 1973.

———. *A History of Negro Slavery in New York*. New York: Syracuse University Press, 1966.

McNeil, John T. *The History and Character of Calvinism*. New York: Oxford University Press, 1954.

Malone, Dumas. "Under the Auspices of the American Council of Learned Societies." *Dictionary of American Biography* 28 (1936): 59–60.

Marrant, John. *A Narrative of the Lord's Wonderful Dealings with John Marrant, a Black*. 1785. Reprint. New York: Garland Publishing, 1978.

Marty, Martin E. *Faith of Our Fathers: Religion, Awakening and Revolution*. 4 vols. College Park, Md.: McGrath Publishing, 1977.

Mather, Cotton. *Bonifacius: An Essay upon the Good*. Cambridge: Belknap Press of Harvard University Press, 1966.

———. *Diary of Cotton Mather, 1709–1724*. Boston: Published by The Massachusetts Historical Society, 1912.

————. *The Negro Christianized.* 1706. In *Racial Thought in America,* ed. Louis Ruchames. Amherst: University of Massachusetts Press, 1969.

————. *On Witchcraft.* Mount Vernon, N.Y.: Peter Pauper Press, 1950.

————. *Rules for the Society of Negroes.* 1693. Reprint. New York: n.p., 1888.

————. *The Wonders of the Invisible World.* London: John Russell Smith, 1862.

Mather, Samuel. *The Figures or Types of the Old Testament.* New York: Johnson Reprint, 1969.

Mathews, Donald G. "Religion and Slavery: The American South." In *Anti-Slavery, Religion, and Reform: Essays in Memory of Roger Anstey,* ed. Christine Bolt and Seymour Drescher. Hamden, Conn.: Archon Books; Folkestone, Kent: William Dawson and Sons, 1980.

Matlack, Lucius C. *The History of American Slavery and Methodism from 1780 to 1849.* New York: n.p., 1849.

Mays, Benjamin. *The Negro's God.* New York: Russell and Russell, 1968.

Medlicott, Alexander. "In the Wake of Mr. Edwards' 'Most Awakening' Sermon at Enfield." *Early American Literature* 15 (Winter 1980/1981): 217–21.

Meier, August, and Elliot Rudwick, eds. *The Making of Black America: Essays in Negro Life and History.* Vol. 1. New York: Atheneum, 1971.

Miller, Kelly. *Out of the House of Bondage.* 1914. Reprint. New York: Schocken Books, 1971.

————. *Race Adjustment: Essays on the Negro in America.* 1909. Reprint. New York: Neale Publishing, 1910.

Miller, Perry. *The American Puritans: Their Prose and Poetry.* New York: Doubleday Anchor Books, 1956.

————. *The New England Mind: From Colony to Province.* Cambridge: Harvard University Press, 1953.

————. *The New England Mind: The Seventeenth Century.* New York: Macmillan, 1939.

Mitchell, Henry H. *Black Preaching.* Philadelphia: J. P. Lippincott, 1970.

Moore, George H. *Notes on the History of Slavery in Massachusetts.* New York: D. Appleton, 1866.

More, Paul E., and Frank L. Cross. *Anglicanism: The Thought and Practice of the Church of England.* Milwaukee: Morehouse, 1935.

Morgan, Edmund S. *The Puritan Family.* 1944. Reprint. New York: Harper and Row, 1966.

————. *Visible Saints.* New York: Harper and Row, 1963.

Morgan, Edwin Vernon. "Slavery in New York: The Status of the Slave under the English Colonial Government." *Papers of the American Historical Association* 5 (1891): 3–16.

Morse, W. H. "Lemuel Haynes." *Journal of Negro History* 4.1 (January 1919): 22–32.

Moulton, Phillips. "John Woolman's Approach to Social Action as Exemplified in Relation to Slavery." *Church History* 40.4 (December 1966): 399–410.

Nell, William C. *The Colored Patriots of the American Revolution.* New York: Arno Press, 1968.

Newlin, Claude M. *Philosophy and Religion in Colonial America.* New York: Philosophical Library, 1962.

Niebuhr, Richard. "The Idea of Covenant and American Democracy." *Church History* 23.2 (June 1954): 126–35.

Olson, Edwin. "Social Aspects of Slave Life in New York." *Journal of Negro History* 26 (January 1941): 66–77.

Overton, Jacqueline. *Long Island Story.* New York: Country Life Press, 1929.

Ovington, Mary White. *Half a Man: The Status of the Negro in New York.* New York: Hill and Wang, 1969.

Oxley, Thomas L. G. "Survey of Negro Literature, 1760–1929." *Messenger* (February 1927): 37–39.

Palmer, R. Roderick. "Jupiter Hammon's Poetic Exhortations." *CLA Journal* 18.1 (September 1974): 22–27.

Pasco, C. F. *An Historical Account of the Society for the Propa-*

gation of the Gospel in Foreign Parts, 1701–1900. London: Published at the Society's Office, 1901.

Pauck, Wilhelm. "Calvin's 'Institutes of the Christian Religion.' " *Church History* 15.1 (March 1946): 17–27.

Peare, Catherine Owens. *John Woolman: Child of Light.* New York: Vanguard Press, 1954.

Pease, William, and Jane H. Pease. "Anti-Slavery Ambivalence: Immediatism, Expediency, Race." *American Quarterly* 17 (Winter 1964): 682–95.

Pettit, Norman. *The Heart Prepared: Grace and Conversion in Puritan Spiritual Life.* New Haven: Yale University Press, 1966.

Pierre, C. E. "The Work of the Society for the Propagation of the Gospel in Foreign Parts among the Negroes in the Colonies." *Journal of Negro History* 1.4 (1916): 349–60.

Poole, Matthew. *Poole's Annotations in Two Volumes upon the Holy Bible.* London: Thomas Parkhurst, 1685.

Pope, Robert G. *The Halfway Covenant.* Princeton: Princeton University Press, 1969.

Porter, Dorothy. *Early Negro Writing, 1760–1837.* Boston: Beacon Press, 1971.

Prime, Nathaniel S. *A History of Long Island: From Its First Settlement by Europeans.* New York: Congress, 1845.

Quarles, Benjamin. *The Negro in the American Revolution.* 1961. Reprint. New York: Norton Library, 1973.

———. "The Revolutionary War as a Black Declaration of Independence." In *Slavery and Freedom in the Age of the American Revolution,* ed. Ira Berlin and Ronald Hoffman. Charlottesville: University Press of Virginia, 1983.

Raboteau, Albert J. *Slave Religion: The "Invisible" Institution in the Antebellum South.* New York: Oxford University Press, 1978.

Ransom, Stanley Austin, ed. *America's First Negro Poet: The Complete Works of Jupiter Hammon of Long Island.* Port Washington, N.Y.: Kennikat Press, 1970.

Rawick, George P., ed. *God Struck Me Dead.* Vol. 19 of *The American Slave: A Complete Autobiography.* 19 vols. 1941. Reprint. Westport, Conn.: Greenwood, 1972.

Rawley, James A. *The Transatlantic Slave Trade: A History.* New York: Norton, 1981.

Redding, J. Saunders. *To Make a Poet Black.* College Park, Md.: McGrath Publishing, 1939.

Redding, Saunders, and Arthur P. Davis, eds. *Cavalcade: Negro American Writing from 1760 to the Present.* Boston: Houghton Mifflin, 1971.

Reese, Carolyn. "From Jupiter Hammon to LeRoi Jones." *Changing Education* 1 (Fall 1966): 30–34.

Remy, Nicholas. *Demonolatry.* London: John Rodker, 1930.

Richmind, M. A. *Bid the Vassal Soar: Interpretive Essays on the Life and Poetry of Phillis Wheatley and George Moses Horton.* Washington, DC: Howard University Press, 1974.

Riddell, William Renwick. "The Slave in Early New York." *Journal of Negro History* 13.1 (1928): 53–86.

Robinson, William H. *Critical Essays on Phillis Wheatley.* Boston: G. K. Hall, 1982.

———. *Early Black American Poets.* Dubuque: Wm. C. Brown, 1969.

———. *Phillis Wheatley in the Black American Beginnings.* Detroit: Broadside Press, 1975.

Rosenberg, Bruce A. *The Art of the American Folk Preacher.* New York: Oxford University Press, 1970.

Ruchames, Louis, ed. *Racial Thought in America from the Puritans to Abraham Lincoln.* Amherst: University of Massachusetts Press, 1969.

Rudwin, Maximillian. *The Devil in Legend and Literature.* New York: Open Court, 1970.

Rush, Benjamin. *An Address to the Inhabitants of the British Settlements in America, upon Slavekeeping.* Philadelphia: n.p., 1773.

Rutman, Darrett B. *American Puritanism: Faith and Practice.* New York: J. B. Lippincott, 1970.

———. ed. *The Great Awakening: Event and Exegesis.* New York: John Wiley and Sons, 1970.

Saffin, John. "A Brief and Candid Answer to a Late Printed Sheet, Entitled, *The Selling of Joseph.*" 1701. In *Racial Thought in America,* ed. Louis Ruchames. Amherst: University of Massachusetts Press, 1969.

———. *The Notebook of John Saffin, 1665–1708.* New York: Harbor Press, 1928.

Schafer, Thomas A. "Jonathan Edwards' Conception of the Church." *Church History* 24.1 (1955): 51–66.

Schenell, Kempes. "Anti-Slavery Influences on the Status of Slaves in a Free State." *Journal of Negro History* 50.4 (October 1965): 257–73.

Scherer, Lester B. *Slavery and Churches in Early America, 1619–1819.* Grand Rapids: W. B. Eerdmans, 1975.

Schneider, Herbert Wallace. *The Puritan Mind.* New York: Henry Holt, 1930.

Seiss, Joseph A. *The Parable of the Ten Virgins: In Six Discourses and a Sermon on the Judgeship of the Saints.* Philadelphia: Smith, English, 1863.

Sewall, Samuel. *The Selling of Joseph.* 1700. Reprint. New York: Arno Press/New York Times, 1969.

———. *The Selling of Joseph: A Memorial,* ed. Sidney Kaplan. 1700. Reprint. Amherst: University of Massachusetts Press, 1969.

Shea, Daniel B. *Spiritual Autobiography in Early America.* Princeton: Princeton University Press, 1968.

Shepard, Thomas. *The Works.* Vol. 2, ed. John Adams Albro. 1853. Reprint. New York: Georg Olms Verlag, 1971.

Silverman, Kenneth. *Selected Letters of Cotton Mather.* Baton Rouge: Louisiana State University Press, 1971.

Slater, Peter Gregg. *Children in the New England Mind in Death and in Life.* Hamden, Conn.: Archon Books, 1977.

Smith, Abbot Emerson. *Colonists in Bondage.* Chapel Hill: University of North Carolina Press, 1947.

Smith, Warren B. *White Servitude in Colonial South Carolina.* Columbia: University of South Carolina Press, 1961.

Snowden, Frank M. *Before Color Prejudice.* Cambridge: Harvard University Press, 1983.

———. *Blacks in Antiquity.* Cambridge: Harvard University Press, 1970.

———, et al., eds. *The Image of the Black in Western Art.* Vol. 1. New York: William Morrow, 1976.

Southern, Eileen. *The Music of Black Americans.* New York: Norton, 1983.

Spalding, Thomas Alfred. *An Essay on Elizabethan Demonology.* 1879. Reprint. London: Caxton Press, 1880.

Steele, David N., and Curtis Thomas, eds. *The Five Points of Calvinism: Defined, Defended, Documented.* Philadelphia: Presbyterian and Reformed Publishing Co., 1963.

Stein, Stephen J. "Providence and the Apocalypse in the Early Writings of Jonathan Edwards." *Early American Literature* 13.3 (Winter 1978/1979): 251–67.

———, ed. *The Works of Jonathan Edwards.* Vol. 5. New Haven: Yale University Press, 1977.

Stephen, Sir Leslie, and Sir Sidney Lee, eds. *The Dictionary of National Biography.* London: Oxford University Press, 1900.

Stoddard, Solomon. *The Safety of Appearing at the Day of Judgement, in the Righteousness of Christ: Opened and Applied.* Boston: Samuel Green, for Samuel Phillis, 1687.

Stowe, Harriet Beecher. *A Key to "Uncle Tom's Cabin."* 1853. Reprint. Boston: John P. Jewett, 1854.

Stuckey, Sterling. *The Ideological Origins of Black Nationalism.* Boston: Beacon Press, 1972.

Taylor, John M. *The Witchcraft Delusion in Colonial Connecticut.* 1647. New York: Grafton Press, 1967.

Thomas, Latta R. *Biblical Faith and the Black American.* Valley Forge, Pa.: Judson Press, 1976.

Thompson, Benjamin F. *History of Long Island from Its Discovery and Settlement to the Present Time.* 3 vols. New York: Robert H. Dodd, 1918.

Thurman, Howard. *Deep River.* 1945. Reprint. New York: Kennikat Press, 1969.

Tichi, Cecelia. "The Puritan Historians and Their New Jerusalem." *Early American Literature* 6.2 (Fall 1971): 143–56.

Tipson, Baird. "Invisible Saints: The 'Judgement of Charity' in the Early New England Churches." *Church History* 44.4 (December 1975): 460–71.

Towner, Lawrence W. "The Sewall-Saffin Dialogue on Slavery." *William and Mary Quarterly* 21.3 (1964): 40–52.

Tracy, Joseph. *The Great Awakening: A History of the Revival of Religion in the Time of Edwards and Whitefield.* Boston: Tappan and Dennent, 1842.

Trumbull, Hammond J. *The True Blue Laws of Connecticut and New Haven and the False Blue Laws.* Hartford: American Publishing, 1876.

Tucker, W. H. *Here After and Judgement.* London: Elliot Stock, 1894.

Turner, Nat. *The Confessions of Nat Turner.* Baltimore: Thomas R. Gray, 1831.

Twombly, Robert C., and Robert H. Moore. "Black Puritan: The Negro in Seventeenth-Century Massachusetts." In *The Making of Black America,* ed. August Meier and Elliott Rutwick. New York: Atheneum, 1971.

Twynham, Leonard. "He Was First to Speak Up on Slavery." *Opportunity: A Journal of Negro Life* 17.6 (June 1939): 176–77, 190–91.

Ullendorff, Edward. *Ethiopia and the Bible.* London: Oxford University Press, 1968.

Van Etten, Henry. *Men of Wisdom: George Fox and the Quakers.* New York: Harper Torchbooks, 1959.

Vartanian, Pershing. "Cotton Mather and the Puritan Transition into the Enlightenment." *Early American Literature* 8.3 (Winter 1973): 214–23.

Vassa, Gustavas. *See* Edwards, Paul; Equiano, Olaudah.

Veysie, Daniel. *The Doctrine of Atonement: Illustrated and Defended in Eight Sermons.* London: Sotheby, 1975.

Vibert, Faith. "The Society for the Propagation of the Gospel in Foreign Parts: Its Works for the Negroes in North America before 1783." *Journal of Negro History* 18.2 (April 1933): 171–212.

Walker, David. *See* Stuckey, Sterling.

Walker, Williston. *The Creeds and Platforms of Congregationalism.* Boston: Pilgrim Press, 1960.

Walsh, James P. "Solomon Stoddard's Opening Communion: A Re-examination." *New England Quarterly* 43.1 (March 1970): 97–114.

Washington, Joseph R., Jr. *Black Religion: The Negro and Christianity in the U.S.* Boston: Beacon Press, 1964.

Weatherford, W. D. *American Churches and the Negro.* Boston: Christopher Publishing, 1957.

Wegelin, Oscar. "Was Phillis Wheatley America's First Negro Poet?" *Literary Collector* (August 1904).

Weimer, Cecil G. "Christianity and the Race Problem." *Journal of Negro History* 16.1 (January 1931): 67–78.

Wheatley, Phillis. *The Poems of Phillis Wheatley,* ed. Julian D. Mason, Jr. Chapel Hill: University of North Carolina Press, 1966.

Whitefield, George. *George Whitefield's Journals.* New York: Banner of Truth Trust, 1960.

Whitney, Janet. *John Woolman: American Quaker.* Boston: Atlantic Monthly Press, 1942.

———. *The Journal of John Woolman.* Chicago: Henry Regnery, 1950.

Wigglesworth, Michael. *The Day of Doom: Great and Last Judgement.* New York: American News, 1867.

Willard, Samuel. *A Complete Body of Divinity.* New York: Johnson Reprint, 1969.

Woodson, Carter G. *The American Negro: His History and Literature.* New York: Arno Press/New York Times, 1968.

———. *The Education of the Negro prior to 1861.* New York: Arno Press/New York Times, 1968.

————. *The History of the Negro Church*. Washington, DC: Associated Publishers, 1921.

————. *The Mind of the Negro as Reflected in Letters Written during the Crises, 1800–1860*. Washington, DC: Association for the Study of Negro Life and History, 1926.

————. *The Negro in Our History*. Washington, DC: Associated Press, 1922.

Woolman, John. *The Journal of the Life, Gospel, Labors and Christian Experiences of that Faithful Minister of Jesus Christ*. 1903. Reprint. New York: Macmillan, 1910.

————. *The Journal and Major Essays*. New York: Oxford University Press, 1971.

Woolsey, Melancthon Lloyd. *The Lloyd Manor of Queens Village*. Reprint. New York: Stearns and Beale, 1951.

Worrall, Arthur J. *Quakers in the Colonial Northeast*. Hanover, N.H.: University Press of New England, 1980.

Wright, Richard. *Uncle Tom's Children*. New York: Harper and Row, 1938.

Zilversmit, Arthur. *The First Emancipation: The First Abolition of Slavery in the North*. Chicago: University of Chicago Press, 1967.

Zook, George Frederick. "The Company of Royal Adventurers Trading Into Africa." *Journal of Negro History* 4.2 (April 1919): 175–216.

Zorn, Roman J. "The New England Anti-Slavery Society: Pioneer Abolition Organization." *Journal of Negro History* 63.3 (July 1957): 157–77.

Index

About the Author

Sondra A. O'Neale (A.B., Asbury College; M.A., Ph.D., University of Kentucky) is the Chair and Associate Professor of the Women's Studies Department at the University of Wisconsin-La Crosse. She has taught at Emory University, at the University of California in San Diego, and at the University of Kentucky in Lexington. Dr. O'Neale has published extensively in professional journals and edited texts on the works of African-American slaves of the 18th and 19th centuries, on the works of African-American women from the 18th through the 20th centuries, and on the phenomenon of religion and biblical typology in modern American culture.